The phrase

ANNUIT COEPTIS

NOVUS ORDO SECLORUM

as found on the top and bottom of

the reverse side of

the Great Seal of the United States

as displayed on the back of the

American Dollar bill is Latin for

ANNOUNCING THE BIRTH OF

THE NEW WORLD ORDER

THE
NEW WORLD ORDER

by
A. Ralph Epperson

NOTICE
(written in February, 2000)

The book that you are about to read was completed in June, 1989 and was based upon the research that I have done for 27 years. All of the signs that I was reading about indicated that THE NEW WORLD ORDER was scheduled to start on January 1, 2000. This obviously did not happen on that date.

However, that does not mean that my research was incorrect. It means that another date has been selected and that this date has truly been kept secret from honest researchers such as myself.

Let me impress upon you: these people are committed to achieving their goal, and THE NEW WORLD ORDER will occur, but at a future date. Let me add that I still believe that this date is very near.

the author

Other works
by
A. Ralph Epperson

THE UNSEEN HAND
An Introduction to the
Conspiratorial View
of History

GOD EXISTS!
There Is No Other Option!

THE NEW WORLD ORDER

TABLE OF CONTENTS

DEDICATION

To my God, who gave me the ability to reason, hence my ability to know Him;

and

To my mother and father who gave me my life, hence my ability to experience the joys of His creation;

and

To the founding fathers, who gave me a nation in which I could express my thoughts, even those that are as controversial as these;

and

To Jim, an old friend, who urged me to start on my search for the truth;

and

To Willy Solis, (1962-1984) a freedom fighter from Costa Rica who loved freedom so much that he was willing to pay the ultimate price for it, and he did;

I dedicate this book.

ABOUT THE AUTHOR

When I finished writing my book entitled THE UNSEEN HAND, and was preparing it for publication, I decided that I would add a brief page describing a little about me and the reasons that I had written it. I felt that it would assist the reader in understanding my material if I included some brief comments about my personal background. I have become an avid reader since my graduation from college and I have noticed that many of the works I read frequently failed to provide some of this background information.

So I feel that I must include similar information in this, my second book.

I started reading in 1963 when a friend of mine noticed that even though I was a college graduate, my knowledge of history, political science and economics was woefully lacking. I started reading at his insistence, and I haven't stopped since. Reading in one subject got me interested in another, and the process led me ultimately into the esoteric world of secret societies and their concealed symbols. (The word esoteric is defined as a word or understanding that is intended for or understood by only a chosen few, as an inner group of disciples or initiates.)

As I continued my reading, I started noticing that I was discovering the evidence of an enormous truth; a truth that had escaped almost all of yesterday's historians. There was no question that some of these researchers had been moved to expose a part of this truth, but I was unable to find the one book that would put the entire story all together. My search for that elusive volume continued, but I simply couldn't find it.

About a year ago, I started feeling the need to write that volume myself.

However, feeling extremely inadequate for a task as important as this one, I decided that I would redouble my efforts to locate the one volume that would put it all together into one easily understood text. I continued my search into the writings of others, hoping to find someone who had performed this task before me, but I continued to be unsuccessful.

Since I was unable to find that one book, I decided that I had to write it myself.

This is that effort.

So, please accept this modest work for what it is: an honest attempt to put 26 years of research into one volume, by an individual who feels completely inadequate for the task! I can assure the reader that my self-perceived inadequacy is only because of the importance of the information discovered.

The chore seems to be doubly difficult: not only must my research be thorough, but I must also make the information I have uncovered believable. However, I do feel that I have succeeded as far as my meager talents have allowed me.

There is no question that the research I conducted was not as exhaustive as it could have been. The more that I read, the more that I realized I had to read because the evidence to support the conclusions of this book appeared to be nearly limitless. However, there comes a time when every researcher must conclude that the material that has been already located is adequate enough to convince even the most ardent skeptic and that any additional material uncovered would only duplicate that which had already been found.

In addition, there are several things I would like the reader to know. Quite often I have quoted the comments of several writers when one or two would probably have made my point. However, there is a reason for this.

My intention is to make certain that the skeptical reader could not claim that I had cited only one writer and that he or she could not speak for the others in his or her field. I wanted the reader to know that there were several authors who made the same point with their writings. In other words, I have endeavored to truly document my conclusions by exposing the reader to as many writers as possible. I believe that the reasons I have endeavored to do this will become clear as the reader progresses through this book.

Secondly, the authors that I have quoted were either those that I discovered had a part in the events described in this book, or were those who had convinced me that they had personally researched the original works of the authors they cited. In other words, I am attempting to prove my contentions from the writings of those who were either directly involved or have thoroughly documented their own research. The reader will soon discover that the writers I have cited are many of the principal writers in the area of this volume.

The reason that I have done this is simply because I believe that the information that I have uncovered is extremely important to the future of the world, and that it must be presented in a manner that is as believable as is possible. I want the reader to believe this information because it comes from the experts in their respective areas of expertise. I also believe that the reader will begin to understand why I have resorted to this strategy as they peruse my book.

And lastly, I would like the reader to understand that I have attempted to keep my comments and or opinions to a minimum in this book. I believe that the evidence that I will present stands on its own and should be adequate to convince even the most ardent skeptic. It will need little if any explanation from me.

In summary, then, I am hopeful that the reader will agree with me that I have succeeded in exposing a monumental truth that has escaped the overwhelming majority of the historians of the past.

ABOUT THE MATERIAL

I am convinced that the average reader will find it difficult to accept the conclusions in this book. However, that does not mean that the evidence is incorrect; it merely indicates that most people will consider those conclusions to be simply too incredible to be believed.

But, because of the implications for the future of not only the United States but of the world, if I am correct, it is imperative that this material be considered by as many as is possible. For this reason, I have attempted to keep the contents of this book as readable as I could.

I am hopeful that each reader will be as dutiful as the average jury member. Anyone who has served on a jury will remember being admonished by the judge to remain open as they consider the evidence to be presented throughout the trial. The juror is instructed to ignore any previous prejudices and to carefully weigh the evidence presented.

I can ask no more.

My goal is to have a positive impact on reversing the plans of those who are altering our future. Obviously, to accomplish that task, I must convince as many as I can that I am correct in my assertions.

I am therefore hopeful that each reader of this material will accept my challenge and remember the admonition of the judge: be honestly open and dutifully consider the evidence that will presented.

INTRODUCTION

Something is wrong in America!

Today's newspapers are full of stories about the rampant rise in divorce rates; the increasing abuse of children by some parents; increases in the incidence of rape; pornography being read by an increasing number of people; more crimes against property; demands for world government; urgings for national borders to fall; Christian churches being closed because they will not seek licensing by the state; etc.

But why are these things happening? Why are all of the legacies of the past, the family, national borders, the right to practice any chosen religion, the right to private property, amongst other things, under such attack? Is it possible that there are actually people and organizations who really want to change the basic order of things?

Clues to the answers to these questions can be gleaned from some comments made by people and organizations that are talking about these wide-reaching changes in the nature of our lifestyle.

An Associated Press dispatch on July 26, 1968 reported:

"New York Governor Nelson A. Rockefeller says as President he would work toward international creation of 'a new world order' ...." [1]

On January 30, 1976, a new document called The Declaration of Interdependence was introduced to the American people. It was signed by 32 Senators and 92 Representatives in Washington D.C. and read in part:

"Two centuries ago our forefathers brought forth a new nation; now we must join with others to bring forth a new world order." [2]

Another individual who has commented is Henry Kissinger, former Secretary of State. According to the Seattle Post-Intelligence of April 18, 1975, Mr. Kissinger said:

"Our nation is uniquely endowed to play a creative and decisive role in the new order which is taking form around us." [3]

President George Bush gave the commencement address at Texas A & M University on May 12, 1989, and he used similar words as well. His speech was on the subject of Soviet-American relations and he was quoted as saying, in part:

"Ultimately, our objective is to welcome the Soviet Union back into the world order.
Perhaps the world order of the future will truly be a family of nations." [4]

Historian Walter Mills maintained that prior to World War I, Colonel Edward Mandell House, the major advisor to Woodrow Wilson, the President at the time, had a hidden motive for involving America in the war. The historian wrote:

"The Colonel's sole justification for preparing such a batch of blood for his countrymen was his hope of establishing a new world order of peace and security." [5]

INTRODUCTION

Adolf Hitler, a Socialist, and the head of the German government prior to and during that nation's involvement in World War II, is quoted as saying:

"... National socialism will use its own revolution for the establishing of a new world order." [6]

He confided to Herman Rauschning, the President of the Danzig Senate:

"National Socialism is more than a religion; it is the will to create superman." [7]

Hitler added this thought:

"Well, yes! We are barbarians, and barbarians we wish to remain. It does us honor. It is we who will rejuvenate the world.
The present world is near its end. Our only task is to sack it." [8]

Another book on his background quoted his comments that his NAZI (National Socialist) Party had a hidden purpose, one that was not perceived by the world at large. Mr. Hitler was quoted as saying:

"He who has seen in National Socialism only a political movement has seen nothing." [9]

The Humanist religion issued a manifesto in 1933 stating its beliefs about the world in general. It took the following position about the need for the wealthy governments to share their wealth with the less fortunate nations:

"It is the moral obligation of the developed nations to provide -- through an international authority -- ... economic assistance ... to the developing portions of the globe." [10]

The April, 1974 issue of Foreign Affairs, the quarterly periodical issued by the Council on Foreign Relations in New York, had an article in it by Richard N. Gardner, the former Deputy Assistant Secretary of State for International Organizations in the Lyndon Johnson and John Kennedy administrations. He stated:

> "... we are likely to do better by building our
> 'house of world order' from bottom up rather than
> from the top down ....
> ... an end run around national sovereignty,
> eroding it piece by piece, is likely to get us to world
> order faster than the old-fashioned assault." [11]

Even the Communist Party is voicing similar thoughts. The People's Daily World for Thursday, March 9, 1989, contained an article written by Angela Davis. Those familiar with Miss Davis will remember that she was the Vice Presidential candidate for the Communist Party a few years ago. She currently is a member of the National Committee of the Communist Party of the United States. She is quoted in the paper as saying:

> "One underlying effect of anti-communism in this
> respect is to encourage a certain hesitancy to embrace
> solutions which call for deep, structural, socio-economic
> transformation." [12]

Another Communist, Alexei Kovylov, spoke at an evening meeting held at Windstar, Colorado in August, 1985, and gave the participants in attendance a surprise presentation.
He spoke about the 12th World Festival of Youth and Students held in Moscow a few months prior to his lecture. He said:

> "There were three programs. The first was political and dealt with the various issues of peace and
> disarmament.
> The second was dedicated to environmental [issues] and to the new international economic order." [13]

The alleged need for a change in the basic way things are done is consistent with the teachings of the "father of Communism," Karl Marx. When he co-authored the COMMUNIST MANIFESTO with Frederick Engels in 1848, Mr. Marx wrote that the Communists:

"...openly declare that their ends can be attained only by the forcible overthrow of all existing social conditions." [14]

Nesta Webster, a writer on the subject of conspiratorial organizations in the past, wrote this in her book entitled SECRET SOCIETIES:

"... the revolution desired by the leaders [of world revolution] is a moral and spiritual revolution, an anarchy of ideas by which all standards set up throughout nineteen centuries shall be reversed, all honoured traditions trampled under foot, and above all the Christian ideal finally obliterated." [15]

Some of the Catholic Popes in the past have commented on the major changes coming in the future. One such Pope was Pope Pius XI, who wrote the following in 1937:

"Communism has behind it occult forces which for a long time have been working for the overthrow of the Christian Social Order ...." [16]

One of the Popes who preceded him, Pope Pius IX, wrote this in November, 1846 about the changes that he saw in the future:

"That infamous doctrine of so-called communism ... is absolutely contrary to the natural law itself, and, if once adopted, would utterly destroy the rights, property and possessions of all men, and even society itself." [17]

Another individual who wrote about the future was Dr. Jose Arquelles, of an organization known as the Planet Art Network. Dr. Arguelles wrote:

"Also implicit in all these events is a call for another way of life, another way of doing things, ... a redistribution of global wealth ... in short, a New World Order." [18]

Just what the future society was that these people are talking about was described, in a brief manner, by Marilyn Ferguson in her book entitled THE AQUARIAN CONSPIRACY. She wrote:

"The new world is the old -- transformed." [19]

Another clue about what is in store for the future world was offered by Dr. James H. Billington, who received his doctorate as a Rhodes Scholar at Oxford University, and has taught at Harvard and Princeton Universities. He wrote this in his book entitled FIRE IN THE MINDS OF MEN:

"This book seeks to trace the origins of a faith --
perhaps THE faith of our time.
What is new is the belief that a perfect secular
[meaning worldly] order will emerge from the forcible
overthrow of traditional authority." [20]

That these future changes would involve force and slavery was confirmed by B. F. Skinner, chairman of the Psychology Department at Harvard University, in his book entitled BEYOND FREEDOM AND DIGNITY. Dr. Skinner has been called "... the most influential of living American psychologists" by Time magazine. So the world should listen to the professor when he speaks. The magazine told the reader what the message of Professor Skinner's book was:

"We can no longer afford freedom, and so it must
be replaced with control over man, his conduct and his
culture." [21]

Another student of these changes is Alvin Toffler, who wrote this in his book entitled THE THIRD WAVE:

"A new civilization is emerging in our lives ....
This new civilization brings with it new family styles;
changed ways of working, loving and living; a new
economy; new political conflicts; and beyond all this an
altered consciousness as well.
The dawn of this new civilization is the single
most explosive fact of our lifetimes." [22]

Another scientist involved in commenting upon the future changes was Dr. Carl Sagan. He has observed:

"It's clear that sometime relatively soon in terms of the lifetime of the human species people will identify with the entire planet and the species ...." [23]

The reason why these changes are necessary was explained by Manly P. Hall, perhaps the world's leading authority on esoteric words and language. He wrote in his book entitled LECTURES ON ANCIENT PHILOSOPHY:

"The time has not yet arrived when the average man is strong enough or wise enough to rule himself." [24]

And he explained who he considered worthy enough to rule those on the world considered by the experts to be incapable of governing themselves. He wrote:

"Never will peace reign upon the earth until we are ruled by the fit." [25]

Mr. Hall even indicated that these changes would occur soon. He wrote this comment in his book previously cited:

"One hundred years ago [meaning in 1884] it was predicted that within a few centuries men would revert to the gods of Plato and Aristotle ....
We may all look forward with eager anticipation to that nobler day when the gods of philosophy once more shall rule the world ...." [26]

Aldous Huxley, in his book called BRAVE NEW WORLD REVISITED, quotes a character called the Grand Inquisitor in one of Feodor Mikhailovich Dostoevski's parables as saying:

"In the end they [the people] will lay their freedom at our [the controller's] feet and say to us 'make us your slaves, but feed us.'" [27]

The Tucson Citizen newspaper of November 3, 1988 printed a photograph of a some people involved in a "march for literacy," and it clearly demonstrated that at least some people in America are now asking their government to make them their slaves. The picture showed a demonstrator carrying a picket sign that read:

"Uncle Sam, we want you to support us." [28]

Mr. Huxley gave us a date when we could expect these changes to occur. He wrote the following in his book written in 1958:

"... the twenty-first century ... will be the era of World Controllers ...." [29]

And then he told us why these "controllers" would not fail:

"The older dictators fell because they could never supply their subjects with enough bread, enough circuses enough miracles and mysteries.
Under a scientific dictatorship education will really work -- with the result that most men and women will grow up to love their servitude and will never dream of revolution.
There seems to be no good reason why a thoroughly scientific dictatorship should ever be overthrown." [30]

Someone who might have given the world the date for the commencement of these predicted changes was Zbigniew Brzezinski, President Jimmy Carter's National Security Advisor during his four year administration. He wrote the following in his book entitled BETWEEN TWO AGES:

"Either 1976 or 1989 -- the two hundredth anniversary of the Constitution -- could serve as a suitable target date for culminating a national dialogue on the relevance of existing arrangements, the workings of the representative process, and the desirability of imitating the various European regionalization reforms and of streamlining the administrative structure." [31]

So, the people of the world can now determine what those changes are that those in the positions of implementing changes have in store for them. In summary, then, these changes are:

The old world is coming to an end. It will be replaced with a new way of doing things.

The new world will be called the "New World Order."

This new structuring will re-distribute property from the "have" nations and will give it to the "have-not" nations.

The New World Order will include changes in:

the family:
homosexual marriages will be legalized; parents will not be allowed to raise their children (the state will;) all women will be employed by the state and not allowed to be "homemakers"; divorce will become exceedingly easy and monogynous marriage will be slowly phased out;

the workplace:
the government will become the owner of all of the factors of production; the private ownership of property will be outlawed;

religion:
religion will be outlawed and believers will be either eliminated or imprisoned; there will be a new religion: the worship of man and his mind; all will believe in the new religion;

The United States will play a major role in bringing it to the world.

World wars have been fought to further its aims.

Adolf Hitler, the NAZI Socialist, supported the goal of the planners.

The majority of the people will not readily accept "the new world order" but will be deceived into accepting it by two strategies:

1. Those in favor of the changes will have become seated in the very thrones of power, generally without the public realizing that fact;

2. The "old world order" will be destroyed piece by piece, by a series of planned "nibbles" at the established format.

The Communist Party is actively supporting the changes to the "new world order."

The basic tenets of Christianity, which were the base for the "old world order," will have to be eliminated.

If the slower, methodical techniques of change do not function, violence will be introduced and controlled by the planners.

The people of the world will give up their freedom to the "controllers" because there will be a planned famine, or some other serious occurrence, such as a depression or war.

The change to the "New World Order" is coming shortly, perhaps beginning after 1989. However, if that is not the year, it will be introduced one step at a time, so that the entire structure will be in place by the year 1999.

The
Great Seal
of the
United States

**Obverse
Side**

Reverse
Side

Chapter 1
Tomorrow's Rulers

Something is indeed wrong in America!

And many sense that changes in this nation's lifestyle are occurring.

The newspapers are saturated with articles reporting the activities of those advocating increased governmental spending for a variety of unconstitutional purposes; organizations supporting a globalism concept urge the world to adopt a one world government; psychologists preaching the destruction of the family unit and recommending that the society rear the nation's children; governments closing private schools; and nations forming regional governments under which national borders are scheduled to disappear.

Since these changes appear to be part of the new philosophy known as "the new world order," anyone desiring to know the future has to become familiar with this new phrase and what it portends for the world of tomorrow.

As an indication that major changes are coming in tomorrow's world, one of the current trends mentioned is the call for a "one-world government." One of those supporting this leap forward is Norman Cousins, President of the World Federalist Society. He is on record as saying:

> "World government is coming. In fact, it is inevitable. No arguments for it or against it can change that fact." [32]

The goal of a one world government is not a new thought. One of the earliest formal organizations that supported the concept of that goal was the Illuminati, founded on May 1st, 1776, by Adam Weishaupt, a teacher of Canon Law at the University of Ingolstadt in Bavaria, now part of Germany. Professor Weishaupt was quoted as saying:

> "It is necessary to establish a universal regime and empire over the whole world ...." [33]

A more modern organization that supports the coming changes is the Masonic Order called, simply, the Freemasons or the Masons. This world wide fraternity has members in America, as will be discussed, and they, too, support a call for a one world government. One who has written about this secret organization is Paul Fisher, and he says this about them in his book entitled BEHIND THE LODGE DOOR:

> "Masonry will eventually rule the world." [34]

Albert Pike, the Sovereign Grand Commander of the Scottish Rite of Freemasonry here in the United States from 1850 to 1891 wrote a book entitled MORALS AND DOGMA. Mr. Pike has been praised by his fellow Masons as a member almost without parallel in the history of the Masonic Order. Carl Claudy, himself a Masonic writer of great esteem, wrote this about him:

> "Albert Pike: one of the greatest geniuses Freemasonry has ever known. He was a mystic, a symbolist, a teacher of the hidden truths of Freemasonry." [35]

So, the outsider can know that whenever Mr. Pike speaks, he speaks with authority and knowledge. He is perhaps the greatest Masonic writer of all time. His book is given to each Scottish Rite Southern Jurisdiction Freemason who is asked to read it. (There seems to be a difference of opinion as to whether or not this book is still required reading for each Scottish Rite Mason. This writer was told that it was given to each Scottish Rite Mason in Tucson. Other Masons say that that is not true.) In it, he informs the new Mason about the moral teachings of the Masonic Lodge. He instructs the Masonic reader that the Order will eventually be asked to rule the entire globe. He wrote:

"... the World will soon come to us for its Sovereigns [apparently referring to its governmental leaders] and Pontiffs [apparently meaning its religious leaders.]
We shall constitute the equilibrium of the universe, and be rulers over the Masters of the World." [36]

He wrote this supportive statement in a book entitled LEGENDA:

"And thus the warfare against the powers of evil that crushed the Order of the Temple goes steadily on, and Freedom marches ever onward toward the conquest of the world." [37]

The Order of the Temple Mr. Pike was writing about was the Knights Templar, which was, according to him,

"devoted to the cause of opposition to the tiara [the Pope's triple crown] and the crowns of Kings ...." [38]

Mr. Pike said that the Catholic Church was a "power of evil ..." because it had "crushed" the Templars, even though he admitted that they were "devoted" to opposition to the Church and its leader, the Pope.
But the major point of that quote is that these forces of opposition, presumably meaning the Masons, are marching "onward toward the conquest of the world."

Mr. Pike repeated his devotion to the conquest of the world, with this comment at the end of his book entitled MORALS AND DOGMA:

"Such, my Brother, is the TRUE WORD of a Master Mason; such the true ROYAL SECRET, which makes possible, and shall at length make real, the HOLY EMPIRE of true Masonic Brotherhood." [39]

But, the major worldwide movement that champions a one world government, under a religious leader, is a new phenomena occurring worldwide called The New Age Movement. Texe Marrs, a researcher into this new religion, has written two books on the subject. Both of these books are excellent primers for those who wish to know more about the beliefs of this religion. The two books are entitled DARK SECRETS OF THE NEW AGE, and MYSTERY MARK OF THE NEW AGE. He has written:

"The New Age Movement has undeniably taken on the definite form of a religion, complete with an agreed-upon body of doctrine, printed scripture, a pattern of worship and ritual, a functioning group of ministers and lay leaders." [40]

Another writer who has written two books on the New Age religion is Constance Cumbey. Her two books are called THE HIDDEN DANGERS OF THE RAINBOW, and A PLANNED DECEPTION. She has written this:

"The New Age Movement is a religion complete with its own Bibles, prayers and mantras, Vatican City/Jerusalem equivalents, priests and gurus, born-again experiences (they call it 'rebirthing,') spiritual laws and commandments, psychics and prophets and nearly every other indicia of a religion." [41]

The new religion has a series of leaders. One is a woman named Alice Bailey, a prolific writer on the subject of the New Age. She was the founder of an organization called the Arcane School, one of the major Lucis Trust divisions. The Lucis Trust was a major publisher of books supporting the religion. In her book entitled THE EXTERNALIZATION OF

THE HIERARCHY, she told her readers who the organizations were that were going to bring the New Age religion to the world. She identified them as being:

> "The three main channels through which the preparation for the New Age is going on might be regarded as the Church, the Masonic Fraternity and the educational field." [42]

(The main thrust of this book will to be to examine only one of the three organizations mentioned by this author, that being the Masonic Fraternity. There are numerous works by other writers exposing the involvement of the Church and the educational field in the New Age Movement, so this writer will not attempt to duplicate those efforts. However, only a few are aware of the involvement of the Masons, and that is why I have chosen to concentrate on that organization.)

Another major writer on the New Age Movement is Benjamin Creme, and he admitted in his book entitled THE REAPPEARANCE OF THE CHRIST AND THE MASTORS OF WISDOM that:

> "The new religion will manifest, for instance, through organizations like Masonry. In Freemasonry is imbedded the core of the secret of the occult Mysteries." [43]

So Masonry conceals a great mystery inside its temples, one that is connected somehow to the New Age Movement.

The Masons admit in some of their writings that they too are anticipating a new age, a series of major changes. Henry Clausen, the past Sovereign Grand Commander (the equivalent of their President) of the Scottish Rite of Freemasonry, has been quoted as saying:

> "We look towards a transforming into a New Age using, however, the insight and wisdom of the ancient mystics." [44]

The Masons claim that the things that they believe in are as old as the ancient civilizations. They also claim that these "mystics," the ancient philosophers, had the wisdom of all ages, and that somehow this knowledge has become lost through the centuries. Humanity today does not possess this knowledge, but it has become the task of the Masons, and other "truth" seekers, to rediscover these principles for the benefit of all of mankind. Those possessing this knowledge will correct the world's current problems. Some of the Masons also claim to have identified the cause of these problems.

One of the most prolific writers on the subject of this "lost" truth is Manly P. Hall, a 33rd degree Mason.

(For those unfamiliar with the Masonic degrees, all Masons in America start through what is called the Blue Lodge, consisting of three degrees. The initiate into this lodge goes through three separate and different initiation ceremonies, one for each degree. After completing these ceremonies, he may stay where he is, or choose to affiliate himself with either the York Rite or the Scottish Rite. The latter is divided into two separate jurisdictions, the Southern and the Northern. These are based primarily on state borders, and whether one joins one or the other depends on where the initiate lives. The two Scottish rites have an additional 29 degrees, making for a total of 32. There is one more degree, called the 33rd degree, which is honorary, and only a few are invited into that degree.

The York Rite has a total of nine degrees. However, since little has been revealed about this order, the author will concentrate on only the Scottish Rite, and in particular, the Southern Jurisdiction.)

Mr. Hall has written a book entitled LECTURES ON ANCIENT PHILOSOPHY in which he talks a great deal about the Masonic fraternity. This is his comment about the coming changes:

> "A new day is dawning for Freemasonry. From the insufficiency of theology and the hopelessness of materialism, men are turning to seek the God of philosophy." [45]

Notice that Mr. Hall has said that current "theology," obviously current "religion," has proven insufficient. Also, he feels that "materialism," meaning the right to private property, is also a failure. But more importantly, he points out that this new "God" of the Freemasons is somehow different from the God of the Jews and Christians. As will be illustrated later, some of the Masons believe that the God of the Bible is a God of evil.

Helena Petrovna Blavatsky, perhaps the founder of the current New Age movement, has also determined that the Masons are somehow supportive of her religious views. She wrote this in her book entitled THE SECRET DOCTRINE:

> "... at the end of the eighteenth and the beginning of the nineteenth centuries many Freemasons travelled to Tibet where they were initiated into the esoteric [defined as intended for or understood by only a chosen few, as an inner group of disciples or initiates] order of the Masters of wisdom." [46]

It should be expected that she would support the Masonic fraternity. In 1875, she founded an organization called the Theosophical Society, basically dedicated to teaching the world about her new secret religion. One of the earliest members of that organization was Albert Pike, later to become the Sovereign Grand Commander of the Scottish Rite of Freemasonry. [47]

Albert Pike, who later became a 33rd degree Mason, the highest degree attainable, also saw that there were some significant changes coming, and that he was supportive of those changes. He wrote the following in his book entitled MORALS AND DOGMA:

> "... we can look on all the evils of the world, and see that it is only the hour before sunrise, and that the light is coming." [48]

If Mr. Hall is right, the "evils" that his fellow Mason Albert Pike saw are connected to current religion, and that which is coming is somehow different from those religious views.

Mr. Hall, who as mentioned previously is another 33rd degree Mason, also wrote that a new day was coming, and that it was not too far into the future:

> "A new light is breaking in the east; [the significance of the location, "the east," will be pointed out later] a more glorious day is at hand. The rule of the

philosophic elect -- the dream of the ages -- will yet be realized and is not too far distant." [49]

So, Mr. Hall is also expecting that these changes are about to occur in the not too distant future.

Someone who attempted to zero in on when these changes were expected to occur was Alice Bailey, previously mentioned. She wrote about when she thought the New Age would arrive:

"Eventually, there will appear the Church Universal, and its definite outlines will appear towards the close of this century." [50]

Since she wrote early in the 20th century, we can see that she was predicting the eventual arrival of the New Age, sometime around the 1990's. This estimate of that date is not too far wrong, as will be demonstrated later in this book.

Whatever is coming in the future, some New Agers have told us that they expect that it will last for a long time. One such writer is Ruth Montgomery, who wrote that she saw that the new religion would rule the earth for a thousand years. She wrote the following in her book entitled HERALD FOR THE NEW AGE:

"The New Age, the millennium [a millennium is a period of one thousand years], will see an end to that strife, at least for a thousand years." [51]

Just what is the New Age religion that will last for at least one thousand years on the earth?

One who attempted to answer that question was Constance Cumbey in her book entitled THE HIDDEN DANGERS OF THE RAINBOW. She wrote that these were the basic tenets of the new religion:

1. "The Plan" for the future includes the installation of a New World "Messiah," the implementation of a new world government and new world religion under Maitreya (an individual who will be examined later in this book).

2. A universal credit card system will be implemented.
3. A world food authority will control all of the world's food supply.
4. A universal tax.
5. A universal draft.
6. They intend on utterly rooting out people who believe the Bible and worship God and to completely stamp out Christianity. [52]

As was discussed prior to this summary, certain people have indicated that they see the Catholic Church as an enemy. Here Mrs. Cumbey says that they see not only Catholicism as the enemy, they also see all of Christianity as an enemy.

Whatever the New Agers believe in, it appears to be growing in popularity. Bantam Books, one of this nation's leading publishing houses, has reported that the sales of their New Age titles has increased tenfold in the past decade. Time magazine reports that the number of New Age bookstores has doubled in the past five years, to a total of about 2,500. [53]

According to an article in Forbes magazine,

"publishers estimate that total sales of New Age titles today are at least $100 million at retail." [54]

So, whatever they believe in, many believe in it.

But perhaps the most insightful comment about the nature of what the New Age religion believed in, and who they worshipped as their god, was written by Mrs. Cumbey in her book entitled THE HIDDEN DANGERS OF THE RAINBOW. She wrote that they had:

"... the intent of bringing about a New World Order -- an order that writes God out of the picture and deifies Lucifer." [55]

So, if Mrs. Cumbey and the other writers on the subject are right, the New Age Movement needs to be studied in some depth.

Chapter 2
The New Age Movement

The New Age Religion appears to be the exact opposite of the Old Age Religion, meaning the religion of the Jews and the Christians. These are the two religions that set the United States on its course because these religions taught that mankind had some basic human rights. They held that the family was the basic unit in all of the world; they believed in the right to private property; they believed in the inalienable (defined as being incapable of being surrendered) right to life; they held that each person had the right to worship their god; and they held that all had the right to freedom of association. As shall be documented in this study, these positions, which were deemed to be "self-evident" by those who wrote the American Declaration of Independence and the Constitution, became the cornerstones of the American civilization. (The term "self-evident" means that these human rights were not worthy of debate because they stood on their own simply because they were true. They couldn't be debated.)

Yet, today, these cornerstones of American life are no longer "self-evident." They are being publicly discussed: people and organizations are now debating whether an individual has the basic human rights to life, liberty and property. Friedrich Wilhelm Nietzsche, a German philosopher, and one of the teachers of many of the world's leading communist revolutionaries, put the argument quite succinctly, in this statement:

"I condemn Christianity. I raise against the Christian Church the most terrible of all accusations that any accuser uttered. It is to me the highest conceivable corruption." [56]

Texe Marrs, an author who has written in opposition to the New Age, wrote this about their hatred of the Christians:

"The New Age believer is told, 'You could be a god in the next instant if only those horrible Christians weren't around with their poisonous attitudes." [57]

That thought was illustrated by another of the important New Agers, David Spangler, who wrote this in his book entitled REFLECTIONS ON THE CHRIST:

"We can take all the scriptures and all the teachings and all the tablets and all the laws, and all the marshmallows and have a jolly good bonfire and marshmallow roast, because that is all they are worth." [58]

So the New Age, like the Masons, feel that Christianity is the enemy, a force to be countered, not by open debate, but by contempt and ridicule, and as shall be illustrated later, by even murder.

Other parties wish to join the debate. In 1911, the Socialist Party of Great Britain published a pamphlet entitled SOCIALISM AND RELIGION, in which they placed their position about religion into the arena:

"It is therefore a profound truth that Socialism is the natural enemy of religion. A Christian Socialist is in fact an anti-Socialist. Christianity ... is the antithesis of Socialism." [59]

So the Socialist, the New Ager, and the Mason have declared war on the Christians. And, as in every war, the enemy must be defeated, even by bloodshed if necessary. This war is no different. Bloodshed is anticipated by all parties in the battle.

LaVedi Lafferty and Bud Hollowell, two New Agers, started the discussion about how their religion sanctions the use of violence against the Christian community. They wrote the following in their book entitled THE ETERNAL DANCE:

"This is a time of opportunity for those who will take it [apparently the New Agers.] For others, [apparently the Christians] if the earth is unsuitable for them, [if they will not accept the New Age religion] they will go on to other worlds." [60]

Another New Age spokesman, Maharishi Mahesh Yogi, the "guru" sought out by the rock 'n roll group known as the Beatles, has been quoted as saying:

"There has not been and there will not be a place for the unfit [apparently the Christians.] The fit will lead, and if the unfit are not coming along, [if they will not accept the New Age religion] there is no place for them.

In the Age of Enlightenment there is no place for ignorant people. Nonexistence of the unfit has been the law of nature." [61]

Another example of New Age thinking on this vital issue came from a pamphlet available in a bookstore selling New Age material. It was published by something called the Guardian Action Publications of New Mexico, and it was entitled Cosmic Countdown. It alleged that it had received these thoughts from something called "Higher Intelligence," and it directed its attention to the hunger/disease problem in the third world. The pamphlet stated:

"The world should be forewarned to be on the lookout for diseases which have been suppressed for

years, suddenly rearing their ugly heads and deci-
mating populations already on the verge of starvation in the Third World Nations.

Although these peoples will eventually be replaced
by the new root race about to make its appearance
in a newly cleansed world; nevertheless, for the moment, this is a tragedy." [62]

The words reveal an incredible scenario: those people in
the Third World nations are going to be entirely replaced by
a "new root race." That eventuality will not be a tragedy; the
tragedy is that these people are dying now due to starvation
and disease.

The concept that a new race of people will inhabit the
world in the New Age millennium has been expressed by
other believers in the religion. Ruth Montgomery, previously
mentioned, has written about that change:

"Those who survive the shift will be a different
type of people from those in physical form today,
freed from strife and hatred, longing to be of service
to the whole of mankind.

... the souls who helped to bring on the chaos of
the present century [apparently the Christians and
the Jews] will have passed into spirit to rethink
their attitudes." [63]

To show that the New Agers are talking about the
physical death of the "enemy," one must only search the
writings of other New Agers. Another believer to write on the
subject of the destruction of those who will not accept the
new religion was Ruth Montgomery. She has been quoted as
saying in a transcribed interview carried by a magazine
called Magical Blend:

"Millions will survive and millions won't. Those
who won't will go into the spirit state, because there
is truly no death." [64]

Estimates of the number to perish have been made by
some New Agers. One who has made such an estimate is
John Randolph Price, who was quoted by Texe Marrs in his
book about the New Age. He said that:

"John Randolph Price was told by his spirit guide
that up to two and one-half billion might perish in
the coming chaos." [65]

That estimate is about half of the current world population.

Another estimate of the number required to die because
they will not accept the new religion was offered by the so-
called "Tibetan master," Djwhal Khul, who has said in one of
his channelling experiences, that one third of all humanity
must die by the year 2000. [66] That would be about 2 billion
people.

Channelling is one of the strange activities occurring
inside the New Age religion. Some of the believers claim that
they have the ability to call forth the deceased spirit of
someone who lived many years before. Quite often these
spirits claim to be "ascended masters," those who have gone
on to discover the eternal truths of all of creation. One such
believer who claimed to be in touch with a "master" was Alice
Bailey, previously mentioned. Her spirit called himself Djwhal
Khul, and she claimed he spoke through her, saying:

"Death is not a disaster to be feared; the work of
the Destroyer is not really cruel or undesirable ....
Therefore there is much destruction permitted by the
custodians of the Plan and much evil turned into
good." [67]

Just what "The Plan" constituted was told to the world
by Benjamin Creme, another New Age leader. He placed an
advertisement in about 20 newspapers all over the world on
April 25, 1982, that defined the term. The ad read, in part:

"What is The Plan? It includes the installation of
a new world government and new world religion
under Maitreya." [68]

But perhaps the most startling example of the teachings
of this new religion came from the pen of Barbara Marx
Hubbard, one of their most articulate writers. She wrote in
her book entitled HAPPY BIRTHDAY PLANET EARTH:

"The choice is: do you wish to become a natural Christ, a universal human, or do you wish to die?" [69]
"People will either change or die. That is the choice." [70]

So the people of the world will be given a choice: they will choose to accept the new religion, or they will choose to die!

The battle lines are drawn!

Choices will have to be made.

Some of the leading Socialists of the past have shown that they too have chosen up sides. One such individual was Adolf Hitler, the head of the German government during World War II, who held no conviction that the murder of over 50 million people during that war was wrong. He considered himself to be an agent of this unseen god in reducing the population of people that he held to be undesirable. He wrote:

"I have the right to exterminate millions of individuals of inferior races, which multiply like vermin." [71]

And he did what he considered acceptable inside his religion. Those who did not believe in his new religion had no choice, and they perished. (The evidence that Adolf Hitler was a New Ager will be presented later in another chapter.)

Another of the leading spokesmen for the Socialist position was George Bernard Shaw, a well-known writer during his day. He wrote a book entitled THE INTELLIGENT WOMAN'S GUIDE TO SOCIALISM, in which he stated:

"I also made it quite clear that Socialism means equality of income or nothing, and under Socialism you would not be allowed to be poor.
You would be forcibly fed, clothed, lodged, taught and employed whether you like it or not. If it were discovered that you had not the character and industry enough to be worth all this trouble, you might be executed in a kindly manner, but whilst you were permitted to live, you would have to live well." [72]

The Masonic writer, Albert Pike, placed the Masonic order into the discussion, when he wrote this in his book MORALS AND DOGMA:

"It is not true to say that 'one man, however little, must not be sacrificed to another, however great, to a majority or to all men.'

That is not only a fallacy, but a most dangerous one.

Often one man and many men must be sacrificed, in the ordinary sense of the term, to the interest of the many.

... the interest and even the life of one man must often be sacrificed to the interest and welfare of his country." [73]

The religious view is that the "sacrifice" of one life for the interest of the "many" is murder, and those who believe in the God of the Bible are told not to commit this act. The commandment against this practice is contained in Exodus 20:13 of the Old Testament, and in Matthew 5:21 in the New, and is simply expressed in the words: "Thou shalt not kill." The principle is easy to understand: no person has the right to take the life of another. This understanding is nearly worldwide (there are, of course, cultures that have determined that human sacrifice, cannibalism and murder are acceptable forms of behavior, but these are rare in the history of man.) But, here we are being exposed to a whole new religious view, one growing daily in size and stature, that openly advocates the wholesale slaughter of entire races of people.

Adam Weishaupt, the founder of the Illuminati, has also endorsed this new conviction that murder was not improper by including it in the initiation ceremony into the Order. He has his initiator tell the initiate:

"Behold our secret .... If in order to destroy all Christianity, all religion, we have pretended to have the sole true religion, remember that the end justifies the means, and that the wise ought to take all the means to do good which the wicked take to do evil." [74]

The initiate was told that he may use whatever means, murder included, to achieve the goals of the association that he was joining. And that the major goal of the Illuminati was the destruction of all religion, including Christianity. That meant that if Christians physically stood in the way, they could be removed by simply murdering them.

Weishaupt even went so far as to say that anyone not willing to take the life of another was unfit to join the Illuminati. He wrote the following in a letter to a fellow member in 1778:

"No man is fit for our Order who is not ... ready to go to every length ...." [75]

Weishaupt wrote that again, this time using different words:

"This can be done in no other way but by secret associations, which will by degrees, and in silence, possess themselves of the government of the States, and make use of those means for this purpose which the wicked use for attaining base ends." [76]

Weishaupt was aware of the enormous power of government and he desired its power for his members. He committed his organization to its infiltration. Then, he committed it to unspeakable purposes: anything that would further the goal of the Illuminati.

He even went on to grant permission to his members to distort the truth by lying if it would further their goals. He wrote:

"There must not a single purpose ever come in sight ... that may betray our aims against religion and the state.
One must speak sometimes one way and sometimes another, but so as never to contradict ourselves, and so that, with respect to our true way of thinking, we may be impenetrable." [77]

Perhaps a perfect example of an oath that these initiates take somewhere along the road to the pinnacle inside the secret society was given in a book written by George Orwell entitled 1984. Mr. Orwell has an initiate into a secret society called The Brotherhood in his story asked these questions:

> "Are you prepared to give your life?
> Are you prepared to commit murder?
> Are you prepared to commit acts of sabotage which may cause the death of hundreds of innocent people?
> Are you prepared to betray your country to foreign powers?
> Are you prepared to cheat, to forge, to blackmail, to corrupt the minds of children, to distribute habit-forming drugs, to encourage prostitution, to disseminate venereal diseases -- to do anything which is likely to cause demoralization and weaken the power of the [people?]
> Are you prepared to commit suicide, if and when we order you to do so?" [78]

This is an example of the philosophy that "the ends justify the means." The initiate should do as he was required, as long as the act benefited the Brotherhood. There is no morality under such an oath.

So murder of the unfit, those unwilling to adopt the new religion, will be acceptable. And those who do the annihilating are to feel no remorse. In the view of the New Age religion, the murderers have served mankind well.

But, this callous disregard for the right to life of every human on the face of the earth has been predicted before. In the New Testament, John was moved to write in John 6:12:

> "Yea, the time cometh, that whosoever killeth you will think that he doeth God service."

The New World Order will sail in on a sea of blood.

Chapter 3
Lord Maitreya

The New Age religion will have a worldwide leader, an individual that they call Lord Maitreya. This individual has not made his public appearance yet, but the New Agers claim that he is on the earth at the present time. They claim that he came to live with the Asian community in East London, England, in July, 1977, by "descending" from his ancient retreat in the Himalaya Mountains along the border of India and Tibet. They further believe that "his imminent emergence into full public view is assured."

They also claim that this individual is the one that the Christians call Christ, the Jews call the Messiah, the Buddhists call the Fifth Buddha, the Hindus call Krishna, and the Muslims call the Imam Mahdi. In other words, all of the major religions of the world are awaiting the arrival of this one individual. It is their claim that this one individual living now in London is the one expected by all of these religions. And he is on the earth now, patiently waiting for the appointed time to reveal his existence to the peoples of the world. He will apparently assume the leadership of all of these religions, and when he does, he will create a one-world religion.

The New Agers have written that in the esoteric tradition (previously defined as being intended for or understood by only a chosen few as an inner group of disciples or initiates) the word "Christ" is not the name of an individual, but the name of an office, or function, within the Spiritual Hierarchy of Masters. The masters are a group of perfected men who have guided human evolution from behind the scenes for centuries. And they believe that this Lord Maitreya is that Christ.

Manly P. Hall has written of this individual, by identifying him as:

"... the way, the truth, and the life which, coming to every life, redeems all who accept it." [79]

Texe Marrs has quoted this individual as saying:

"My Army is ready for battle, My masters of Wisdom and Myself at the head. That battle will be fought for the continuance of man on this earth. Rest assured that my Army shall triumph." [80]

It appears that the battle to be fought between the followers of Lord Maitreya and the rest of humanity is still in the future. But at least one of the participants has an army already prepared.

One who claims to have seen the birth in a "vision" of someone who seems to fulfill the requirements of this Maitreya was astrologer Jeanne Dixon. Her major claim to being a "prophet" is her prediction, reportedly made before the event, of the assassination of President John Kennedy in 1963. However, her credentials were dealt a serious blow in 1968 when she also "prophesied" that the Soviet Union would be the first to put a man on the moon. Another of her "prophecies" was that the Republican Party would be victorious in 1968 (and it was with the election of Richard Nixon, a Republican,) but she also predicted that "within the following decade (1970-1979) the two-party system as we have known it will vanish from the American scene. [81]

She further predicted that Richard M. Nixon had "excellent vibrations for the good of America" and would "serve [the] country well." [82]

Those who question her inability to correctly predict that America, not the Soviet Union, would become the first to place a man on the moon; and that the two-party system has not vanished from the scene; and that President Nixon apparently did not have "good vibrations" for this nation and would later be removed from office by the event commonly referred to as "Watergate," can only presume that she must have been given "inside" information about the assassination of the President Kennedy. And that would account for her knowing, at least in that event, the true future.

Secondly, one can only wonder why this "non-prophet" should be listened to about anything after her appalling record on "prophecies," but there is reason to believe that she might have been asked to write an account of this "vision" of an important birth by the New Age religion because they wanted the official imprimatur of someone commonly referred to as a "prophet." In other words, her "prophecy" might have been written to legitimize his claim to be a man-god so that when this individual made his public appearance himself, the public would marvel at the fact that his birth had fulfilled a "prophecy."

But, in any event, Ruth Montgomery wrote a book about her, entitled THE GIFT OF PROPHECY, in which she wrote about the very revealing and intriguing vision that Jeanne Dixon allegedly had:

"The vision which [Jeanne] considers the most significant and soul-stirring of her life occurred on February 5, 1962.
She saw the brightest sun she had ever seen. [The reader is asked to remember this reference to "the sun."]
Stepping out of the brightness were a Pharaoh and Queen Nefertiti. [Remember here that these two individuals were Egyptians. This will become significant later on in this study.] The couple ... thrust forth [a] baby, as if offering it to the entire world." [83]

Jeanne looked at the baby and then said, according to the author:

"I knew 'Here is the beginning of wisdom.'" [84]

So what Ruth Montgomery wrote can be summarized as follows:
A sun deity gives the world a child, from Egypt, who possesses enormous "wisdom." And this event allegedly took place on February 5, 1962. The interpretation of these symbols will be discussed later and their alleged significance will be developed.
Jeanne then says:

"A child, born somewhere in the Middle East shortly after 7 a.m. (E.S.T.) on February 5, 1962, will revolutionize the world. Before the close of the century he will bring together all mankind in one all-embracing faith.

Mankind will begin to feel the great force of this man in the early 1980's, and during the subsequent ten years the world as we know it will be reshaped into one without wars and suffering. His power will grow greatly until 1999 |this year is extremely significant as will also be developed| at which time the peoples of this earth will probably discover the full meaning of the vision." [85]

So, according to this "vision," a child, born on February 5, 1962, will grow up to bring a one-world religion onto the face of the earth, and his efforts will be successful in 1999.
The New York Times newspaper ran three consecutive articles on the conjunction of five planets, the sun, the moon and an "invisible body that astrologers call Khetu," starting on February 4, 1962. The first article stated that the various bodies moved into "rough alignment in the constellation Capricorn at 7:05 A.M., New York time," and that they would "remain in that alignment until 7:17 A.M., New York time, Monday." [86]
However, the article went on to say that most of the people in India became alarmed, because most astrologers were making "predictions of disasters." There were a few astrologers who were predicting good for the world as a result of this alignment, but "few Indians appear[ed] to be paying them much heed."

Astronomers did not consider the event to be rare, however, and the article went on to report that "the same configuration [had] occurred several times in the past," the last time being in April, 1821, and then it occurred twice. The article reported that Dr. Kenneth L. Franklin of the Museum of Natural History-Hayden Planetarium in New York had commented that that year does not seem to be a year of any remembered disasters. He was then quoted as saying: "And that year isn't famous for anything, as far as I know." [87]

Dr. Franklin also commented on the body the astrologers call Khetu. He "speculated that it may be some sort of astrological addition used to make everything come out right." He then added that he believed Khetu "to be the invisible planet that is frequently taken into account in astrological reckonings, but that he had no idea how it was possible to keep track of something that no one could see."

The Times carried another article the next day, Monday, February 5, 1962, and it repeated the concern of the Hindu astrologers. In fact, that headline read "Hindu Astrologers Still Say It's Doomsday." And the sub-headline read "Peaceful Beginning of Planetary Event Is Viewed Gravely."

The third article in the series ran on Tuesday, February 6, 1962, and carried the headline "'Doomsday' in India Uneventful." The article reported that the Indian astrologers had "predicted a variety of disasters, earthquakes, tidal waves, devastating fires, and warfare, to name a few," but that none of these events had occurred. Furthermore, the article reported that Hindu priests had claimed that the reason nothing had happened was because their prayers to their god had been answered.

But, none of these three articles mentioned the birth of anyone on these three days. Furthermore, none but a few astrologers had believed that something good was going to happen, and that only a few in India had listened to them.

Only Jeanne Dixon, another "astrologer," had seen a vision of something beneficial, in this case the birth of a baby "full of wisdom," at about the midpoint of the three day affair.

One can only wonder if, once again, she missed the mark, and was involved in another error.

In any event, these people claim that the Lord Maitreya will appear shortly to the entire world and start everyone off on a road to a world religion. Helena Petrovna Blavatsky in her book entitled THE SECRET DOCTRINE, called him "the dragon of wisdom." So it appears that the one call that Jeanne Dixon made that appears to match other comments is her statement that the baby she saw in her "vision" was "full of wisdom." If the baby she claimed to have seen in her vision was "Lord Maitreya," then she was right, because others have claimed that Lord Maitreya is "full of wisdom."

However, there is still reason to believe that she was given "inside" information by some New Agers who wanted to have this "Lord's" birth "prophesied' so that when he did surface, the New Agers could claim that his birth had been "a fulfilled prophecy."

So the world awaits the visible appearance of Lord Maitreya.

Chapter 4
The Ancient Mysteries

"The One Who Knows The Secret Does Not Speak.
The One Who Speaks Does Not Know The Secret."

Alice Bailey, one of the key members of the New Age religion, wrote:

> "There is no question therefore that the work to be done in familiarizing the general public with the nature of the Mysteries is of paramount importance at this time. These Mysteries will be restored to outer expression through the medium of the Church and the Masonic Fraternity." [88]

The question of just what the Ancient Mysteries were was answered, in part, by Albert G. Mackey, another 33rd degree Mason, in his two volume work entitled ENCYCLOPAEDIA OF FREEMASONRY. He wrote this under the subject of the Ancient Mysteries:

"Each of the pagan gods ... had, besides the public and open, a secret worship paid to him to which none were admitted but those who had been selected by preparatory ceremonies called Initiation.
This secret worship was termed the Mysteries." [89]

The student of the Masonic Order can know that when Mr. Mackey writes, his writings can be relied upon. He is considered to be one of the premier Masonic authors of all time. These are the comments from the biographical information presented on Mr. Mackey in the front of his ENCYCLOPAEDIA:

"... his writings are universally esteemed for their sincerity, honest records and common sense. [He was] a leader in research ... who valued accuracy." [90]

Carl Claudy, another Mason who writes on the subject of the Lodge, also has words of praise for Mr. Mackey:

"[He was] one of the greatest students and most widely followed authorities the Masonic world has ever known." [91]

And in his book entitled INTRODUCTION TO FREEMA-SONRY, he praised Mr. Mackey with these words:

"Albert Gallatin Mackey: one of the greatest students and most widely followed authorities the Masonic world has known. [He is] the great Master of Freemasonry." [92]

So Mr. Mackey can be believed when he tells his readers that the worship of pagan gods had a secret, non-visible worship besides the public one. The reader can believe him when he identifies the name of this secret worship. He told his readers:

"This secret worship was termed the Mysteries."

Another who has written about the subject of the Ancient Mysteries was Manly P. Hall, another 33rd degree Mason. He has written in his book entitled WHAT THE ANCIENT WISDOM EXPECTS OF ITS DISCIPLES:

"In the remote past the gods walked with men and ... they chose from among the sons of men the wisest and the truest.
With these specially ordained and illumined sons they left the keys of their great wisdom, which was the knowledge of good and evil. [This will be examined later.]
... these illumined ones, founded what we know as the Ancient Mysteries." [93]

He wrote additional comments about these mysteries in another of the books he has written, called THE SECRET TEACHINGS OF ALL AGES:

"The arcana [defined as being a secret or hidden knowledge] of the Ancient Mysteries were never revealed to the profane [defined as those not initiated into the inner mysteries] except through the media of symbols. Symbolism fulfilled the dual office of concealing the sacred truths from the uninitiated and revealing to those qualified to understand the symbols."[94]

Mr. Hall dedicated the latter book to:

"the proposition that concealed within the emblematic figures, allegories and rituals of the ancients is a secret doctrine concerning the inner mysteries of life, which doctrine has been preserved in toto [in the whole] among a small band of initiated minds since the beginning of the world." [95]

He went on to mention that the Mysteries:

"were secret societies, binding their initiates to inviolable secrecy, and avenging with death the betrayal of their sacred trusts." [96]

Mr. Hall told the reader that no one is to know the identity of those who have received the secrets. He wrote:

"The true Adept and Initiate shall reveal his identity to no man, unless that one is worthy to receive it." [97]

He further explained where some of these initiates lived, when he wrote:

"... no reasonable doubt can exist that the initiates of Greece, Egypt, and other ancient countries possessed the correct solutions to those great cultural, intellectual, moral, and social problems which in an unsolved state confront the humanity of the twentieth century." [98]

He further amplified that thought when he added:

"Neo-Platonism [defined by Mr. Hall as a school founded by Plotinus around 240 A.D., concerning itself with the problems of metaphysics, the study of knowledge] recognized the existence of a secret and all-important doctrine which from the time of the earliest civilizations had been concealed within the rituals, symbols and allegories of religions and philosophies." [99]

So, in summary, it is possible to understand what these Ancient Mysteries were. There appear to be at least four truths gleaned from the information provided in the comments made above. Those truths appear to be:

1. The Ancient Mysteries had two forms of worshipping the same god.
2. The knowledge of the true god was reserved for those who had been entrusted with the secrets.
3. Those who understood those secrets were sworn to the strictest secrecy.
4. Those who had knowledge of the secrets claimed to possess all of the answers to all of the problems of mankind.

There was an additional secret for the secret bearers: they had to be initiated in a private initiation ceremony. Albert Pike wrote a little about it:

"Initiation was considered to be a mystical death; and the perfect Epopt was then said to be regenerated, newborn, restored to a renovated existence of life, light and purity." [100]

In fact, this "new born" experience is similar to the experience the "born again" Christians go through. The Christians call their experience a second birth, just as the Masons do. In fact, Albert Pike calls a similar ceremony a "born again" experience. He wrote:

"In the Indian Mysteries, the Third degree, the Initiate is said to be 'born again.'" [101]

The ceremony in the ancient mysteries has been described by the Masonic writer Manly P. Hall:

"In the ancient system of initiation, the truth seeker must pass through a second birth, and those who attained this exalted state were known thereafter as 'the twice born.'
This new birth ... must be personally earned through a complete regeneration of character and conduct." [102]

This "new birth" ceremony involves a symbolic death, according to the Mason Kenneth Mackenzie. He wrote:

"In the ancient mysteries, the aspirant could not participate in the highest secrets until he had been placed in the Coffin.
In this he was symbolically said to die, and his resurrection was to the light." [103]

Modern day Masons participate in an almost similar ceremony to the one described by these Masonic writers. In the Third Degree, called the Master Mason degree, inside the Blue Lodge, the candidate is actually knocked off of his feet by several of the Masons in attendance. He is wrapped up in a blanket and moved to the western end of the Temple. There, after further ceremony, he is "raised up" by a secret grip called "The Master's grip, or the lion's paw." [104]

Those who learned the mysteries also learned that they had a secret project, one that was described by Albert Pike in his book entitled MORALS AND DOGMA. Mr. Pike wrote:

"Behold our object, the end, the result, of the great speculations ... of antiquity; the ultimate annihilation of evil, and restoration of Man to his first estate, by a Redeemer, a Masayah, a Christos, the incarnate Word, Reason, or Power of Deity." [105]

Mr. Hall told his readers that those who had been initiated into the mysteries were the secret power behind the governments of the past. He wrote this about these ancient initiates in his book entitled WHAT THE ANCIENT WISDOM EXPECTS OF ITS DISCIPLES:

"[they] ... are the invisible powers behind the thrones of earth, and men are but marionettes, dancing while the invisible ones pull the strings. We see the dancer, but the master mind that does the work remains concealed by the cloak of silence." [106]

Other writers have confirmed the thoughts of Mr. Hall. A Masonic scholar named George Steinmetz also acknowledged that these mysteries exist, and that some of the members inside the Masonic lodges are custodians of the secrets. He has written this in his book entitled FREEMASONRY, ITS HIDDEN MEANING:

"Ancient secret doctrine, which is concealed in Masonic allegory and symbolism .... It was but to preserve these truths for future generations that Masonry was perpetuated." [107]

Another who has officially connected the Ancient Mysteries to the Masonic Order was Manly P. Hall, who wrote this:

"Much of the ritualism of Freemasonry is based on the trials to which candidates were subjected by the ancient hierophants [defined as the high priests of the mysteries] before the keys of wisdom were enthroned to them." [108]

The Ancient Mysteries had a beginning, according to Mr. Mackey. He wrote about where they started:

"The first of which ... are those of Isis and Osiris in Egypt. The most important of these mysteries were the Osiric in Egypt." [109]

Another writer, Edmond Ronayne, an ex-Mason, confirmed that the Masons were involved in the worship of Osiris, when he wrote this in his book entitled THE MASTERS CARPET:

Masonry's "... ceremonies, symbols, and the celebrated legend of Hiram in the Master Mason's degree, were directly borrowed from the 'Ancient Mysteries,' or the secret worship of Baal, Osiris or Tammuz." [110]

Albert Pike then detailed where the mysteries went after their beginnings in Egypt. He wrote this in MORALS AND DOGMA:

"From Egypt, the Mysteries went to Phoenicia, and were celebrated at Tyre. Osiris changed his name, and became Adoni or Dionusos, still the representative of the sun. In Greece and Sicily, Osiris took the name of Bacchus ...." [111]

So the Ancient Mysteries conceal an important mystery kept secret from the average person. The mystics claim that this mystery has been concealed from the world for centuries.

Even though they had taken the mystery to other continents, those who believed in this religion were yet to take it to America.

That was yet to come.

Chapter 5
Secret Societies

"An invisible hand is guiding the populace."
Lafayette

Arthur Edward Waite, a prolific writer on secret societies, has written this:

"Beneath the broad tide of human history there flow the stealthy undercurrents of the secret societies, which frequently determine in the depths the changes that take place upon the surface." [112]

Another who wrote about the power just underneath the surface was President Woodrow Wilson, who made this startling statement:

"... there is a power so organized, so subtle, so complete, so pervasive, that they had better not speak above their breath when they speak in condemnation of it." [113]

So these two writers has warned America that secret societies had been arranging the major events of the past. And President Wilson warned those who were quick to condemn these organizations that they had better be cautious. Albert Pike also connected the secret societies with a secret belief in his book entitled MORALS AND DOGMA. He wrote that all secret orders and associations:

"... had two doctrines, one concealed and reserved for the Masters, ... the other public ...." [114]

One such secret society with two doctrines was the Illuminati, and Professor Weishaupt, its founder, boasted of his organization's secrecy. He realized that this secrecy would enable them to decide the fate of nations and because their deliberations were secret, no outsider could interfere. He wrote:

"The great strength of our Order lies in its concealment; let it never appear in its own name, but always covered by another name, and another occupation." [115]

Weishaupt later wrote about that secrecy in a letter to a fellow member of the Illuminati:

"Nothing can bring this about [the new world order] but hidden societies. Hidden schools of wisdom are the means which will one day free men from their bonds [the "bonds" of religion, as will be detailed later.] Princes and nations shall vanish from the earth." [116]

So the secret societies were created to bring the world to the new society known as the New World Order. The members of these organizations obviously feel that their goals are so noble that they may perform whatever tasks are required of them to bring that goal to fruition. This means that murder, plunder, and lying all become acceptable as long as these methods assist its members in obtaining their goal.

But the Masons want the world to know that they are not one of the societies involved in changing the world's civilization. They are quick to rush to their own defense. Albert G. Mackey attempted to clear the air about those who had been charging them with some of these activities. He wrote in the ENCYCLOPAEDIA OF FREEMASONRY:

> "There is no charge made more frequently against Freemasonry than that of its tendency to revolution, and conspiracy, and to political organizations which may affect the peace of society or interfere with the rights of governments.
>
> It has been the unjust accusation of every enemy of the Institution in all times past, that its object and aim is the possession of power and control in the affairs of state.
>
> It is in vain that history records no instance of this unlawful connection between Freemasonry and politics; it is in vain that the libeler is directed to the Ancient Constitutions of the Order, which expressly forbid such connections." [117]

So the public is to believe that just because their Constitution forbids such activity, the Masons do not engage in it.

But the evidence that connects the Masonic Lodges to such activity continues to accumulate, Mr. Mackey's denials notwithstanding.

Chapter 6
Concealed Mysteries

"In all time, truth has been hidden under symbols." [118]

"... symbols ... are nevertheless ingenious veils that cover the truth." [119]

Thus wrote Albert Pike, the Sovereign Grand Commander of the Southern Jurisdiction of the Scottish Rite of Freemasonry.

There certainly seems to be a power in knowing something that you can't tell your family, friends, children or business acquaintances. Adam Weishaupt said it best with this selection from his writings:

"Of all the means I know to lead men, the most effectual is a concealed mystery." [120]

CHAPTER 6 CONCEALED MYSTERIES

The power of hidden symbols was alluded to by another writer, this time Foster Bailey in his book entitled THE SPIRIT OF FREEMASONRY:

"A symbol veils or hides a secret, and is that which veils certain mysterious forces. These energies when released can have a potent effect." [121]

There are many who can attest to that simple truth: organizations with concealed or secret initiation ceremonies abound in America. College fraternities and sororities teach the college student to accept secret initiation ceremonies and hidden knowledge at a young age. The Masons, intended for adult males, have similar organizations for their young sons and daughters, and other secret organizations for their wives. All of these organizations tend to prepare their male members for further service in the master secret organization: the Masons.

However, the Masons are quick to point out that they conceal their truths from the general public. Manly P. Hall wrote this :

"It is for the Adepts [an adept is defined by the dictionary as one who is an expert. But, there is an "esoteric" definition that shall be discussed later] one to understand the meaning of the Symbols." [122]

He further instructed his readers that understanding the symbols could make one wise:

"... an understanding of these symbols is the beginning of wisdom" [123]

Max Toth, a writer about the Great Pyramid of Giza in Egypt also wrote about the purpose of symbols:

"The knowledge of the ancient mysteries was never revealed to the layman except through the media of symbols.
Symbolism fulfilled both the need to conceal sacred truths from the uninitiated and to offer a language for those qualified to understand it." [124]

36

Whatever these secrets are, one writer on the subject feels it is time to make them public. Alice Bailey, one of the key writers supporting the New Age movement, wrote this:

"The hour for the ancient mysteries has arrived .... These Ancient Mysteries were ... hidden in numbers, in ritual, in words, and in symbology; these veil the secret ...." [125]

Another writer who writes on the Order, Carl H. Claudy, told anyone who read the Masonic literature that they had best understand the language, or they would miss the true meaning of the words. He wrote:

"He who hears but the words of Freemasonry misses their meaning entirely. [126]

Rex Hutchens, a 32nd degree Mason who has written a book for the Masons, one so important that it was used to replace one written by Henry Clausen, a former Sovereign Commander, also informed his readers that his writings also concealed a secret:

"The word reveal means to 're-veil,' that is, to give one explanation and yet continue to maintain the mystery of the symbol by not explaining it in a full and complete manner." [127]

So, the language code must be broken if one is to learn the truth about the Masonic Order. The reason that this is so is because the Masons have admitted that they have concealed the true meaning of some of their language.

However, it is possible to know the true meanings of at least some of the hidden language. And the reader can be certain that the discovered interpretations are correct because the Masons themselves have revealed the hidden meanings of some of their symbols in some of their own literature.

The secret societies that have concealed their purposes in hidden meanings, concealed writings, and private initiation ceremonies, are admittedly powerful. One who recognized that power was Benjamin Disraeli, the Prime Minister of England in the late 1880's, who said this in the House of Commons on July 14, 1856:

> "There is in Italy a power which we seldom mention in this House .... I mean the secret societies .... It is useless to deny, because it is impossible to conceal, that a great part of Europe -- the whole of Italy and France and a great portion of Germany, to say nothing of other countries -- is covered with a network of these secret societies ....
> ... what are their objects? They do not want constitutional government; ... they want to change the tenure of the land, to drive out the present owners of the soil and to put an end to ecclesiastical [meaning religious] establishments." [128]

The Masons know about concealing secrets from the rest of the world. Carl Claudy, a Masonic writer, told his readers that secrets are inside secrets which are inside other secrets. He wrote:

> "Cut through the outer shell and find a meaning; cut through that meaning and find another; under it if you dig deep enough you may find a third, a fourth -- who shall say how many teachings?" [129]

And even the Communists use concealment.
Nikolai Lenin, the Marxist Communist who communized the Russian nation in the years following the Russian Revolution of 1917, wrote this:

> "We have to use any ruse, dodge, trick, cunning, unlawful method, concealment, and veiling of the truth." [130]

The use of secrecy to conceal thoughts from certain of the members of an organization or from the public is the device of those who have something to hide.
That something is so horrible, so terrible, that knowledge of that secret must be kept from those who would have the most to lose by knowledge of that secret.
In the case of the secret societies, it is a belief in Lucifer, also known as Satan, the devil.

In the case of Communism, it is the truth that the people living in a Communist nation know that the system does not work. But those in a non-Communist nation targeted for a Communist government are not to learn that simple truth. They are to be told that the system is the culmination of man's upward search for a perfect society. And they must be deluded into believing that there is no cost in the change from their current form of government to the Communist form. But history has recorded the brutality of the Communists and the fact that millions of people have had to die as the Communists installed that form of government.

The evidence to support that contention will be discussed later in this study.

Secrecy is certainly not a part of the Chrisian religion. It is possible to know that nothing that Jesus said has been hidden from the Christians. He told the high priest in John 18:20:

"... and in secret have I said nothing."

The intentional concealing of an organization's beliefs and purposes by the use of hidden language and concealed symbols is reserved primarily to the secret societies, and the nationwide Masonic Lodges are indeed a secret society.

The Masons know that they must conceal their horrible secret from the people.

That secret is simply the fact that certain of their members worship Lucifer. And that they keep that secret from the overwhelming majority of their own members. And certainly the public is not to know this fact.

And the evidence to support that conclusion is ample.

But only to the one who cares enough to look for it.

Chapter 7
Serpents, Stars and Suns

So the student of history has to discover the hidden meanings behind the symbols in the Masonic literature and in the secret initiation ceremonies to understand the Masonic Order.

One of the first symbols that needs to be examined is the symbol of the serpent, also called a snake or dragon.

Manly P. Hall wrote that the use of this symbol is as old as early man when he wrote this in his book entitled THE SECRET TEACHINGS OF ALL AGES:

"Among nearly all these ancient peoples the serpent was accepted as a symbol of wisdom ...." [131]

Here Mr. Hall states that the serpent was a symbol of "wisdom." It will be remembered that Lord Maitreya, the future New Age leader, also claimed to possess "wisdom."

Mr. Hall continued:

"Serpent worship in some form has permeated nearly all parts of the earth."

"The serpent is the symbol and prototype of the Universal Savior, who redeems the world by giving creation the knowledge of itself and the realization of good and evil." [132]

And then Mr. Hall links the serpent with the Ancient Mysteries previously discussed. He continues with the comment that the serpent was worshipped by the priests of that religion:

"The priests of the Mysteries were symbolized as a serpent, sometimes called Hydra." [133]

He then pointed out that the Ancient Mysteries have been passed on to various other cultures, and that they have been brought forward to the present day:

"The Serpent Kings [notice that Mr. Hall capitalized the two words, as one would do for a deity or for royalty] reigned over the earth.

It was these Serpent Kings who founded the Mystery Schools which later appeared as the Egyptian and Brahmin Mysteries .... The serpent was their symbol .... They were the true Sons of Light, and from them have descended a long line of adepts and initiates duly tried and proven according to the law." [134]

Another writer, Wilfred Gregson, informed his readers why Mr. Hall capitalized the two words "Serpent Kings" when he wrote:

"One symbol of great prominence throughout all ancient civilizations is the snake of serpent, where it has symbolized 'Divine Wisdom.'" [135]

So. Mr. Hall had reason to capitalize the words, because he had discovered that the serpent represented divinity. Notice also that Mr. Gregson, even though he chose not to capitalize the word "serpent," confirmed that Mr. Hall's use of the capital letter was correct when he stated that there was a connection between "Divine Wisdom" and the serpent.

Mr. Hall made the same connection in these comments:

"The serpent is true to the principles of wisdom, for it tempts man to the knowledge of himself." [136]
A serpent is "often used by the ancients to symbolize wisdom." [137]

The symbol of the serpent has another concealed truth, according to Kenneth Mackenzie. He identified that truth in this quote when he described a Brazen Serpent:

"It was a type of Mediator, and a promise of redemption."

The word Brazen is defined as "bold, or impudent." And Impudent is defined as "shamelessly bold or disrespectful."
It will be remembered that Lucifer was an anoited cherub in heaven, who fell because he sought godly power. The story is covered in Isaiah 14: 12-14 of the Old Testament:

"How are thou fallen from heaven, O Lucifer, son of the morning! How art thou cut down to the ground ....
For thou hast said in thine heart, I will ascend into heaven, I will exalt my throne above the stars of God: ... I will be like the most High."

Therefore, it can be safely said that Lucifer would be considered to be "shamelessly bold" and "disrespectful."
It appears that the Brazen Serpent could be Lucifer!
Another author, John Anthony West, wrote a book entitled SERPENT IN THE SKY, in which he also connected the serpent with "wisdom." He wrote:

"... the serpent represents intellect, the faculty by which man discriminates. There is a higher and a lower intellect.
Thus, symbolically, there is a serpent that crawls, and the higher intellect, that which allows man to know God -- the heavenly serpent, the serpent in the sky." [138]

The somewhat veiled worship of this serpent in the sky inside the Masonic lodges was alluded to by another Masonic writer, Kenneth Mackenzie, in his book entitled THE ROYAL MASONIC CYCLOPAEDIA. He wrote this:

"Among the charges preferred against the Order of Knights Templar, for which Jacques de Molay suffered martyrdom, was that of worshipping an idol or image called Baphomet.

It has been suggested that Baphomet is none other than the Ancient of Days, or Creator.

More cannot be said here without improperly revealing what we [meaning we Masons] are bound to hele, conceal and never reveal." [139]

So, according to this Mason, the snake or serpent is somehow a symbol of the subject of the Masonic worship, and apparently this fact is the secret that the Masons cannot reveal to the rest of the world.

A Christian minister, Reverend Alexander Hislop, wrote a book that included some discussion on the subject of serpent worship. In that book, entitled TWO BABYLONS, he explained that serpent worship was not something that is recent in time. It was an ancient practice.

"Along with the sun [this symbol will be discussed later,] as the great fire-god, and, in due time, identified with him, was the serpent worshipped. In the mythology of the primitive world, the serpent is universally the symbol of the sun.

... as the sun was the great enlightener of the physical world, so the serpent was held to have been the great enlightener of the spiritual, by giving mankind the 'knowledge of good and evil." [140]

He then discussed a coin minted in Tyre, the center of the ancient Phoenician culture. (This coin was also the subject of an article in the September, 1986 issue of The Good News magazine.) It depicted a serpent entwined around a tree stump. To the left of the stump stood an empty cornucopia, and to the right a flourishing palm tree. The snake on the coin is the symbol of the powerful god whom the Romans called Aesculapius. The name means "the man-instructing snake, or the "snake that instructs man."

The article then reported:

"In mythology, Aesculapius was believed to be the child of the Sun, and thus the 'enlightener' of mankind. As the legend goes, Aesculapius was ultimately struck down by a thunderbolt thrown by an angry Zeus, king of the gods, and cast into the underworld." [141]

The tree stump represented the fallen "god" and his ruined kingdom. In the mythologies of many ancient civilizations, the image of a fallen tree was used to symbolize the cutting off of a great god or hero, someone cut off in the midst of their power. The snake on the coin was shown twisting itself around the dead stump, exerting its power in an attempt to restore his fallen kingdom.

The cornucopia is an ancient symbol of plenty, but it was empty on the coin. This has been interpreted as meaning that the abundance had been cut off because the great "god" has been cut off. However, the implication is that the horn of plenty will return when the fallen "god" is restored to his "rightful" position.

The palm tree shown on the coin is a well known symbol of victory. So it appears that the coin was minted to depict the anticipated return of the fallen snake-god to the world.

The Bible talks about a fallen serpent in the book of Revelation, chapter 12, verse 9. However, in this case, the snake is connected to another symbol of the serpent: "a great dragon."

"And the great dragon was cast out, that old serpent, called the Devil, and Satan ...."

Is the serpent worshipped in the Ancient Mysteries and a symbol in the Masonic ceremonies a symbol of Satan, the devil? As has already been discussed, there is indeed evidence that this is the case.

Another symbol that needs to be analyzed is the star.

On the page opposite page 124 in Mackey's ENCYCLOPAEDIA is a drawing illustrating the "symbols of Freemasonry." Included in the twenty or so Masonic symbols is a drawing of a shooting star.

It can be fairly claimed that a blazing or shooting star would be one that was on the move inside the universe. One of the directions it could move would be towards the earth. If it was moving towards the earth, it could be called a "falling star."

Lucifer is a "fallen angel," according to Isaiah, an Old Testament prophet, who wrote this in Isaiah 14:12:

"How art thou fallen from heaven, O Lucifer ...."

Notice that Isaiah also said that Lucifer fell from heaven. And other parts of the Bible report that he fell to the earth.

So, it is conceivable that the symbol of the "falling" or "blazing" star could be a symbol of Lucifer.

A variety of authors have used their writings to discuss the star as a symbol. Professor Adam Weishaupt, the founder of the Illuminati, was one who explained what he considered the star to be a symbol of:

"... the Flaming Star is the Torch of Reason." [142]

Mr. Mackey wrote that the star:

"was a symbol of God."

He then connected the blazing star to another symbol when he wrote:

"The Blazing Star ... refers us to the sun ...." [143]

And then he connected it with the secret initiation ceremonies inside the Masonic lodge:

"In the Fourth Degree of the same Rite [the Scottish Rite of Freemasonry] the [Blazing Star] is again said to be a symbol of the light of Divine Providence pointing out the way of truth." [144]

And Mr. Hutchens, the Masonic writer who has authored the recent book on Masonry, further interpreted the symbol of the star:

"The star as a type of the myriad suns that light other countless systems of worlds is an emblem of that Masonic Light in search of which every Mason travels -- the correct knowledge of the Deity, and of His laws that control the universe." [145]

Closely allied with the symbol of the star is the symbol of the sun. Albert Pike identified it with the worship of the past in this collection of quotes from his writings:

"The worship of the sun became the basis of all the religions of antiquity." [146]

"... thousands of years ago, men worshipped the Sun .... Originally they looked beyond the orb to the invisible God .... They personified him as Brahma, Amun, Osiris, Bel, Adonis, Malkarth, Mithras, and Apollo. Krishna is the Hindu Sun-God." [147]

"... the Gauls worshipped the Sun under the name of Belin or Belinis." [148]

"The sun is the ancient symbol of the life-giving and generative power of the Deity. The Sun was His manifestation and visible image." [149]

"The Sun is the hieroglyphical sign of Truth, because it is the source of Light." [150]

So, Mr. Pike identified the sun as a symbol of a deity that should be worshipped. He chose to capitalize the first letter in the word, the "s," as one would in recognizing the name of a deity.

Albert Mackey repeated Mr. Pike's contentions with comments like these about "sun worship:"

"... [it was] the oldest and by far the most prevalent of all the ancient religions. Eusebius says that the Phoenicians and the Egyptians were the first who ascribed divinity to the sun."

"Hardly any of the symbols of Masonry are more important in their signification or more extensive in their application than the sun as the source of material light, it minds the Mason of that intellectual light of which he is in constant search.

The sun is then presented to us in Masonry first as a symbol of light, but then more emphatically as a symbol of sovereign authority." [151]

So, the sun was a symbol of something that only the believers in the religion known as the Ancient Mysteries understood. These believers, called adepts, certainly knew that the people would not accept their mystery religion, so they had to conceal it from them. So the task became one of creating a religion around a belief that they knew the people would accept, because it would make some sense, at least as far as the adepts would explain it. But their basic purpose was to create a popular religion as a cover for their secret worship.

The secret religion would be built around a belief in the sun.

The sun would be a perfect thing to build a religion around because of its basic nature. It is very visible, and has a very important role in man's life. It rises in the morning (it appears to be born) and then sets during the evening, (it appears to die) and then appears to be "born again" the next morning. It also appears to wander in the sky, setting further north (or south) each night. It then returns back to any given position twice a year.

So the sun appears to have a major birth or death twice each day and twice each year.

It would be very easy for the adepts to explain to the people that only something bigger than mankind, a god, had the ability to die and come back to life. So, the adepts would teach the people that they had to pray to the god or it would choose not to return. They encouraged a worship of the sun so that it would return to mankind again, either once a day, or once every six months.

Albert Pike confirmed this view with this explanation of why early man worshipped the sun:

"To them [meaning early man] ... the journeyings of the Sun, were voluntary and not mechanical ...." [152]

So early man considered the sun to be something that moved voluntarily. In other words, the sun did not have to return each morning. Man must have quickly determined that since the sun did not have to return, man should start asking it to return. Man certainly must have figured out just how important the sun was to his life and well-being and he certainly must have determined that if the sun chose not to return, all of mankind would perish. So it was an easy jump from a belief that the necessary sun was an entity that chose to move across the daytime sky, to a belief that it would return only if man prayed to it to return.

But there is something even more interesting to be considered that Pike didn't explain with that comment.

Obviously, to make the new religion work, the believers would have to be able to predict the movements of the sun. It wouldn't be too long before some of the common people would start noticing that the sun was neither an actual being nor a god to be worshipped, but something that moved according to precise laws. If the common people figured that out, they would not need the adepts who had computed the sun's periodic cycles. So, to keep their power intact, they would teach the people that if they did not accommodate their wishes, they would make certain that the sun did not return. They could even predict, as their measurements became more sophisticated, the exact time and date when the moon would go between the sun and the earth, causing the sun to "disappear." They could then fool the people into believing that they were the cause of the disappearance. They could then explain to the people that if they did not continue to pay them sort sort of tribute, they would not intercede in their behalf, and the sun would not reappear.

To keep the minds of the common people away from figuring out that the whole religion was a scam, the adepts would conduct beautiful and ornate ceremonies around the worship of the sun. And they would expect the people to pay them for the elaborate rituals. And to make their rituals valid, the adepts would always claim that the sun obeyed their prayers, thereby convincing the people of their need to keep the adepts around. The people would continue to pay tribute to these adepts as long as they appeared to be successful.

Now, if the adepts knew that the sun was a symbol of something that the people would not support, such as a belief that Lucifer, the devil, was the god that they worshipped, they would have to continue with their charade, so that the people would not decide to stop worshipping. Because if the people figured it out, they would no longer support their activities. They would have to keep their beliefs from the people, and conceal their secret worship in hidden symbols. So sun worship as a religion prospered. Mr. Hutchens discussed that position in his book:

> "In the Tabernacle the brethren, clothed in black, mourn Osiris, who is representative of the sun, of light, of life, of good and beauty. They reflect upon the way the earth may again be gladdened by his presence." [153]

Mr. Pike connected the sun to Osiris, mentioned by Mr. Hutchens as worthy of being mourned:

> "The three lights at the Altar [inside the Masonic Temple] represent Osiris, Isis and Horus. Osiris was represented by the Sun." [154]

Mr. Mackey went a little further and informed his readers that:

> "Osirus was the sun ...." [155]

In his book entitled INTRODUCTION TO FREEMA-SONRY, Carl H. Claudy, the author, himself a Mason, connected the sun worship with the ceremonies inside the Masonic Lodge:

> "The lodge ... sets him [meaning the initiate] upon the path that leads to Light but it is for him to ... travel the winding path to the symbolic East." [156]

The physical sun rises in the east, and the Masons explain that their search for light begins in the east. And notice that Mr. Claudy capitalizes the word "East," apparently in reverence to the spot where they believe that this god resides.

The Masons tell the world that they circumambulate (defined as walking around) the Temple floor during their initiation ceremonies. Mr. Claudy explains why this rite is performed:

> "When the candidate first circles the lodge room about the altar, he walks step by step with a thou-

sand shades of men who have thus worshipped the Most High by humble imitation.

Thus thought of circumambulation is no longer a mere parade but a ceremony of significance, linking all who take part in it with the spiritual aspirations of a dim and distant past." [157]

He further instructs his readers as to why this ceremony is part of their ceremony:

"Early man circled altars on which burned the fire which was his God, from east to west by way of the south [notice that the north is not included in the ceremony. The significance of that omission will be discussed later.] Circumambulation became a part of all religious observances."

In another part of his book, entitled INTRODUCTION TO FREEMASONRY, Mr. Claudy reported that this style of walking was traceable to the ancient religions of the past. He wrote:

"Circumambulation ... was in the ceremonies of ancient Egypt." [158]

So, this practice of the modern Masons is based upon the ancient religious practices of the Ancients.

So the Masons are telling us that early man walked around in a circle because he was worshipping the sun. Then they tell us that they are doing it for the same reason.

There are reasons that the north as a location to be visited in their walk around the temple floor is not included in their initiation rites, and six of the great Masonic writers have told us why this is so.

Captain William Morgan offered his readers this explanation with this comment from his book:

"... we, therefore, Masonically, term the north a place of darkness." [159]

Mr. Mackey confirmed that statement in his book:

"The north is Masonically called a place of darkness." [160]

And Mr. Pike confirmed the comments made by the other two Masons with this declaration:

"To all Masons, the North has immediately been the place of darkness, and of the great lights of the Lodge, none is in the North." [161]

And Kenneth Mackenzie added his confirming thoughts:

"The North was always esteemed a place of darkness." [162]

Mr. Hutchens became the fifth Masonic writer to confirm this detail:

"As in other degrees, the closing ritual provides a summary of the lessons taught in the degree. We hear in the West the eagles gather and the doom of tyranny is near. In the South, truth struggles against error and oppression. In the North, fanaticism and intolerance wane. In the East, the people begin to know their rights and to be conscious of their dignity and that the sun's rays will soon smite the summits of the mountains." [163]

Mr. Hutchens informed his readers that the North was where "fanaticism and intolerance" resided. What he meant by this and what the symbol of the North represents will be explored in later paragraphs of this study.

And the sixth Masonic writer who confirmed that the North was a place of darkness was Carl Claudy, who wrote this in his book entitled INTRODUCTION TO FREEMASONRY:

"... the place of darkness, the North." [164]

And the reason the Masons do not include the North in their rites is found in the Bible in Isaiah 14:13:

"I [meaning Lucifer] will exalt my throne above the stars of God: I will sit also upon the mount of the congregation in the sides of the north."

The God of the Bible sits in the North, and Lucifer hopes one day to acquire the throne of God for his throne. But, until then, the "North is a place of darkness."

But, while the north is an excluded territory, the east is the "place of light," and is to be revered. Mr. Hutchens tells his readers why that is so:

"... the East -- the source of light and thus knowledge." [165]

Albert Mackey quotes Etienne Francois Bazot, a French Masonic writer in his ENCYCLOPAEDIA:

"The veneration which the Masons have for the East ... bears a relation to the primitive religion whose first degeneration was sun-worship." [166]

Rex Hutchens then tells his readers that the Masons deploy lights around the Lodge room during the initiation ceremony for the 25th degree, called the Knight of the Sun. He writes:

"The ceiling should be decorated to represent the heavens with the moon, the principal planets and the constellations Taurus and Orion. A single powerful light, a great globe of glass, representing the sun, is in the South.
In a physical sense the greater light comes from the sun and the transparencies provide lesser light ... symbolically, the sun or great light is the Truth and the lesser lights are man's symbolic representation of Truth." [167]

Mr. Mackey further discusses this Rite of Circumambulation, as he calls it, in his ENCYCLOPAEDIA. He says that the rite:

"... exists in Freemasonry.

... the people always walked three times round the altar while singing a sacred hymn. In making this procession, great care was taken to move in imitation of the course of the sun." [168]

He then assisted the reader with understanding this practice in the Masonic temples:

"This Rite of Circumambulation undoubtedly refers to the doctrine of sun-worship ...." [169]

However, in another of the books that he wrote, Mr. Mackey directly states that the rite is connected to sun worship. This is what he wrote in a book entitled MANUAL OF THE LODGE:

"The circumambulation among the pagan nations referred to the great doctrines of Sabaism or sun worship." [170]

Sabaism is defined by Mr. Mackey in his ENCYCLOPAEDIA as:

"SABAISM: The worship of the sun, moon and stars, 'the host of heaven.' It was practiced in Persia, Chaldea, India and other Oriental countries, at an early period of the world's history." [171]

He then added this rather cryptic comment:

"... and although the dogma of sun-worship does not of course exist in Freemasonry, we find an allusion to it in the Rite of Circumambulation which it preserves ...." [172]

One can understand what Mr. Mackey meant by that comment: the Masons do not worship the sun, they worship the Sun!

So he was telling the truth, but concealing it in a symbolic language.

Mr. Hutchens then volunteered the information that in the 12th of the 32 degrees the Rite of Circumambulation is preserved. He writes:

"In all the Scottish Rite Degrees thus far, the candidate has made twenty-one prescribed circuits around the altar; this degree adds seven for a total of twenty-eight.
This practice, called circumambulation, is derived from the ancients and existed among the Romans, Semites, Hindus, and others.
It is thought to have been a rite of purification. The sun was believed to travel around the earth; the initiates imitated the movement of the sun when they made circuits around the altar." [173]

Furthermore, in the ninth degree, other symbols of the sun are involved in the ceremony. Mr. Hutchens tells his readers:

"After the obligation is taken, the nine candles of yellow wax are lit.
Yellow is representative of the sun, hence light and knowledge." [174]

In the tenth degree, further symbols representing the sun are utilized, according to this author:

"There are three sets of five lights: the wax is yellow, meaning knowledge and also, as the color of the sun, represents the Deity." [175]

Other clues that the sun and the serpent are both known symbols of the Masonic Lodge are given by the titles of two of the 32 degrees inside the Masonic Lodge.
The 25th degree initiate is called a Knight of the Brazen Serpent, and the 28th degree initiate is called a Knight of the Sun.
There is another symbol of the sun inside the Masonic Lodge. The Worshipful Master, the equivalent of the President of the Lodge, sits in the east side of the temple. We are told why that is:

"The Worshipful Master represents the sun at its rising, the Senior Warden [another officer of the Lodge] represents the sun at its setting, and the Junior Warden [still another officer of the Lodge] represents the sun at meridian [the half-way point.]" [176]

Other individuals and organizations besides the Masonic Lodges are also involved, in varying degrees, with sun worship, or with an acknowledgement that the sun plays a central role in their understanding of the nature of the world. Elizabeth Clare Prophet has been described as being a leader in the New Age Movement, and she has written this in a newsletter she publishes called THE COMING REVOLUTION:

"the healing of the nations begins with the healing of ourselves. We must draw forth from the Great Central Sun -- that eternal Light with which we were anointed from the beginning." [177]

Adolf Hitler, the head of the German government prior to and during World War II, and who was directly responsible for the murder of over 50 million people, was also a sun-worshipper. Very early in his life, he joined a secret organization called the Thule Society. And forty years after the war, some historians are finally delving into its strange beliefs. Two of these writers, Michel Bertrand and Jean Angelini, have produced a book entitled THE OCCULT AND THE THIRD REICH, and one of their conclusions is:

"In the Nazi cosmology the sun played a prime role ... as a sacred symbol of the Aryans, in contrast to the feminine and magical symbolism of the moon, revered by the Semitic peoples."

The Nazi Party was the name of the National Socialist German Workers' Party, the party that Mr. Hitler joined. It became the controlling party of the German government prior to and during the war.

... the Fuhrer [German for leader, in this case meaning Mr. Hitler] saw in the Jewish people, with their black hair and swarthy complexion, the dark side of the human species, while the blond and blue-eyed Aryans constituted the light side of humanity. Hitler undertook to extirpate [meaning to eliminate] from the material world its impure elements ... to lead it back to glory." [178]

But sun worship, as the Masons point out, is not new. The Bible talks about it as well.

Ezekiel was an Old Testament prophet writing sometime during the period of 571 to 592 B.C. He tells about how he was taken by God to see a practice occurring near the Temple. This is what he wrote in Ezekiel 8:15-16:

"And He [the Lord God] brought me into the inner court of the Lord's house, and behold, at the door of the temple of the Lord, between the porch and the altar, were about five and twenty men, with their backs toward the temple of the Lord, and they worshipped the sun toward the east."

And Ezekiel points out that the Lord God considered this practice "an abomination."

There is another reference to sun worship in the Old Testament, this time in Deuteronomy 17: 2-4, 7. That reference reads as follows:

"If there be found among you, ... man or woman ... that ... hath gone and served other gods, and worshipped them, either the sun, or moon, or any of the host of heaven ...

and it be true ... that such an abomination is wrought in Israel ... so thou shalt put the evil away from among you."

So the God of the Bible has made it clear that sun worship is something that He does not want His creatures practicing. The Bible even went so far as to say, in both instances, that He considered the practice to be an "abomination" or an "evil."

But to show just how far this practice has invaded the Christian community, the following "prayer" was offered up at a recent funeral in a local Christian church:

"Now you will feel no rain, for your Mother, the earth, will fold her arms around you.

Now you will feel no cold, for your Father, the Sun, will always warm you."

Sun worship continues.
Because some Christian churches pray to the Sun god in their church services.
And don't understand who they are praying to.
Simply stated, the Sun god that they were praying to is Lucifer!

Chapter 8
The Author's Clarification

The student of esoteric language and concealed symbols must study the being referred to as Lucifer, Satan or the devil in the Bible.

But before that study commences, the author has to take an unusual step and attempt to clarify his position on the subject.

I have endeavored to write this book as an historian, carefully basing my conclusions on my own research into the writings of the people involved. I have literally read hundreds of works on the subject of this book, and have attempted to record those comments as accurately as was possible.

Although I am a Christian, I have tried not to let my religious views color my thinking on the subject of this book. As I said, I have tried to write this book not as a religious writer, but as an historian who has discovered that history has been a series of planned events led by a conspiracy based upon a worship of Lucifer. I believe that it is possible to show that this is a fact of history, not as a religious writer, but as an historian. And that is what I have attempted to do in this book.

I have, on occasion, quoted the Bible, and will do so in the remaining material whenever the context seems to warrant it. At the very least, for the skeptic, the Bible is a magnificent record of the history of a particular group of people during particular periods of the past. I have used the Bible as I have used any other book, as a book of history. But it has always been to make a counterpoint in a specific instance where the historical facts seem to indicate that the use of the Bible warranted it.

In this instance, it becomes important to start with a reading of a particular section of the Bible, and then show how others, not known for their belief in the God of the Bible, have also chosen to believe that section as well.

It is hoped that the reader can understand the significance of what I have just written. It will make the reading of the remaining material a little easier to understand.

Chapter 9
Lucifer Worship

The Bible discusses a being called Lucifer in both the Old and New Testaments. Other names for this creature are Satan, and the devil.

One of the first explanations of just who this being known as Lucifer is, is found in the Old Testament in a book written by the prophet Isaiah, who wrote around 740 B.C. He wrote that Lucifer was created "full of wisdom," and was "perfect." He was created the "anointed cherub that covereth the throne of God," and that he actually was "upon the holy mountain of God." He later "corrupted [his] wisdom by reason of [his] brightness." The Bible then records that God "cast [him] to the ground."

Isaiah wrote this in Isaiah 14:12:

"How art thou fallen from heaven, O Lucifer, son of the morning! How art thou cut down to the ground which didst weaken the nations!"

Notice that the fall of Lucifer weakened the "nations of the world." This will be examined in other chapters of this study.

"For thou hast said in thine heart, I will ascend into heaven. I will exalt my throne above the stars of God: I will sit also upon the mount of the congregation in the sides of the north.
I will ascend above the heights of the clouds; I will be like the most High."

Luke, a writer in the New Testament, records in Luke 10:18, that Jesus said that he beheld "Satan [Lucifer's new name] as lightning fall from heaven." Peter records in II Peter 2:4 that God has "spared not the angels [who were involved in Lucifer's revolt against God] that sinned, but cast them down" as well.
Paul, another New Testament writer, wrote this about Lucifer in II Corinthians 11:14, in about 57 A.D.:

"And no marvel, for Satan is transformed into an angel of light".

And in II Thessalonians 2:9, Paul wrote that Satan was capable of working "lying wonders."
In around 90 A.D., John, the author of the book known as Revelation, wrote in Revelation 12:9, that Satan was a "dragon."
Lucifer shows up in the original site of human habitation on earth, called the Garden of Eden. The creator God placed Adam, the first man (and later Eve, the first woman) in this garden, but told them that there were certain rules that they had to abide by. These are spelled out in Genesis 2:16-17:

"And the Lord God commanded the man, saying, Of every tree of the garden thou mayest freely eat: but of the tree of the knowledge of good and evil, thou shalt not eat of it; for in the day that thou eatest thereof thou shall surely die. "

Later, Lucifer spoke through a serpent to Eve, but in reality, to both men and women:

"Yea, hath God said: Ye shall not eat of every tree of the garden? And the woman said unto the serpent: We may eat of the fruit of the trees of the garden: But of the fruit of the tree which is in the midst of the garden [the tree of the knowledge of good and evil] God hath said, Ye shall not eat of it, lest ye die.

And the serpent said unto the woman, Ye shall not surely die. For God doth know that in the day ye eat thereof, then your eyes shall be opened, and ye shall be as gods, knowing good and evil."

So, from the above information, it is possible to glean a little knowledge about the nature of Lucifer:

1. He was cast down from heaven, because he desired to ascend directly into the seat of heavenly power, the throne of God.
2. He is referred to as the "son of the morning." This appears to be a reference to Lucifer being similar to the sun, which also arises every morning.
3. His desire is to sit on the north side of the mountain of God.
4. Lucifer can deceive the world, because he has been transformed into an "angel of light."
5. Lucifer can work "lying wonders."

Now, with those basic understandings of Lucifer in place, it will be possible to examine the views of others about this fallen entity.

However, not all agree with a picture of Lucifer being evil. Albert Pike wrote:

"... there is no rebellious demon of Evil, or Principle of Darkness and in eternal controversy with God. [179]

In fact, Mr. Pike believes that Lucifer was not a force of evil, but could be a force for good. He wrote this in MORALS AND DOGMA:

"For the Initiates [those initiated into the true secrets of Masonry] this is not a person, but a force, created for good, but which may serve for evil." [180]

To further amplify that belief of Mr. Pike's, it becomes important to quote a letter that he wrote on July 14, 1889 to the 23 Supreme Councils of the world. Judging from the contents of this letter, it appears that Mr. Pike was attempting to tell the leaders of the various Supreme Councils all over the world that they were to know that Lucifer was the secret god of the Masons.

This letter clearly indicates that he believed the position that Lucifer was a god who had come to earth for the good of mankind. He wrote:

"That which we must say to the crowd is [presumably Mr. Pike meant that the "crowd" was all of the non-Masons, or the public at large] We worship a God, but it is the God that one adores without superstition."

It appears that one of the purposes of this letter was to advise all of the top ranking Masons that they were to concoct a story that the Masons worshipped the "traditional" God, so that none could ever accuse them of worshipping a cherub, a non-god, by the name of Lucifer. In other words, they were to deny that Lucifer was their god whenever an outsider was smart enough to break through all of the secrets and figure it out.

So the secret inside the Masonic Order is that Lucifer is their secret god.

Any non-Mason today who attempts to explain to any of their Masonic friends or relatives that this is the secret inside the Lodge will be met with an instanteous denial. Every Mason, whether they know the secret of the Lodge or not, will obviously deny the accusation.

Mr. Pike continued:

"You may repeat it to the 32nd, 31st and 30th degrees -- The Masonic religion should be, by all of us initiates of the high degrees, maintained in the purity of the Luciferian doctrine."

Here Mr. Pike seems to indicate that it is the 30th, 31st and 32nd degrees that are to be taught the "Luciferian doctrine." The direct evidence that the honorary 33rd degree is formally taught that Lucifer is the Great Architect of the Universe will be presented later. But, here Pike seems to say that that lesson is to be taught at an earlier degree.

> "If Lucifer were not God, would Adonay [the God of the Christians and the Jews] and his priests calumniate [defined as spreading false and harmful statements about or to slander] him?"

Pike makes two incredible statements about Lucifer:

1. He is considered to be a god! and
2. The priests, and the rabbis, have it all backwards, and are all slandering his name.

As has been illustrated, the Bible states that Lucifer is nothing more than a fallen cherub. He is not a god. Yet Mr. Pike clearly states that Lucifer is a god!

And secondly, those who claim that he is the "wicked one" are "slandering" him. Those individuals have it all wrong!

Mr. Pike continued:

> " ... the true and pure philosophic religion is the belief in Lucifer, the equal of Adonay;"

Adonay, also spelled Adonai, is the Hebrew word for God. To show that Pike was referring to the God of the Bible, he wrote this in his book entitled MORALS AND DOGMA:

> "... Adonai, the rival of Bal and Osiris." [181]

As has been illustrated, Osiris is the sun-god, and the sun has been shown to be a symbol of Lucifer. Adonai is the "rival" of Lucifer, both in the Bible, and in the writings of Albert Pike.

> "but Lucifer, God of Light and God of Good, is struggling for humanity against Adonay, the God of Darkness and Evil." [182]

Here once again Mr. Pike writes that Lucifer and Adonay are rivals, and that the religious world has it all backwards:

Lucifer is the "good god," and Adonay is the God of "evil and darkness."

(The author would like to interrupt the narrative to make an observation.

That authenticity of that letter by Albert Pike that was just quoted has been questioned by a variety of writers.

It has been reported that Mr. Pike made these comments in a "encyclical" hand carried to the a meeting of 23 Supreme Councils of the world on July 14, 1889 in Paris, France.

This author is willing to concede that the only evidence for the contents of this "encyclical" consists of it being quoted in a book written by Frenchman named A.C. de la Rive entitled LA FEMME ET L'ENFANT DANS LA RANC-MACON-NERIE UNIVERSELLE. That title translated from French to English means THE WOMAN AND CHILD IN UNIVERSAL FRENCH MASONRY. A copy of that page that contains that quote, and the cover of the book has been supplied to this author by a concerned researcher who had someone locate the book in France for him and make copies of the pertinent pages.

The author has read another book that contains the English translation of that "encyclical." That book is entitled OCCULT THEOCRASY and was written in 1933 by Edith Starr Miller. She cites the book by Mr. de la Rive as her source.

She obviously believed that the letter was true and contained the actual thoughts of Mr. Albert Pike.

In other words, the only source for the letter is a Frenchman who quotes it in his book and not Mr. Albert Pike himself. It must be assumed that Mr. Pike, if he were alive today and was asked whether the letter was his, would deny that he ever wrote such an "encyclical," whether or not he had written it. But, the reader is admonished to remember that if he did indeed worship Lucifer, and wrote the "encyclical," he would certainly have to deny it. So that answer would tell the researcher nothing.

It is the contention of this writer, and others who are attempting to decipher the secret symbols of the Masonic Order, that a small percentage of the Masons know that all of the symbols inside the Lodge refer to Lucifer. And it must be remembered that these Masons must of necessity do all that they can to deny that fact.

And certainly anyone today who believes that the contents of the letter are a fraud would do all that they could to discredit anyone who said that the thoughts were the actual thoughts of Pike.

However, this writer is of the opinion that Mr. Pike did indeed worship Lucifer, and is not basing that conclusion on just this one letter. Notice that Mr. Pike has written elsewhere that he considered Lucifer to be the secret god of the Masonic Lodge.

So, it is not essential to this writer's position that this "encyclical" be proven to be valid. It is the author's contention that there is ample evidence from other sources, including from Masons other than Mr. Pike, that the secret god inside the Masonic lodges is Lucifer.

That evidence is available to anyone who cares to locate it.)

But there is another Mason who knows that Lucifer is the "good god" of a particular segment of the Masons. Pike's fellow 33rd degree Mason, Manly P. Hall, also felt that this "god" was a "god of good." He wrote in his book entitled THE SECRET TEACHINGS OF ALL AGES:

"Sun worship played an important part in nearly all the early pagan Mysteries.

The Solar Diety ... was slain by wicked ruffians, who personified the evil principle of the universe. By means of certain rituals and ceremonies, symbolic of purification and regeneration, this wonderful GOD OF GOOD was brought back to life and became the saviour of His people." [183] (emphasis by author.)

This "god" who came back to life is not the Jesus of the Bible, because Mr. Hall refers to him as "The Solar Diety." He is referring to the death and resurrection of Osiris, covered in detail in the Masonic rituals.

Manly P. Hall has further identified Lucifer as the god of some of his fellow Masons. He has written this in his book entitled THE LOST KEYS OF FREEMASONRY:

"When the Mason learns the key to the warrior on the block is the proper application of the dynamo of the living power, he has learned the mystery of his Craft.

The seething energies of Lucifer are in his hands and before he may step onward and upward, he must prove his ability to properly apply energy." [184]

Mikhail Bakunin, the Russian anarchist, also addressed this question of evil and good gods. He wrote:

"The Evil One is the satanic revolt against divine authority, revolt in which we see the fecund [defined as meaning fertile] germ of all human emancipations, the revolution.

Socialists recognize each other by the words 'In the name of the one to whom a great wrong has been done.'

Satan [is] the eternal rebel, the first freethinker and the emancipator of worlds.

He makes men ashamed of his bestial ignorance and obedience; he emancipates him, stamps upon his brow the seal of liberty and humanity, in urging him to disobey and eat of the fruit of knowledge." [185]

That thought that Lucifer was a "good" spirit, to whom a "great wrong" was done, is the basic thought that holds the New Age together, according to Texe Marrs, the author of two major books on the subject. He has written:

"Many New Agers commend Lucifer because by tempting Eve he enabled man to evolve toward enlightened knowledge and godhood." [186]

Mr. Marrs discusses the thoughts of a leader in a mystical organization called the Stelle Group, named Eklal Kueshana. He writes that this New Age leader says that:

"Lucifer is the head of a secret Brotherhood of Spirits .... the Brotherhood is named after Lucifer because the great Angel Lucifer has been responsible for the abolishment of Eden in order that men could begin on the road to spiritual advancement." [187]

So, there is a basic disagreement about the nature of Lucifer, also known as Satan or the devil. The Bible depicts

him as a force for evil, and Mr. Pike, and others, pictures
him as a force for good.

But the connection between Lucifer and the Ancient Mysteries needs to be further amplified.

The Mysteries had a purpose: to create a super man, one
capable of understanding the true nature of the universe, and
to worship the "true" god.

W.L. Wilmshurst, a Mason, wrote these thoughts in his
book entitled THE MEANING OF MASONRY:

"This -- the evolution of man into superman --
was always the purpose of the ancient Mysteries, and
the real purpose of modern Masonry is, not the social
and charitable purposes to which so much attention is
paid, but the evolution of those who aspire to perfect
their own nature and transform it into more god-like
quality." [188]

He amplified this thought a little later in his book:

"Man who has sprung from the earth [meaning
that he was not created by a creator God] and developed through the lower kingdoms of nature to his
present rational state, has yet to complete his evolution by becoming a god-like being and unifying his
consciousness with the Omniscient -- to promote which
is and always has been the sole aim and purpose of
Initiation." [189]

"No higher level of attainment is possible than
that in which the human merges in the Divine consciousness and knows as God knows." [190]

So, just as Satan tempted mankind with the ability to
know good and evil themselves just like God, without His
assistance, now the Masons are teaching that they too could
become a god through an initiation into the Ancient Mysteries.

John Anthony West, in his book SERPENT IN THE SKY,
wrote this in support of Mr. Wilmshurst's statement:

"Egypt started with the concept of divine attributes within man. The gods are not brought down to
earth; rather man is raised to the gods." [191]

Others besides the above mentioned Masons, like Louis Feuerbach, have joined the discussion with similar thoughts. He was a nineteenth century philosopher, and a hero of the Communists like Karl Marx. In fact, Frederick Engels, the co-worker with Karl Marx during the time Marx wrote THE COMMUNIST MANIFESTO, wrote this about his friend:

"All the Communists of 1845 were followers of Feuerbach ...." [192]

The reason that the Communists supported the ideas of Feuerbach is apparent when the student reads his writings. He wrote:

"Man alone is our God, our father, our judge, our redeemer, our true home, our law and our rule, the Alpha and Omega of our life and of our political, moral, public and domestic activity. There is no salvation, save through the medium of man." [193]

John Denver, the well known popular singer, has adopted this same philosophy about his divinity. He has been quoted as saying this after his new conversion:

"It's the single, most important experience of my life -- I can do anything. One of these days, I'll be so complete I won't be human; I'll be a god." [194]

Mr. Hall, the Mason, stated a similar thought when he wrote this in his book entitled LECTURES ON ANCIENT PHILOSOPHY:

"We may study the star intellectually, but we have never attained consciousness until we are the star." [195]

But this idea that man could become a god is not new. The Bible anticipated it, and Isaiah wrote about it back in 741 B.C. This is what he wrote in Isaiah 43:10:

"Thus saith the Lord ....
... understand that I am He: before me there was no God formed, neither shall there be after me."

And once again, in Isaiah 45:5:

"I am the Lord, and there is none else, there is no God beside me ...."

The Bible teaches that there is but one God, and that mankind has no possibility of sharing His godhead.

One who apparently has not believed those statements in the Bible is Shirley MacLaine, who has become a spokesman for the position that man can become a god. She has written several books on the subject of her support of the New Age (Newsweek magazine described her as "the New Age evangelist.") She wrote the following statement in her book entitled DANCING IN THE LIGHT:

"... we are part of God ..." [196]

and this elsewhere in the same book:

"... if one says audibly I am God, the sound vibrations literally align the energies of the body to a higher atunement." [197]

If each man is a god, mankind is capable of making decisions for their own welfare. Each man has complete control of his decision-making, according to Miss MacLaine. In fact, man's control has extended into areas few have ever claimed for mankind. These are the thoughts of Miss MacLaine:

"I think we choose to be together .... We choose our parents, and I think the parents choose the children they want to have before they ever come into an incarnation." [198]

She went on further to record another strange thought, when she wrote this:

"... there was no such thing as reality, only perception." [199]

One can only wonder where Miss MacLaine got these bizarre thoughts from. Several clues that can assist the student in understanding her have been given by either her own revelations or from some articles that have appeared about her in the media.

In her book entitled OUT ON A LIMB, she wrote about her meetings with her married lover in her apartment. She commented that he looked at her shelf of books on, amongst other subjects: "Marxist theory," including a "biography of [Karl] Marx." [200]

PARADE magazine of December 18, 1988 had an article on Miss MacLaine in which it revealed that her den had "lots of framed pictures: Shirley with [Communist] Fidel Castro, and with [Communist] Nikita Khrushchev [amongst others.]" [201]

The magazine reported how Shirley and her lover:

"talked about Democratic-Socialist principles and how it was possible to have them both at the same time if the rich would only share their wealth more." [202]

Elsewhere in her book, she wrote about how much of a hypocrite she was when she added this contradictory statement:

"... wanted to talk to him [her lover] about how I had made a lot of money and that it made me feel elite in a world that was broke to know I could buy just about anything I wished for." [203]

However, nowhere in her book did she say that she had freely donated any of her own wealth to the relief of the poor. Apparently she believes that the Communist ideas about wealth sharing are acceptable only as long as she does not have to share her wealth like she wants the other rich to do.

Miss MacLaine has since gone on a nationwide tour promoting her new found religious views to the public. Newsweek magazine reported in 1987 that she had made a great deal of money explaining her new thoughts to others:

"Since MacLaine began her tour in January [1987,] more than 10,000 people in 15 cities have paid the $300 admission fee." [204]

10,000 times $300 equals 3 million dollars.

Obviously, Shirley's tours have proven to be both popular and lucrative. The Newsweek article on her seminar mentioned a little of what she teaches in them. The following are a few of her comments:

> "'The earth is moving off its axis,' she says, and only the 'collective consciousness' of mankind can right it.
>
> For the spiritually inclined, 'a window of light' will appear on those days [August 16 and 17, 1987] that MacLaine says will 'allow us to rise to a higher plane of cosmic understanding.'" [205]

"Evangelist" MacLaine became "Doctor" MacLaine when she reported some of her new cures for two of the world's most serious medical problems: AIDS and cancer of the abdomen. According to the Newsweek article, she told her audience:

> "They [those who paid to hear her in the 15 cities on the tour] all got to hear MacLaine's pronouncements on such subjects as AIDS (she thinks sufferers are sick because they have been 'bereft of love necessary to sustain the balance' of health); and cancer (for cancer of the abdomen, she advises 'putting patients in a yellow room because yellow is the color 'frequency' of that part of the body.')" [206]

And to think her "patients" only have to pay $300 for such wisdom!

But "Doctor" MacLaine is not as dumb as one might think. The Newsweek magazine article reported:

> "... everyone who attended had to sign waivers absolving the seminar's organizers from responsibility for psychological injury." [207]

So someone in charge of arranging her seminars is aware that her ideas might cause psychological damage to those attending, and they have moved to protect her from malpractice lawsuits.

Not only was this "New Age evangelist" making money on her personal lecture tours, she was also making money on her best selling books.

As of July, 1987, her book entitled OUT ON A LIMB, had sold 3 million copies, and her other major seller, DANCING IN THE LIGHT had sold 2.2 million. Time magazine reported that her "five books on self-exploration and self-promotion have run to more than 8 million copies." [208]

It appears as if selling the New Age religion can be very profitable!

But, in summary, perhaps the most cogent comment about the battle between the New Age and the Christians was made by Nesta Webster in her book entitled SECRET SOCIETIES:

> "The war now begins between the two contending principles: the Christian conception of man reaching up to God, and the secret society [Miss Webster wrote too early for her to know about the New Age Movement] conception of man as God, needing no revelation from on high and no guidance but the law of his own nature.
>
> And since that nature is in itself divine, all that springs from it is praiseworthy, and those acts usually regarded as sins are not to be condemned." [209]

The battle lines are drawn between those who believe in a creator God, and those who believe that man can become god.

These are the two opposing positions. And the battle between them has begun.

Chapter 10
Becoming a God

What does the New Age religion offer to its believers? As was covered in the last chapter, it is simply the promise of personally becoming a god!

But there is another bait. It is unlimited knowledge of the entire universe!

Fred Gittings wrote this in his book entitled SECRET SYMBOLISM IN OCCULT ART:

> "... it is claimed that, after Lucifer fell from Heaven, he brought with him the power of thinking as a gift for mankind." [210]

Manly P. Hall added these comments about this belief system:

> "In the secret teachings it is written that mind is the Savior-God." [211]

"... where reason reigns supreme, inconsistency cannot exist. Wisdom ... lifts man to the condition of Godhead." [212]

"Even in man's present state of imperfection it is dawning upon his realization that he can never be truly happy until he is perfect, and that of all of the faculties contributing to his self-perfection none is equal in importance to the rational intellect.

... only the illumined mind can, and must, lead the soul into the perfect light of unity." [213]

"Philosophy is indeed a mystical ladder up which men climb from ignorance to reason." [214]

"... the philosopher soon becomes fabulously wealthy in that most priceless of all possessions: reason." [215]

But the Masons are not the only ones preaching the need for man's reason to solve all of man's problems.

The Humanist Religion (this will be examined more carefully in a later chapter) that is currently becoming America's major religious view of mankind, also has a plank in its platform about the total dependence on man's reason. Their fourth plank in their 1933 HUMANIST MANIFESTO reads:

"Fourth: Reason and intelligence are the most effective instruments that humankind possesses." [216]

And the members of the Illuminati share the similar views of both the Masons and the Humanists. Professor Weishaupt wrote these two statements:

"This is the great object held out by this Association: and the means of attaining it is Illumination, enlightening the understanding by the sun of reason." [217]

"When at last Reason becomes the religion of men, then will the problem be solved." [218]

Perhaps the position that reason is man's last hope for a perfect world can be summed up with these comments from members of the Masonic Lodge.

Harold J. Bolen wrote this in the New Age Magazine, the official magazine of the Scottish Rite of Freemasonry:

"Freemasonry believes it is more holy to live by reason than to live by faith, for reason is a bridge of understanding while faith is only a bridge of hope.

Reason challenges our minds, while faith might give comfort without achievement." [219]

Mr. Hall then added this confirming statement:

"The secret doctrine that flows through Freemasonic symbols has its source in three ancient and exalted orders, one of which is the Dionysial artificers [Dionysus was identified by the Romans with Bacchus, the "god" that Albert Pike and Albert Mackey have identified with the sun-god Osiris.]

The Dionysians also first likened man to a rough ashlar which, trued into a finished block through the instrument of reason, could be fitted into the structure of that living and eternal Temple built without the sound of hammer, the voice of workmen, or any tool of contention." [220]

Albert Pike added additional comments to the record, the first of which claimed that Masonry had its own Ten Commandments. The first of those commandments was:

"1.   God is the Eternal, Omnipotent, Immutable Wisdom." [221]

Wisdom is defined as the power of judging rightly based upon knowledge and man gets wisdom through the use of his reason. In fact, Mr. Pike went so far as to deify man's mind. He wrote:

"Reason is The Absolute, it is in IT we must believe.... [222]

"Masonry propagates no creed except its own most simple and Sublime One; that universal religion, taught by Nature and by Reason." [223]

"The structure itself will be overthrown, when, in the vivid language of a living writer, 'Human reason leaps into the throne of God and waves her torch over the ruins of the Universe.'" [224]

Masonry has deified reason, the ability of man to make his own decisions in all of his affairs without concern of the moral absolutes imparted by the God of the Bible. No one would be impudent enough to suggest that man not use his mind at all. What these New Agers, Masons, Humanists, and members of the Illuminati are saying is that they wish to use the mind exclusively. That means, for those who believe that there is no God, man can have "the knowledge of good and evil," and make up his own moral code as he goes along. For those who believe in a God, He is to have no say in the future determination of what is right or wrong. Therefore man should have the right to decide for himself in all moral, religious, political and economic decisions, whether or not there is a God.

But the truth of life is that the existing God gave man moral laws to follow, primarily in the Old Testament. These are called "moral absolutes," and spell out just what is right and wrong. According to these individuals and organizations, man has the right to ignore these teachings, and to decide for himself what is right and wrong.

This new "morality" is not new. It is as old as man himself. The Bible teaches that man decided to eat the "fruit of the tree of the knowledge of good and evil," and that is what these organizations have done.

Where these decisions of men's "reason" leads mankind will be discussed later in this material.

But it is possible to know what the God of the Bible thinks about these decisions.

Proverbs 1:7 of the Old Testament Bible teaches:

"The fear of the Lord is the beginning of knowledge: but fools despise wisdom and instruction."

The Bible says that there is a true wisdom, and that it springs from the mind of God. The Humanists, New Agers, Communists and the Masons say that wisdom springs solely from the mind of man, and that man's mind teaches that he can become a god himself, having the ability to decide for himself in all things.

And Proverbs 3:5 directs man to:

"Trust in the Lord with all thine heart; and lean not unto thine own understanding."

But some men "reason" that they are too wise for that. And mankind has had to pay for their impudence.

Chapter 11
Sons of Light

If early man first worshipped the sun and then the star as a symbol of that sun, it would be the next logical step to worship the light that comes from that sun. And this is the progression that is taught by history.

Albert Mackey wrote:

> "... light always constituted a principal object of adoration, as the primordial source of knowledge ..."[225]

John White, called "another New Age theologian" by Texe Marrs in his book entitled DARK SECRETS OF THE NEW AGE, wrote that man is not only to seek light but to become light:

> "First you go toward the light.
>
> Next you're in the light.

Then you are the light." [226]

Adam Weishaupt, the founder of the Illuminati, (which means The Illuminated Ones) wrote this in 1778:

"Let there be light, and there shall be light." [227]

And on August 17, 1984, the Lucis Trust sent this letter to an inquiring citizen who wanted an explanation of the origin of the name Lucis Trust. This is the explanation he received:

> "Lucis is the genitive case of the Latin word Lux. We would translate it 'of light.'
> The Trust has always been Lucis right from its incorporation in 1923. The publishing company, however was called at first the Lucifer Publishing Company as authored by H. P. [Helena Petrovna] Blavatsky earlier.
> Lucifer as here used means 'bringer of light or the morning star' and has no connection whatsoever with Satan as conventional wisdom would have it." [228]

But there is someone else who is making the claim to being the "morning star." That claim is made in the book of Revelation, chapter 22, verse 16 of the New Testament of the Bible:

> "I Jesus ... am the root and offspring of David, and the bright and morning star."

So the Lucis Trust claims that Lucifer is "the morning star," and Jesus Christ makes the same claim. Only one can correctly be what they both claim to be.

But the Lucis Trust attempted to make an important distinction between Lucifer and Satan, one that should be made again at this juncture.

Lucifer was the name of the being that was in heaven with the God of the Bible, until he rebelled. He was punished and sent to earth, where it appears that his name was changed to Satan. These New Agers, some of the Masons, and members of the Illuminati worship the being that was in heaven before he fell, not the being known as Satan.

Albert Pike added this explanation of their belief in the being that emanates light to mankind. He wrote this in MORALS AND DOGMA:

> "And the Mason is familiar with these doctrines ... that the Supreme Being is a centre of Light whose rays or emanations pervade the Universe; for that is the Light for which all Masonic journeys are a search, and of which the sun and moon in our Lodges are only emblems." [229]

Notice that Mr. Pike says that this light-bringer is a god; in fact he capitalizes the "s" and the "b" in "Supreme Being." He further deifies "Light" by capitalizing the letter "l." And then he added these thoughts about the nature of this "Light:"

> "Behold, it said, the light, which emanates from an immense centre of Light, that spreads everywhere its benevolent rays; so do the spirits of Light emanate from the Divine Light." [230]
> "Masonry is a march and struggle toward the Light." [231]

To show the reader that these are not just the thoughts of one Mason, but are the thoughts of all of Freemasonry, it becomes important to quote other Masonic writers.

Kenneth Mackenzie in his book entitled THE ROYAL MASONIC CYCLOPAEDIA, written in 1877, said this after the entry: SONS OF LIGHT:

> "Masons by their tenure are necessarily Sons of Light, and are so accepted even by their opponents, who are Sons of Darkness." [232]

This is an important revelation. Those who are opposed to the Masons and what they stand for are told that they are "Sons of Darkness." If "Light" is a deity, and it must be because Mr. Mackenzie capitalizes the word, then "Darkness" is also a god. At least this Mason recognizes that there are two gods in the universe: one of Darkness and one of Light. The evidence that other Masons are aware of this distinction will be offered later in this study.

Another source of revelations on the subject of the Masonic religion is a book entitled FREEMASONS REPOSITORY, which is a collection of articles written by Masons. The particular one used in the following reference was published in 1882-1883. Here the writer was moved to comment:

"'Let there be light' is a phrase of small import as some have heard it when kneeling at Masonic Altars. Its breadth of meaning has not been understood.

These are the true Craftsmen who are followers of the light in every deed; they are pledged to oppose whatever is of darkness, ignorance and sin; they have entered upon that illumined way which leadeth to God and to heaven, and they may rightly be called 'Sons of Light.'"

"Thus has light been regarded in all the philosophies and religions of the world. In this respect Masonry but maintains the symbolism which has found general acceptance." [233]

"Light is the sign of a presence and power deserving of devout recognition. God may be said to reveal himself in the light. He dwelleth in light inaccessible -- yet he reveals himself to give knowledge to the minds of men, while by the illumination of his presence and his truth he imparts to the human world a condition of true spiritual life ...."

"The creation of the earth ... was, at the first, 'without form and void.' It was a shapeless and desolate mass of matter. In that condition of primeval chaos, there was an entire absence of light.

Then it was the Spirit of God manifested itself as the great quickening principle of a new order, communicating light and life to the hitherto desolate and disordered creation." [234]

To show the reader that most people do not understand the esoteric meaning behind the symbol of "light," Mr. Mackey wrote these comments in his ENCYCLOPAEDIA:

"Freemasons are emphatically called the 'sons of light,' because they are, or at least are entitled to be, in possession of the true meaning of the symbol."

"Light is an important word in the Masonic system. It conveys a far more recondite [defined as being beyond the grasp of the ordinary mind] meaning that it is believed to possess by the generality of readers. ... it contains within itself a far more abstruse [defined as being hard to understand] allusion to the very essence of Speculative Masonry." [235]

Perhaps the very reason that the Masons conceal a great truth in the word "light," or "Light," can be best summarized in this single statement of Albert Pike in his book entitled MORALS AND DOGMA:

"... Light will finally overcome Darkness." [236]

So, if the student of "esoteric knowledge" wishes to understand the language, it becomes important to determine, if possible, who the "light-bearer" is. And the student can know for certain who that is, because one of the greatest "seekers of light" has told the world. That writer is Albert Pike, a Mason, and he has described who this individual is in his book entitled MORALS AND DOGMA. Mr. Pike identified the "light-bearer" on page 321 of that book:

"Lucifer, the Light-bearer!

Lucifer, the Son of the Morning!

Is it he who bears the Light ...?

Doubt it not!" [237]

Albert Pike has admitted that the Masons seek Light! He has now admitted that the "Light-bearer" is Lucifer! The Masons ask for "Light" from the "Light-bearer" Lucifer!

But Mr. Pike is not the only Mason who has admitted that in easily understandable language. Another Masonic writer is Manly P. Hall, and he has said basically the same thing in his book entitled THE LOST KEYS OF FREEMASONRY. The skeptic can know that this book has been included in a "list of the best Masonic books available" in a Masonic magazine called THE ROYAL ARCH MASON. The list says that "it [the list] is the finest basic library available to Freemasons." So the student can know that this book is approved reading for the Masonic Order. This is that comment, as found on page 48 of his book:

"The seething energies of Lucifer are in his hands |the Master Mason's hands] and before he may step upward [through the remaining degrees?] he must prove his ability to properly apply energy." [238]

So the energies of Lucifer are in the hands of the Master Mason! The god of some of the Masons is Lucifer! There can be no doubt, because some of the best known Masonic writers have told the reader in their own words!

Mr. Hall added this comment on page 55 of the same book:

"The Master Mason is in truth a sun, a great reflector of light ....

He stands before the glowing fire light [the sun?] and the world.

Through him passes Hydra, the great snake [Lucifer?], and from its [the snake, as a symbol of Lucifer] mouth there pours the light of God.

His [Hydra's, the great snake's?] symbol is the rising sun ...." [239]

Albert Pike confirmed that Hydra was a "serpent" on page 508 of his book entitled MORALS AND DOGMA.

So that quote from Mr. Hall's book confirms that the Mason is the intermediary between the sun-god and man. And through him passes the truth of the sun-god.

Simply stated, once again, Lucifer is the god of some of the Masons!

The Bible has made it clear that Lucifer entered the body of a snake when he approached Adam and Eve in the Garden of Eden.

So, the Masons believe that "Light," the emanations from their god Lucifer, will finally overcome the truth given to man by God inside the Bible.

Albert Pike put another piece of the puzzle into place when he wrote this on page 287 of MORALS AND DOGMA:

"You see, my brother, what is the meaning of Masonic "Light."

You see why the East of the Lodge, where the initial letter of the Name of the Deity overhangs the Master, is the place of Light.

... it is that Light, the true knowledge of Deity [the truth that Lucifer is god!] the eternal Good, for which Masons in all ages have sought.

Still Masonry marches steadily onward toward that Light that shines in the great distance [the coming New World Order, still perceived as being many years in the future] the Light of that day when Evil [this "Evil" will be identified later in this study,] overcome and vanquished, shall fade away and disappear forever, and Life and Light be the one law of the universe, and its eternal harmony." [240]

So, Mr. Pike tells the careful reader that the "Light" that all Masons seek is the true knowledge of the real god. And then he tells the world that Lucifer is the real god of the universe.

The final secret of the Masons is no longer a secret!

The student of the Masons can know that the great secret that the Adept Masons are keeping from the Initiate Masons is that the concealed God of the Masonic Lodge is Lucifer, the "light-bearer!"

But a study of "Light" would not be complete without identifying the individual that the Bible says is the source of the true light. The name of this individual has been recorded in the New Testament, and it was written down by the disciple John, in about 80 A.D. He was an eye witness to many of the events in the New Testament, and he was moved to write the following, in John 8:12:

"Then spake Jesus again unto them, saying I am the light of the world: he that followeth me shall not walk in darkness, but shall have the light of life."

So here we see the exact nature of the battle between the followers of the deceiving "light-bearer," Lucifer, meaning the Masons, the Illuminati and the New Age, and the true light, Jesus. And as has been illustrated, these organizations believe that their god, their light, will finally overcome the true light, Jesus Christ.

The battle lines are indeed drawn, and have been for many centuries.

All are working to insure a victory for their side in the war.

Chapter 12
East and West

In order to understand why "Light" has become an object of worship by the Masons and others, one has to understand some simple laws of the physical universe. It is obvious that the sun rises in the east, and sets in the west. The Masons know that it is in the direction known as the east where the physical sun rises each day.

Mr. Pike indicated that it is in the eastern part of their Lodge that their Worshipful Master, their equivalent of the President, sits. One Mason who explained this fact was Captain William Morgan, a Mason of some 30 years, who exposed the Masonic rituals in a book entitled FREEMASONRY EXPOSED. According to him, the Master sits in the east for a reason:

> "As the sun rises in the east to open and adorn the day, so presides the Worshipful Master in the east to open and adorn his lodge ...." [241]

Albert Pike further discussed that point when he wrote:

"Our Lodges are said to be due East and West, because the Master represents the rising Sun, and of course must be in the East." [242]

Mr. Mackey also wrote about the relationship of the place of the Master's location, and the east:

"The East, being the place where the Master sits, is considered the most honorable part of the Lodge ..." [243]

So the sun, a symbol of Lucifer, the god of some of the Masons, resides in the east. The Masons know this, so they place their Worshipful Master in that area, and then conceal the reasons why they have done so from their fellow Masons.

The significance of this fact will become clear in further chapters of this study.

Chapter 13
The Pyramid of Giza

The Masons have agreed with the Egyptians that Osiris, one of their gods, was a deity. For instance, Albert Mackey wrote "Osirus was the sun ...." [244]

Sun-gods all over the world have had temples erected to their memory, and as a place where they might be worshipped. Osirus was no exception.

The Masons are aware of this penchant for temple building as a place for. god worship. In October 1953, a Mason wrote the following in the NEW AGE MAGAZINE, the magazine published by the Scottish Rite of Freemasonry:

> "If perchance you were to visit the Great Pyramid of Gizeh [also spelled Giza] ... you would be presented with a souvenir stating that Osiris commanded Thalmes to build him a house in the form of a pyramid with certain designated passageways." [245]

Some in Egypt claim that the Great Pyramid was not built as a tomb for a deceased pharaoh, but as a temple for initiation into sun worship. There is now a growing body of evidence to support that claim.

But, it is important to set the stage for that conclusion first by examining that evidence.

(The author would like to make a few comments at this juncture. It is not my purpose to convince the reader that these comments about the purpose of the pyramid are correct. I am only attempting to convince you that these sun-worshippers consider them to be true. And, because they do, they are making plans for our future. And those plans should concern each reader of this material because, as I am attempting to point out, the overall changes they are arranging are going to alter the very way all of us live our lives. And, I for one, do not care for the plans being made.)

There are some who claim that the pyramid was constructed about six thousand years ago, and not about three thousand years ago as most archaeologists believe.

One who makes that claim is Richard W. Noone in his book entitled 5/5/2000. Mr. Noone's book is not about pyramids as such, but about his claims that massive changes will occur on the earth on that date in the year 2000 due to a change in the alignment of five planets near to the earth. This will not be the place to comment on his charges. However, he has done considerable research into the pyramids as part of his studies.

He has pointed out that the word for "pyramid" in ancient Egypt was "glorious light," once again connecting the pyramid with the sun and the sun-god Osiris.

Manly P. Hall stated that he too believed that the pyramid was constructed for some purpose other than for the burial of a pharaoh. He wrote:

"The Pyramids |notice that he capitalizes the word] -- the great Egyptian temples of initiation." [246]

He also wrote that he knew what the initiation ceremony was for:

"... the illumined of antiquity ... entered its portals as men; they came forth as gods." [247]

There are many now who believe that an individual named Khufu built the Great Pyramid. The name, according to Mr. Noone, is

"phonetically similar to the ancient Egyptian word for the Great Pyramid, Khuti, meaning 'Glorious Light.'" [248]

Some writers on the pyramid have indicated that their research has led them to the conclusion that the pyramid has a concealed time table built into its passageways. Max Toth is one of these authors, and he has written this in his book entitled PYRAMID PROPHECIES:

"The prophecies of the ancient masters are located into the pyramid form ...." [249]

It is the opinion of Mr. Noone that there is only one "prophecy" that should be examined, and it is this one:

"Beginning at the geometrical point beneath the pyramid arris edge [defined as two straight lines coming together at an angle] meets the projected floor line of the ascending passage, we have a straight line that runs up the ascending passage and Grand Gallery.
This line measured 6,000 inches." [250]

(For those not familiar with these terms, the pyramid is entered through a passageway called the Descending Passageway. This meets with a passageway, going up into the pyramid, called, obviously, the Ascending Passage, at the end of which are several rooms. So, here the author is describing a line down the Grand Gallery, through the ground under the pyramid, where it meets with a line coming down the outside of the pyramid. The line, from the point where these two lines meet, back up the inside line, and where it meets the rooms at the top of the passageway, measures 6,000 inches. The significance of this measurement will be explained in some of the following paragraphs. The important thing to notice here is that this 6000 inch line is truly hidden: it does not exist in reality. It is hidden under ground with no apparent existence. It is truly a hidden prediction.)

Joseph Carr, a writer on the Nazi Party of Adolf Hitler and its connections with sun worship, wrote about an experience an individual had inside the pyramid:

"In April, 1904 an English Buddhist named Aleister Crowley visited Cairo ....
Rose Edith Crowley [his wife] asked her husband to perform a magical ritual .... [He] obeyed by saying the prayer of invocation to Horus [another Egyptian sun-god.] He later claimed that a being appeared to him during that hour [and] announced to [him] that the old age was passing away, and a New Age was dawning.
Also revealed to Crowley was that the religion of the New Age could not take its place until the old religion [presumably Christianity] was smashed." [251]

So, here we see a connection between the pyramid, sun-worship and the New Age.

One of the proofs that the pyramid was not constructed as a burial chamber is the fact that both of the two large rooms inside the pyramid, the so-called "King's chamber" and the "Queen's chamber," have vent ducts leading from inside the rooms to the outside of the pyramid. This had led many to believe that the ducts were meant to provide air for human occupants. Some of these writers have expressed their opinions in the books that they have written. One of these is Wilfred Gregson, an architect and a 33rd degree Mason, who wrote this:

"Obviously the idea was to get air moving into the pyramid. You can't exist very long breathing stagnant air. So my principle is that this was a temple of initiation." [252]

Manly P. Hall, a fellow Mason, agreed with Mr. Gregson, when he wrote this comment:

"... there seems to be no reason why a legitimate tomb should have air vents going from the King's chamber [as well as the Queen's chamber] out to the surface." [253]

Another writer on the pyramid, Andre Pochan, has written in his book THE MYSTERIES OF THE GREAT PYRAMID:

"If the two conduits [into the King's chamber] were originally ventilation ducts, the unavoidable conclusion is that the Great Pyramid's upper chamber was not the site of the royal sepulcher.
Continuous ventilation would have inevitably resulted in not only the putrefaction of the mummy, but also the rapid destruction of all the funerary furniture indispenable to the deceased for his life to the beyond." [254]

Mr. Noone connected the great pyramid in Egypt with the symbolism of the pyramid in Mexico, called the Pyramid at Chichen-Itza:

"the temple at the East of the quadrangle has a great many repeats of a huge sun burst, from the middle of the sun burst is the huge head of a serpent whose mouth is open.
This needs little explanation.
The sun representing 'God' and the serpent 'His Divine Wisdom,' holds man's head so that he can neither see the serpent 'Divine Wisdom,' nor the Light of God from which it comes." [255]

Mr. Noone is saying that the serpent is attempting to keep man from understanding that the god was Lucifer, in the form of a sun burst.
But there is another mystery concealed inside the Great Pyramid that must be explored.
The pyramid appears to have been built to memorialize the explosion of a great star 4,000 years ago.
Mr. Noone says:

"If the Ascending Passage and Grand Gallery were built to observe this supernova explosion, the Giza complex was built to memorialize a tremendous cataclysm in the earth's planetary system which affected the globe with fire and flood." [256]

"The Grand Gallery, aimed like a giant telescope at a particular celestial body in the earth's southern sky -- before its view of the heavens was blocked by the completion of the building -- points to where radio astronomy has just pinpointed the supernova (or giant stellar explosion) nearest to our solar system ... The Great Pyramid's Grand Gallery is focused at this particular spot in the earth's southern sky." [257]

Then Mr. Noone discussed the research being done to locate the spot in the universe where the Grand Gallery is pointed. He wrote:

"In the late 1960's Dr. Anthony Hewish, 1974 co-recipient of the Nobel Prize in physics, was working at England's Mulard Radio Astronomy Observatory. Hewish began to track a mysterious rhythmic series of pulses, clearly from a point in the earth's southern sky." [258]

Mr. Noone pointed out that Dr. Hewish :

"... demonstrated that the strange rhythmic pulses were radio emissions from a star that had collapsed or blown itself up in the earth's southern sky some time around 4000 B.C., a date memorialized in the mysteries of Freemasonry as Anno Lucis, the Year of Light." [259]

In another part of the world George Michanowsky, author of the book entitled THE ONCE AND FUTURE STAR, was deciphering an incredible message cut, carved, and indented in an ancient cuneiform (meaning a language of wedge-shaped characters used in ancient inscriptions) clay tablet, located in the British Museum.

"The ancient Sumerian cuneiform table Michanowsky was deciphering described a giant star exploding within a triangle formed by the three stars Zeta Puppis, Gamma Velorum, and Lambda Velorum. These three stars are located in the earth's southern sky and unknown to Michanowsky at the time were being tracked by Anthony Hewish.

Michanowsky continued deciphering the Sumerian star catalogue, containing observations going back thousands of years. The remarkably accurate star catalogue now stated that the blazing star that had exploded within the triangle would again be seen by man in 6,000 years." [260]

So two world renowned scientists had independently discovered the results of a large explosion that they both felt had occurred around 6000 years ago.

Mr. Noone then asked the question:

"Is there a Masonic connection between Vela X, a star which exploded within a triangle, and the ancient religious symbolism and star dates of Freemasonry?" [261]

And the Masons have answered it with a positive yes. Albert Mackey, the Mason, in his ENCYCLOPAEDIA, wrote this:

"In the Year of Light; abbreviated A.L.
The date used in ancient Craft Masonry; found by adding 4000 to the Vulgar [meaning the common] Era; thus, 1911 + 4000 = 5,911." [262]

This current book was being written in 1989, A.D., which stands for Anno Domini, the "year of the Lord," meaning since the birth of Jesus. But according to the Masons, the true calendar date should be written 5989 A.L.

Another writer on the Great Pyramid is Tom Valentine, and his book is entitled THE GREAT PYRAMID: MAN'S MONUMENT TO MAN. Mr. Valentine wrote:

"... the Great Pyramid's system of passages and chambers is a chronological graph that begins in 4000 B.C. and continues for six thousand years." [263]

So, according to the Masons, there are only 11 years to the year 6000. But what happens after the 6,000 years? What is next?

The New Agers have told us. Marilyn Ferguson, a New Age believer, has written a book entitled THE AQUARIAN CONSPIRACY, in which she wrote the following:

"... we are entering a millennium of love and light." [264]

A millennium is defined as a thousand year period. So, it appears that sometime in the near future, the New Agers are going to see the beginning of the millennium reign of Lord Maitreya.

This position was confirmed by the Lucis Trust, also a New Age organization, when it wrote the following in a quarterly newsletter for the third quarter, 1982:

"The year 2000 looms before humanity as a gigantic milestone which marks both an ending and a beginning. It marks the end of a volatile millennium which has seen enormous progress and change ....

But more importantly, the year 2000 stands as a symbolic portal through which humanity can pass into a New Age ... if it so chooses." [265]

So something is coming.
And it is coming by the year 2000.
And it is called The New Age.
Or The New World Order.

1 Chapter 14
Obelisks

The Masons have admitted that they use symbols to conceal important truths from their fellow Masons. Previous chapters have examined two of the major Masonic symbols, the star and the sun. Other Masonic symbols need to be examined as well.

One of these symbols is the obelisk. The word is defined by a dictionary as a tall, four-sided stone pillar tapering toward its pyramidal top.

There are three of major importance in the world today: one in Washington D.C., called the Washington Monument; another one in Central Park, in New York City; and the third in the Vatican, located in Rome, Italy.

The first major obelisk is in St. Peter's square in Rome, Italy, and is placed in such a way that every Pope who addresses any crowd in the square, must face the obelisk.

The second major obelisk was brought to New York from its location in Alexandria, Egypt, and placed in Central Park in New York City in 1881. The four sides of this obelisk are covered with Egyptian hieroglyphs and these drawings have been translated by a variety of Egyptologists including some Masonic writers.

The Masons have told the readers of one of its publications that this obelisk was quarried:

"... to praise and adore the divinity of the sun, worshipped by the ancient Egyptians as the source of light and life. It is a representation of the God Ra, or the sun." [266]

So, there is a symbol of the sun in Central Park, in the heart of New York City.

The third major obelisk is the Washington monument, which was constructed to honor George Washington, the first President of the United States. President Washington was an active and public member of the Masonic Lodge. The monument built in his honor:

"is the tallest such monument in the world, 555 feet high, though not truly an obelisk, because it is not quarried from a single piece but put together from 36,000 separate blocks of granite faced with marble." [267]

This obelisk is a symbol that has definite Masonic connections. It was constructed many years after the President's death on December 14, 1799, as it was not until 1833 that the Washington National Monument Society was organized to erect a monument in his memory.

The monument was not completed until 1848, when the 3300 pound capstone was set in place. The weight of the capstone appears to be semi-symbolic, utilizing the number 33 as a reminder of the 33 degrees inside the Masonic Order.

The obelisk was constructed of a total of 36,000 separate blocks and included 188 Memorial Stones inside the monument, donated to the Society by individuals, societies, cities, states and nations of the world. Approximately 35 of these came from Masonic lodges, and the last of these blocks was placed into the monument at the 330 foot level. Once again, the number 33 shows up in the construction of the obelisk, and once again it is semi-concealed in a fact about its construction.

The total cost of the monument concealed another Masonic number, this time the number 13: the cost of the entire monument was $1,300,000.

There are other Masonic secrets concealed in the numbers relating to the eight windows in the monument, two on each side. Six of these windows are of the same size, but the seventh and the eighth, the two facing the east, are larger. It will be remembered that The Masons have stated that it is in the east that their Master sits. So the east has special significance to them.

The eight windows total 39 square feet in size, and 39 is three times the Masonic number 13. But the two windows facing the east conceal another reference to the number 13. The student of geometry will remember that the sum of the squares of the base and perpendicular in a right-angled triangle is equal to the square of the hypotenuse, meaning the third side. The example often cited to prove that truth is the triangle with the three sides being 3 inches, 4 inches, and 5 inches in length. The square of the two sides, the sides that are 3 inches and 4 inches in length, are 9 and 16, and the total of those two squares is equal to the square of the 5 inch side, or 25.

Each of the two windows in the east are 2 feet by 3 feet, and the square of the third side is 13. The square of 2 is four, and the square of 3 is 9. The total of 4 and 9 is 13.

The number 13 appears to be a very symbolic number to the Masons, but finding out why it is has become a difficult chore. One clue is contained in the Bible in the book of Genesis. That book records in Genesis 14:4 that it was in the thirteenth year that an amalgamation of various kings rebelled against their leader. It will be recalled that Lucifer rebelled against God in the heavens, and some historians equate the number 13 with rebellion and Lucifer.

Stan Deyo is one author who explained that the number 13 had a very definite meaning. He wrote this in his book entitled THE COSMIC CONSPIRACY:

"... thirteen is the value [assigned] to represent Satan, [the] serpent, [the] dragon, [the] tempter or rebellion." [268]

So the Washington Monument, dedicated to the memory of a Mason, conceals many Masonic symbols inside its obelisk form. But there is an extremely important meaning that has not been explained by modern historians.

As has been illustrated, the Masons have placed a particular importance on the obelisk, primarily because it has its root in the ancient times in Egypt. However, there is another reason, one that is far more important.

The first connection is to the past. Carl Claudy, the Masonic writer, wrote this:

"... the initiate of old saw in the obelisk the very spirit of the god he worshipped." [269]

So, according to this Masonic writer, the obelisk is a symbol of a god that was worshipped by the believers of the ancient mysteries. It has been shown that those involved in the ancient mysteries worshipped Lucifer.

But a far more important reason was revealed to those careful enough to note the importance of the revelation. Mr. Claudy then added this comment:

"From the dawn of religion the pillar, monolith or built up, has played an important part in the worship of the Unseen.

... in Egypt the obelisk stood for the very presence of the Sun God himself." [270]

He repeated these very words in another section of the same book:

"... in Egypt the obelisk stood for the very presence of the Sun God himself." [271]

He went on to repeat his statement that:

"... the initiate of old saw in the obelisk the very spirit of the God he worshiped." [272]

Mr. Claudy revealed that the obelisk is a symbol of the sun-god, and implied that this very deity is present inside the stone itself.

The obelisk stands for the very presence of the sun-god!
And the sun-god is Lucifer!

Mr. Pike confirmed this statement in his book entitled MORALS AND DOGMA:

"The obelisk was ... consecrated to the Sun." [273]

And Kenneth Mackenzie, a third Masonic writer, added this supporting statement:

"Sun-worship was plainly connected with the erection of obelisks ....
... they were placed in front of the temples of Egypt. [They referred] to the worship of the sun." [274]

And Mr. Mackey, a fourth Masonic writer, offered this comment:

"Obelisks were, it is supposed, originally erected in honor of the sun god." [275]

So, obelisks are a symbol of the "very presence of the sun-god himself." This is an explanation that is not offered to the overwhelming majority of the American people. Yet, one of the major monuments in Washington D.C. is an obelisk. And it was erected to honor George Washington, a very visible member of the Masonic Order. And the Masons have concealed various esoteric numbers inside the blocks of the monument itself.

One of the strange incidents that involved the Washington monument occurred first in 1981, and then again in 1985, when the inauguration ceremony of President Ronald Reagan was moved to the west front of the Capitol from the traditional location, the east front. Every President since George Washington had been sworn in on the east front of the Capitol building, but, for some unexplained reason, someone wanted President Reagan sworn in on the west front.

Newsweek magazine for January 26, 1981, the issue covering the inauguration ceremonies, wrote about this change in the location of the ceremony:

"Swearing in a President on the Capitol's West Front -- for the first time ever -- ...."

The article went on to point out that the reason the move was made was not an aesthetic one:

"But the seldom-used West Front is crumbling, its rickety porticos held up by wooden posts. 'It's not about to fall down,' assured Capitol architect George White, 'but it is in need of structural repair.' Rather than pop for a major repair job, however, the Inaugural committee ordered a hasty coat of white paint -- and draped a gigantic American flag over the unsightly wooden beams."

But the Newsweek magazine article did not explain why the location was moved to that particular side of the Capitol.

But a possible explanation was offered, rather subtly, in a Time magazine picture that accompanied their coverage of the inauguration ceremonies. The picture was a behind the back, over the shoulder, elevated shot showing the President giving his inauguration address. The picture is approximately 7" by 8" in size, and both the President, at the bottom of the picture, and the Washington monument off in the distance, at the top of the picture, appear to be about one inch in height.

But the interesting caption at the bottom of the picture is where it appears the hidden message is contained. The caption reads:

"Before some 150,000 listeners at the West Front of the Capitol, Reagan gazes toward the Washington Monument and delivers his address." [276]

The President gazes at a symbol of the "very presence of the sun-god himself" and gives his inauguration address.

It is unknown if this shift in the location site was for the express purpose of giving a signal to those able to understand the significance of the President "gazing" at the very presence of the sun-god. But it was the first time that any President had been sworn in on that side of the Capitol, and it put him in a position where, if someone had wished to send a signal involving the Washington monument and its esoteric symbology, they could have done so.

The same scene was repeated in President Reagan's second inauguration in 1985. Time magazine wrote this in their coverage of that event in their January 21, 1985 issue:

"A public ceremony will follow on Monday at the West Front of the Capitol ...." [277]

A possible explanation of the significance of these two inauguration ceremonies will be offered in one of the last chapters of this book.

But, for the esoteric minded, it appeared that someone might have wanted some of the American people to know something about President Ronald Reagan.

The move to the west front of the Capitol Building might have had a concealed meaning.

Chapter 15
The Illuminati

The thought that there have been people actually planning the major events of the future in a harmful way has often been expressed by some of the world's leaders. One such individual was Winston Churchill, the Prime Minister of England during World War II. He wrote about what he had discovered when he made his views public in a London newspaper in 1920. These are those thoughts:

> "From the days of Spartacus-Weishaupt to those of Karl Marx, to those of Trotsky, Bela Kun, Rosa Luxembourg, and Emma Goldman, this world wide conspiracy for the overthrow of civilization and for the reconstitution of society on the basis of arrested development, of envious malevolence [defined as being done with malice; spiteful] and impossible equality, has been steadily growing.
>
> It played a definitely recognizable role in the tragedy of the French Revolution. It has been the mainspring of every subversive movement during the

nineteenth century, and now at last this band of extraordinary personalities from the underworld of the great cities of Europe and America have gripped the Russian people by the hair of their heads, and have become practically the undisputed masters of that enormous empire." [278]

Spartacus was the code name that Adam Weishaupt, the founder of the Illuminati, used inside that organization; Karl Marx was, of course, the so-called "father of communism;" Trotsky was Leon Trotsky, one of the major leaders in the Communist Revolution in Russia in 1917; and Bela Kun, Rosa Luxembourg and Emma Goldman were revolutionaries. The French Revolution was in 1789, and many historians have concluded that the Illuminati fomented it with the goal of putting their fellow member of the Illuminati, the Duc d' Orleans, on the throne of France.

Mr. Churchill linked Weishaupt and the Illuminati of 1776 with the Communist Karl Marx of 1848, and Marx with the Russian Communists of 1917. It was his opinion that these individuals had been linked together in a conspiracy lasting for more than 140 years. He then combined this conspiracy with European and American revolutionaries. And his final comment was that their combined purpose was to "overthrow civilization." In other words, Mr. Churchill claimed that their purpose was to bring the world a "New World Order."

He had provided the reader with a brief overview of a long lasting conspiracy. He had told the world that this conspiracy wanted to overthrow civilization.

But, because few knew anything at all about this conspiracy, the world paid no attention to Mr. Churchill's comments.

That was no accident because this conspiracy has, in the main, acted under the cover of concealment. They do not announce their plans before they occur. And they certainly do not announce their involvement after the planned event has occurred.

Professor Adam Weishaupt boastfully stated that his organization would remain concealed from the eyes of the public. He wrote:

"The great strength of our Order lies in its concealment; let it never appear in any place in its own name, but always covered by another name, and another occupation."

He even told the world, in his writings, where he would conceal the Order:

"None is fitter than the three lower degrees of Free Masonry; the public is accustomed to it, expects little from it, and therefore takes little notice of it." [279]

He felt that this secrecy would lead him to success because he felt no one would be able to break into it. He wrote:

"Our secret Association works in a way that nothing can withstand ...." [280]

Another reason that he felt that the Illuminati would succeed was the fact that he was offering his members worldwide power. He felt that this inducement would enable him to draw into his organization only those who would do anything to satisfy that desire for power. He wrote:

"The true purpose of the Order was to rule the world. To achieve this it was necessary for the Order to destroy all religions, overthrow all governments and abolish private property." [281]

The Bavarian government discovered the existence of this secret conspiracy and investigated the Order in 1786. They issued a report in which they concluded:

"... the express aim of this Order was to abolish Christianity, and overthrow all civil government." [282]

As mentioned previously, Weishaupt founded the Illuminati on May 1, 1776, and the selection of that date as the founding date of their Order appears to be no coincidence. Albert Pike wrote that May 1st was a festival day:

"The festival was in honor of the Sun." [283]

The reason that Weishaupt chose the First of May to found his secret, anti-Christian religion has not been satisfactorily explained. However, there are some interesting clues as to why he might have chosen that date.

One possible explanation involves the Roman emperor Diocletian, who reigned from 284-305 A.D.

After the death of Jesus, the Christian world continued to be persecuted by a string of violent Caesers of the Roman Empire. But the violence inaugurated by Diocletian surpassed them all in violence.

An edict requiring uniformity of worship was issued in 303 A.D., and the Christians resisted by refusing to pay homage to the image of the emperor. Diocletian met that resistance with specific retaliation against the Christians: they lost their public and private possessions, and their assemblies were prohibited. Their churches were torn down, and their sacred writings were destroyed.

In addition, many Christians paid for their resistance with their lives: it has been estimated that the victims numbered into the hundreds of thousands.

Finally, Diocletian grew ill, and abdicated on May 1, 305 A.D. The persecution persisted, but never again approached that of the emperor Diocletian.

Is it possible that Professor Weishaupt learned about the date of this abdication and picked up the mantle laid down by Diocletian, and started the persecution of Christians again, some 1400 years later?

The goal of the Illuminati was "man made perfect as a god -- without God." [284] But it was a strange ideal, because Weishaupt permitted his followers to utilize any activity to achieve his goal, including lying. He wrote:

> "One must speak sometimes one way and sometimes another ... so that, with respect to our true line of thinking, we may be impenetrable." [285]

The members did tell the truth when they took the initiation ceremony, however. They took an oath which read, in part:

> "I bind myself to perpetual silence and unshaken loyalty and submission to the Order ...." [286]

Weishaupt claimed that he was shocked when his Order turned into a religion, but that is what he said:

"I never thought that I should become the founder of a new religion." [287]

But his religion had a different base than the traditional religion: his was based upon a worship of reason:

[288] "... then will Reason rule with unperceived sway."

"... Reason will be the only code of Man. This is one of our greatest secrets."
"When at last Reason becomes the religion of man, then will the problem be solved." [289]

Weishaupt's dedication of his organization to "reason" makes some sense when the reader recalls that "reason" has been defined as the "unbridled use of man's mind to solve man's problems without the involvement of God." The Bible calls this "the fruit of the tree of the knowledge of good and evil."
It was this knowledge that God wanted man not to have, and it was the promise made to man by Lucifer that man could have it by eating of "the fruit."
In addition, Weishaupt's religion offered its believers a reward not offered by any other religion: worldwide power! Weishaupt wrote:

"The pupils [members of the Illuminati] are convinced that the Order will rule the world. Every member therefore becomes a ruler." [290]

Weishaupt's religion not only offered power to his believers, but he offered them something else not guaranteed by any other religion: worldly success. He said that once a candidate had achieved the exalted degree of Illuminatus Minor, the fourth of the thirteen inside his Order, his superiors would:

"assist him [the member] in bringing his talents into action, and [would] place him in situations most favorable for their exertion, so that he may be assured of success." [291]

One of those areas where the Illuminati would strive to place their members was inside government. Weishaupt wrote:

"We must do our utmost to procure the advancement of Illuminati into all important civil offices." [292]

Weishaupt's religion also had a rather unusual view of man's nature. Traditional religion teaches all of mankind that man is basically a sinner, and that his way out is to change his bad habits. Weishaupt felt that this position was in error. He wrote:

"Man is not bad except as he is made so by arbitrary morality. He is bad because Religion, the State, and bad examples pervert him." [293]

"Men ... suffered themselves to be oppressed -- gave themselves up to civil societies, and formed states. To get out of this state ... there is no other mean than the use of Reason ....

This can be done in no other way but by secret associations, which will by degrees, and in silence, possess themselves of the government of the States, and make use of those means for this purpose which the wicked use for attaining their base ends." [294]

Professor Weishaupt's religion authorized its members to use any means that would benefit the goal of the Illuminati. That goal was simple: the destruction of all Christianity:

"Behold our secret .... If in order to destroy all Christianity, all religion, we have pretended to have the sole true religion, remember that the end justifies the means, and that the wise ought to take all the means to do good which the wicked take to do evil." [295]

Weishaupt spoke about the Jesuits, an order of priests inside the Catholic Church. He was, it will be remembered, an instructor at a Catholic university in Ingolstadt, Bavaria, run by the Jesuits. He apparently admired their success, because he organized his order in a similar manner. He wrote:

"What these men have done for altars and empires, why should I not do against altars and empires? By the attraction of mysteries, of legends, of adepts, why should I not destroy in the dark what they erect in the light of day." [296]

Some writers in the past have summarized the beliefs of the Illuminati for the future use of historians. One was Nesta Webster, who wrote the following about their aims in her book entitled WORLD REVOLUTION:

1. Abolition of Monarchy and all ordered Government.
2. Abolition of private property.
3. Abolition of inheritance.
4. Abolition of patriotism.
5. Abolition of the family (i.e. of marriage and all morality, and the institution of the communal education of children).
6. Abolition of all religion. [297]

Weishaupt must have felt that his plan would ultimately succeed. He certainly felt that his Order would control the world. And he anticipated that there would be opposition to his goals. He summarized all of these thoughts in this statement:

"By this plan, we shall direct all mankind. In this manner, and by the simplest means, we shall set all in motion and in flames. The occupations must be so allotted and contrived, that we may, in secret, influence all political transactions." [298]

Weishaupt decided that his Illuminati needed a cover, and he successfully infiltrated the Masonic Order in 1782, at the Masonic Congress at Wilhelmsbad. Some Masons became aware of that infiltration and were moved to comment about it. One such Mason was President George Washington who was sent a copy of Professor John Robison's book entitled PROOFS OF A CONSPIRACY by a Christian minister named G. W. Snyder. The President responded to the minister's request that he read the book, and his letter to the minister has been preserved for posterity. Mr. Washington wrote the minister:

"It was not my intention to doubt that the doctrines of the Illuminati, and principles of Jacobinism, had not spread in the United States.

On the contrary, no one is more fully satisfied of this fact than I am. The idea that I meant to convey was that I did not believe that the Lodges of Freemasons in this country had, as societies, endeavored to propagate the diabolical [defined as being of the devil] tenets of [the Illuminati.]

That individuals of them may have done it, or that the founder ... may have had these objects -- and actually, in my view, had a separation of the people from their government, is too evident to be questioned.

I believe ... that none of the Lodges in this country are contaminated with the principles ascribed to the society of the Illuminati." [299]

The President indicated that he was aware that the Illuminati had arrived in America; that its tenets were diabolical, meaning that he recognized that they involved themselves in devil worship; and that they intended to separate man from his government.

The President of the United States had acknowledged the presence of the devil-worshipping Illuminati in America!

The book that the President read was written by a member of the Lodge who had been asked to join the Illuminati. He was a professor of Natural Philosophy at Edinburgh University in Scotland. After his study, he concluded that the purposes of the Illuminati were completely unacceptable, and he wrote his book to expose its goals. He wrote:

"... an Association has been formed for the express purpose of rooting out all the religious establishments, and overturning all the existing governments of Europe." [300]

He discovered that the leaders would:

"... rule the world with uncontrollable power, while all the rest, ... will be ... employed as mere tools of the ambition of their unknown superiors." [301]

James Watt, the inventor of the steam engine, was a contemporary of Professor Robison, and he wrote this about his friend:

"a man of the clearest head and the most science of anybody I have ever known." [302]

But, even with all of these criticisms about the purposes of the Illuminati, there were some Masons who felt that the association between the Masons and the Illuminati was a positive federation. One such Mason, Kenneth Mackenzie, has written that this Masonic infiltration was:

"... an attempt to purify Masonry, then in much confusion." [303]

Another Mason who approved of the merger was Dr. Walter M. Fleming, one of the four founders of the Shrine, an organization that is part of the Masonic fraternity. He and three other Masons formed this organization in 1871, and he assisted in the preparation of a history of the Shrine in 1893. In that book, Dr. Fleming wrote:

"Among the modern promoters of the principles of the Order [the Shrine] in Europe, one of the most noted was Herr Adam Weishaupt ... professor of law in the University of Ingolstadt, in Bavaria ... who revived the Order in that city on May 1, 1776. Its members exercised a profound influence before and during the French Revolution, when they were known as the Illuminati." [304]

Dr. Fleming, a 33rd degree Mason, was recognizing the found-of the Illuminati as a "reviver of the Order." His quote comes from a book entitled PARADE TO GLORY, written by Fred Van Deventer, which appears to be given to each new member of the Shrine.

So Dr. Fleming was supportive of the efforts of Professor Adam Weishaupt, because he had "revived the Order."

Albert Mackey also praised Professor Weishaupt. He wrote these comments in his ENCYCLOPAEDIA OF FREEMA-SONRY:

"... Weishaupt could not have been the monster that he has been painted by his adversaries."

And the reason he couldn't have been a "monster," was because he was:

"... a Masonic reformer." [305]

However, the major support that Weishaupt has received has come from members of the Masonic Order who have attacked those who have been critical of the Professor and the Illuminati he was the founder of.

Albert Mackey, for instance, admitted that John Robison was a fellow Mason, but he wrote these comments about his belief that a conspiracy had infiltrated the Illuminati:

"many of his statements are untrue and his arguments illogical." [306]

"his theory is based on false premises and his reasoning fallacious and illogical ...." [307]

Kenneth Mackenzie in his book entitled THE ROYAL MA-SONIC ENCYCLOPAEDIA also criticized Professor Robison as being:

"The author of a silly and self-contradictory book about Freemasonry ....

... the nauseating nonsense with which Robison decks his book is only to be compared to the more virulent and subtle sarcasm of Barruel." [308]

The individual called "Barruel" by Mr. Mackenzie was in fact the Abbe Barruel who had written a four volume series on the Illuminati in 1798, independently from the book written by Professor Robison. The Abbe's research basically supported the conclusions of Professor Robison.

Obviously, some of the Masons feel that the Abbe, like Professor Robison, was grossly in error.

This is what the Abbe wrote about the Illuminati:

"... a terrible and horrible sect.

"... it has formed for that general Revolution which is to overthrow all thrones, all altars, annihilate all property, [destroy the right to private property] efface [obliterate] all law, and end by dissolving all society." [309]

Another who attacked the Abbe's volumes on the Illuminati was Thomas Jefferson, one of America's founding fathers. Although it appears that he had read only one of the four volumes in the set, Mr. Jefferson commented:

"Barruel's own parts of the book are perfectly the ravings of a Bedlamite." [310]

A Bedlamite was a patient of the Bedlam hospital for lunatics in London, England. So it can be seen that Mr. Jefferson did not care for the Abbe's research. While he charged the Abbe with being a lunatic, Mr. Jefferson praised Adam Weishaupt with these words:

"Weishaupt seems to be an enthusiastic philanthropist. Weishaupt believes that to promote the perfection of the human character was the object of Jesus Christ. His [Weishaupt's] precepts are the love of God and love of our neighbor." [311]

Albert Mackey, one of the greatest Masonic scholars and researchers, praised the Illuminati with these words found in his ENCYCLOPAEDIA:

"The original design of Illuminism was undoubtedly the elevation of the human race." [312]

Mackey also praised the founder as well:

"He is celebrated in the history of Masonry as the founder of the Order of the Illuminati of Bavaria ...." [313]

Other Masonic writers have praised the founder and his conspiratorial society known as the Illuminati as well. Kenneth Mackenzie wrote this:

"Its object was the advancement of morality, education, and virtue ...."
"had the Order been allowed free scope, much good would have resulted ...." [314]

But, whether the critics or the supporters were correct, the Illuminati had come to America. Several researchers into the conspiracy of the Illuminati have provided the student with their evidence that these conspirators had brought their plans to the United States.

Nesta Webster, who wrote in the 1920's, wrote this about her discoveries of where the Illuminati went after their discovery by the Bavarian government:

"Whilst these events [the early stages of the French Revolution of 1789] were taking place in Europe, the New World [meaning America] had been illuminized.
As early as 1786 a lodge of the Order [of the Illuminati] had been started in Virginia, and this was followed by fourteen others in different cities." [315]

In 1798, Jedediah Morse, a minister and the father of Samuel Morse, the inventer of the telegraph, preached a now famous sermon on the Illuminati. He clearly had discovered their presence in America. He said:

"The Order [of the Illuminati] has its branches established and its emissaries at work in America." [316]

And in 1812, the President at Harvard University, Joseph Willard, retired to preach in Vermont. He took the occasion of his retirement on July 4, 1812, to express his concern over the consequences of the then looming war:

"There is sufficient evidence that a number of societies of the Illuminati have been established in this land. They are doubtless striving to secretly undermine all our ancient institutions, civil and sacred. These

societies are clearly leagued with those of the same order in Europe ....

We live in an alarming period . The Enemies of all
order are seeking our ruin. Should infidelity generally
prevail, our independence would fall, of course. Our republican government would be annihilated ..." [317]

Perhaps the next appearance of the Illuminati occurred in
Chicago, Illinois, in 1886, in what has been called the Haymarket Riot. It is uncertain as to whether or not they were
formally involved as an organization, but the whole affair certainly seems to have occurred in a sequence similar to what
they would have orchestrated if they had been involved.

Cyrus McCormick, the owner of a harvester works in Chicago, had refused to accept a union to represent his employ-
ees. When he was pressed by the union, he closed his factory
and opened it later with non-union workers. The strikers and
the non-union workers clashed, and a squad of police arrived.
A bomb was thrown from out of the crowd, and it killed one
and wounded many others. Shooting broke out, and sixty-
eight policemen were wounded and seven of them killed.

After the Haymarket affair, a Captain in the Chicago
police department, Michael J. Shaack, decided that he would
see if he could determine why the disaster had occurred, and
he started a thorough investigation. About a year later, he
issued his report, and these are some of his conclusions:

"All over the world the apostles of disorder, rapine,
[defined as plunder, pillage] and Anarchy are today
pressing their work of ruin, and preaching their gospel
of disaster to all the nations with a more fiery energy
and a better organized propaganda than was ever
known before.

People who imagine that the energy of the revo-
lutionists has slackened, or that their determination to
wreck all the existing systems has grown less bitter,
are deceiving themselves. The conspiracy against society is as determined as it ever was.

Nothing but the uprooting of the very foundations
and groundwork of our civilization will satisfy these
enemies of order ...." [318]

Although Captain Shaak did not specify that the group behind the riot was the Illuminati, he clearly had discovered that the goal of the conspirators was to "uproot civilization," which had been their announced goal for over one hundred years. It appears that his research had uncovered the fact that the Illuminati had been at work in America.

1886 was a big year for those uncovering the evidence that this conspiracy existed. Two other individuals spoke out about the secret societies in the world. One was Henry Edward Manning, Archbishop of Westminster, England, who wrote that the Communist International was:

"the work of secret, political societies, which from 1789 to this day have been perfecting their formation."

He said that this conspiracy:

"is now a power in the midst of the Christian and civilized world, pledged to the destruction of Christianity and the old civilization of Europe." [319]

The other was Abbe Joseph Lane, a respected scholar of the time, who wrote that he had discovered a plan:

"to disorganize at one blow Christian society and the beliefs and customs of the Jews, then bring about a state of things where, religiously speaking, there will be neither Christian nor Jew." [320]

So there were plenty of warnings, but, overall, few in the world listened. And the secret societies continued to prosper.

Chapter 16
Karl Marx, Satanist

Other secret societies prospered as well. And some of the historic figures of the past belonged to them. And the fact that these people belonged to these secret societies has generally not been acknowledged by the historians who have written the "accidental school of history" (the theory that the major events happen by accident. It holds that no one really knows why wars, depressions, inflations, etc. happen. They just do. The opposing view of history is called The Conspiratorial View of History. This view holds that the major events of the past have happened by design. People plan wars, depressions, inflations, and revolutions years in advance.)

One of these individuals was Karl Marx, the so-called "father of communism." Mr. Marx had been born into a religious family. His family was Jewish and had converted to Christianity shortly before his birth. Karl was later baptized into the Protestant faith.

Marx's first written work was called "The Union of the Faithful With Christ," in which he wrote:

"Through love of Christ we turn our hearts at the same time toward our brethren who are inwardly bound to us and whom He gave Himself in sacrifice." [321]

Just a short time later, he wrote this poem he entitled "The Pale Maiden:"

"Thus heaven I've forfeited.
I know it full well.
My soul, once true to God,
Is chosen for hell." [322]

George Jung, a friend of Marx's during this time, added this comment about Marx's attitude:

"Marx will surely chase God from his heaven and will even sue him. Marx calls the Christian religion one of the most immoral of religions." [323]

Marx confirmed this position that something had changed his mind about Christianity with these quotations from his writings:

"The abolition of religion as the illusory happiness of man is a demand for their real happiness." [324]
"I wish to avenge myself against the One who rules above." [325]

Something had indeed changed Marx's view of Christianity. He continued:

"We must war against all prevailing ideas of religion, of the state, of country, of patriotism. The idea of God is the keynote of a perverted civilization.
It must be destroyed." [326]

As can be illustrated by his own writings, something had not only changed his ideas on Christianity, but something had changed his ideas on what God had taught man through the Bible. Marx was now being critical of God's instructions about:

How to worship the Creator;

How to create a nation to protect God-given rights;

Why to establish and maintain national borders;

How to create the conditions under which all could be free to love their Creator.

All of these ideas had a Biblical foundation. All of these principles were taught in the Bible. And each of these ideas had been tested by a variety of civilizations for many centuries, but as can be seen from his writings, Marx wanted to "war against" all of these Biblical principles.

Something had indeed changed his mind.

In addition, Marx had found another bulwark of God's plan for man to be unsatisfactory. He also discovered he had to war against the family.

Marx wrote this in his COMMUNIST MANIFESTO:

"Abolition of the family! Even the most radical flare up at this infamous proposal of the Communists." [327]

His bitterness towards the family unit caused members of his own family to suffer as well:

"Arnold Kunzli, in his book KARL MARX - A PSYCHOGRAM, writes about Marx's life, including the suicide of two daughters and a son-in-law. Three children [of his] died of malnutrition. His daughter Laura, married to the Socialist Lafargue, also buried three of her children; then she and her husband committed suicide together.

Another daughter Eleanor, decided with her husband to do likewise. She died; he backed out at the last minute." [328]

Marx further showed his disdain for the family unit by fathering a child with his own personal maid. She was a gift from his mother-in-law upon the occasion of Marx's wedding. Apparently he found no hypocrisy in the fact that he had a maid at the time he considered himself to be the champion of the working man. Marx railed against the rich and prosperous, those who were wealthy enough to have had maids. But he had one himself.

It is possible to understand a small degree of the utter despair that Jenny von Westphelan, Karl Marx's wife, must have felt being married to a man who allowed such tragedies to occur. Marx was quoted as writing:

"Daily, my wife tells me she wishes she were lying in the grave with the children. And truly I cannot blame her." [329]

But the historians who have probed Marx's background have generally failed to uncover the reason that he had become so bitter against Christianity and all of its teachings. A few honest historians have uncovered the something that changed Marx's views, and that something was Satan worship. Marx had discovered the world of the occult.

Marx had first been brought to the ideas of Socialism by Moses Hess when he was 23. But the most important influence in his young life was the worship of Satan.

Many of his friends had discovered this religion before he had. One was Mikhail Bakunin, a Russian anarchist, who wrote:

"Satan is the first free-thinker and Saviour of the world. He frees Adam and impresses the seal of humanity and liberty on his forehead, by making him disobedient." [330]

Another friend of Marx's was Pierre Proudhon, a French socialist and writer. Marx had been introduced to Proudhon by Hess. Mr. Proudhon "worshipped Satan," according to a book about him and his relationship with Karl Marx. [331]

He had written that God was the prototype for injustice:

"We reach knowledge in spite of him, we reach society in spite of him. Every step forward is a victory in which we overcome the Divine. God is stupidity and cowardice; God is hypocrisy and falsehood; God is tyranny and poverty; God is evil.

Where humanity bows before an altar, humanity, the slave of kings and priests, will be condemned ....

I swear, God, with my hand stretched out towards the heavens, that you are nothing more than the executioner of my reason, the scepter of my conscience .... God is essentially anti-civilized, anti-liberal, anti-human."

Here Proudhon declared God to be evil because he believed that God had denied man his ability to "reason."

Notice that the thoughts of these men were not those of an atheist. Marx and his friends, at this stage of their lives, were not atheists, as present day Marxists describe themselves. That is, while they openly denounced and reviled God, they hated Him while they acknowledged His existence. They did not challenge His existence. They challenged His supremacy.

The thing that changed Marx's views about life was the fact that he had discovered the world of Satan worship.

There is evidence that he had joined a Satanic cult headed by Joana Southcott, a Satanic priestess who considered herself to be in contact with a demon named Shiloh. One of the distinguishing characteristics of his membership in this cult was his long hair and unkempt beard, worn by members of her cult. Proudhon also wore his hair in a similar manner, and it is quite likely that he was a member of this cult as well.

Other Communists have declared their hatred of God. One, a communist named Flourens, wrote this in 1871:

"Our enemy is God. Hatred of God is the beginning of wisdom." [32]

Another notable Communist, Nikolai Lenin, the father of the Communist revolution of 1917 in Russia, also voiced his hatred of God and religion. He wrote the following comments:

"Atheism is an integral part of Marxism. Marxism is materialism. We must combat religion." [333]

"We, of course, say that we do not believe in God. We do not believe in eternal morality. That is moral that serves the destruction of the old society." [334]

"Everything is moral which is necessary for the annihilation of the old exploiting social order [Lenin wished to destroy the Old World Order, and replace it with the New World Order] and for uniting the proletariat."

"We must combat religion. Down with religion. Long live atheism. The spread of atheism is our chief task. Communism abolishes eternal truths. It abolishes all religion and morality." [335]

"Religion is a kind of spiritual intoxicant, in which the slaves of capital drown their humanity, and blunt their desire for decent human experience." [336]

"We shall always preach a scientific philosophy. We must fight against the inconsistencies of the Christians ...." [337]

Lenin, like Marx before him, came from a religious family. His father was a school inspector, and a devout member of the Russian Orthodox Church. But, at the age of eighteen, Lenin started reading Karl Marx and soon was expounding Marxist principles.

He later wrote:

"Atheism is a natural and inseparable portion of Marxism, of the theory and practice of scientific Socialism. Our propaganda necessarily includes propaganda for atheism." [338]

Other Communists have joined the attack on religion. Nikita Khrushchev, a Russian dictator who embraced the Communist theology during the time he spent at the top of the Russian government, wrote this:

"Do not think that the Communists have changed their minds about religion. We remain the Atheists that we have always been; we are doing as much as we can to liberate those people who are still under the spell of this religious opiate." [339]

But notice that Mr. Khrushchev went one step further than some of the other atheists. He stated that the task of the Communist atheists was to "liberate" the God-fearers from their God. This, obviously, is the task not only of the Communists but of the New World Order.

Others, more recently, have praised Marxism. One even served in a high administrative position inside President Jimmy Carter's cabinet. He was Zbigniew Brzezinski, the Special Assistant to the President for National Security Affairs. He was, or is, also Director of the Research Institute on International Change, Professor of Public Law and Government, and a member of the Russian Institute, all at Columbia University.

In 1970, Mr. Brzezinski wrote a book entitled BETWEEN TWO AGES, in which he made some startling observations on the nature of Marxism. Some of these are as follows:

"... Marxism represents a further vital and creative stage in the maturing of man's universal vision."

"Marxism is simultaneously a victory of the external, active man over the inner, passive man and a victory of reason over belief ...."

"... Marxism has served as a mechanism of human 'progress,' even is its practice has often fallen short of its ideals."

"Teilhard de Chardin [a modern day Jesuit theologian and writer] notes at one point that 'monstrous as it is, is not modern totalitarianism really the distortion of something magnificent, and thus quite near to the truth?'"

"... what will probably remain the major contribution of Marxism: its revolutionary and broadening influence, which opened man's mind to previously ignored perspectives and dramatized previously neglected concerns."

"... Marxism, disseminated on the popular level in the form of communism, represented a major advance in man's ability to conceptualize his relationship to the world."

"Marxism ... provided a unique intellectual tool for understanding and harnessing the fundamental forces of our time.

... it supplied the best available insight into contemporary reality." [340]

It is one thing to make all of these favorable comments about Marxism, and it is another to actually test the theory against the reality.

There are nations around the world that have applied Marx's theories. It is now possible to measure the promises against the actuality.

One who has actually attempted to determine the actual practice of Marxism in Communist Russia was Robert Conquest, a famed British Sovietologist. He estimated that at least 21,500,000 human beings had been executed or killed in other ways by the Marxist Communist authorities during and after the Russian Revolution of 1917. Mr. Conquest pointed that out this figure was a low estimate and that the total figure could go as high as 45,000,000.

The revolution in Russia was the first successful attempt to create a government in a nation based upon the theories of Marxism, the "victory of reason over belief."

China as a nation also experienced a similar fate during its Communist revolution of 1923 to 1947. Professor Richard L. Walker in an official government report released by the Senate Subcommittee on Internal Security in 1971 estimated that the total dead in China might go as high as 64,000,000. China, too, had experienced the Marxist "victory of reason over belief."

A tourist who visited China after the United States had established diplomatic relations with that nation in 1973 shared his thoughts about how Marxism had worked in China in an article he wrote for the August 10, 1973 New York Times newspaper. That article was entitled FROM A CHINA TRAVELER, and was written by the tourist, American banker David Rockefeller. This is what he wrote about the Marxism in China:

"Whatever the price of the Chinese Revolution [as many as 64,000,000 killed,] it has obviously succeeded not only in producing more efficient and dedicated administration, but also in fostering high morale and community purpose." [341]

After reading this comment, the student might recall the statement made by Adam Weishaupt:

"Behold our secret ....

... remember that the end justifies the means ..." [342]

No one but Mr. Rockefeller knows what he meant by that comment, but it certainly seems to mean that he must have felt sorry for the 64,000,000 Chinese that were brutally killed by the Marxist Communists, but the results certainly justified their deaths. He was sorry that 64,000,000 Chinese had to die in the Revolution, but it was a small price to pay for "efficient administration and community purpose!" Don't forget, "the end justifies the means."

And, the student is not to forget: Zbigniew Brzezinski wrote that Marxism was a "victory of reason over belief."

Perhaps the best example of someone using "reason over belief" was the story offered by Whittaker Chambers, a former member of the Communist Party in America who decided to break with the Party and come out from it. He has been quoted as saying:

"Communism is what happens when, in the name of Mind, men free themselves from God."

Mr. Chambers had a very interesting break from his beliefs in Marxism and Communism. He related the story in his book entitled WITNESS:

"But I date my break from a very casual happening. I was sitting in our apartment on St. Paul Street in Baltimore.
My daughter was in her high chair. I was watching her eat. She was the most miraculous thing that had ever happened in my life. I liked to watch her

had ever happened in my life. I liked to watch her even when she smeared porridge on her face or dropped it meditatively on the floor.

My eyes came to rest on the delicate convolutions of her ear -- those intricate, perfect ears. The thought passed through my mind: 'No, those ears were not created by any chance coming together of atoms in nature [the view of the Communists.] They could have been created only by immense design.'

The thought was involuntary and unwanted. I crowded it out of my mind. But I never wholly forgot it or the occasion. I had to crowd it out of my mind.

If I had completed it, I should have had to say: Design presupposes God.

I did not then know that, at that moment, the finger of God was first laid upon my forehead."

He later added this thought:

"A Communist [meaning someone who believes that Marxism is a "victory of reason over belief"] breaks because he must choose at last between irreconcilable opposites -- God or Man, Soul or Mind, Freedom or Communism." [343]

Mr. Chambers had figured it out.

Marx, Lenin, Brzezinski and Rockefeller apparently had not.

Chapter 17
Adolph Hitler, Satanist

Another individual who joined a secret society was Adolf Hitler, the head of the Nazi Socialist Party in Germany. He joined a secret society called the Thule Society, termed "the secret prime mover of Nazism." [344] And it is a rare historian who has written about the importance of this group, or the fact that Hitler had joined it.

The authors of a book on this organization wrote:

"It is in the Thule Society that one has to look for the real inspiration of Nazism." [345]

The Thule Society had interesting roots. It was itself:

"but a fragment of a much more important secret society known as the Germanic Order founded in 1912." [346]

That organization had its origin in other secret societies:

"[they had] gathered together certain lodges of the Prussian Freemasonry, as well as a number of openly anti-Semitic associations.
The Thule Society became a particularly active branch of the main society." [347]

The importance of the Thule Society in the formation of the Nazi Party is now being discovered, but not generally by the historians who write the "Accidental School of History."

"The Committee and the forty original members of the New German Workers' Party were all drawn from the most powerful Occult Society in Germany: the Thule Society." [348]

But the most revealing statement made about this Society was that the major leaders all had a common religion:

"The inner core within the Thule Society were all Satanists who practiced Black Magic." [349]

Another writer on the Thule Society is Joseph Carr, who has written a book entitled THE TWISTED CROSS. In it, he makes this observation:

"The inner group which controlled the Thule Society contained men who were self-confessed Luciferians ...." [350]

So, the evidence is that Hitler himself became a Luciferian. He had absorbed the works of the tragic philosopher, Friedrich Nietzsche:

"whose powerful dissertation on 'the Genealogy of Morals' sought to make a 'Revaluation of all values' in the proof that so-called evil was good, and what was habitually believed to be good was evil." [351]

Here is that thought again that the God of the Bible is "evil," and somehow the "god" considered to be evil is "good."
And that what was needed was a "re-evaluation of morals." In other words, that which has been taught by the

Biblical "good" God has to be eliminated, and a new system substituted therefor.

These thoughts will be examined later in this study.

But Hitler also acknowledged the role of Freemasonry in his life:

"In Hitler's observations, published ... under the title HITLER SPEAKS ... one can rediscover the important role played by German Freemasonry as a model for esoteric structuring of the Nazi Party." [352]

Just like so many other secret societies, the Thule Society had an "esoteric structuring." That must have meant that there were two classes of members, those who knew what the secret was and those who didn't.

But there is evidence that Adolf Hitler was one of the members of the Society that knew.

The man who played the most important role in Hitler's life was Dietrich Eckart, one of the original seven who founded the Nazi Party and who was in fact called the "spiritual founder of Nazism." One writer wrote just how important Eckart was in Hitler's life:

"Adolf Hitler himself considered Eckart as the most important influence on his life." [353]

It is known that Eckart had experimented with numerous drugs in an attempt to reach "higher consciousness." It is now being discovered that Hitler also attempted the same thing:

"... Hitler attained higher levels of consciousness by means of drugs and made a penetrating study of medieval occultism and ritual magic ...." [354]

Eckart has been called:

"a dedicated Satanist ... and the central figure in a powerful and wide-spread circle of occultists -- the Thule Society." [355]

But he was also believed in the future appearance of Lord Maitreya, the hoped for New Age Messiah. Eckart participated in a series of seances with two Russian generals who had left their native land to come to Germany.

"During these seances, Eckart and his associates were told of the imminent appearance of the German messiah, a 'Lord Maitreya.'" [356]

And he deliberately guided the career of Hitler into the occult world of Satan and Lucifer worship. When he lay dying, he told those gathered at his bedside:

"Follow Hitler! He will dance, but it is I who have called the tune! I have initiated him into the 'Secret Doctrine,' opened his centres in vision and given him the means to communicate with the Powers.
Do not mourn for me: I shall have influenced history more than any other German." [357]
"Eckart claimed to his fellow adepts in the Thule Society that he had personally received a kind of Satanic annunciation [meaning announcement] that he was destined to prepare the vessel of the Anti-Christ, the man inspired by Lucifer to conquer the world and lead the Aryan race to glory." [358]

Another of the links of the Thule Society with Lucifer worship is the emblem chosen as the symbol of the Nazi Party itself: the swastika. The dictionary defines a swastika as a cross with its four equal arms bent back in a right angle extension. There are two forms of the symbol: one with its arms bent to the left, and one with the arms bent to the right. The former is universally a symbol of good, while the latter is universally a symbol of evil.

"Hitler personally selected the final design of the Nazi Blood Flag [the one carrying the swastika as an emblem representing the Nazi Party.] He reversed the swastika [from the one proposed] to the form that represents evil ...." [359]

Hitler had a model to base his selection on: the swastika was the symbol of the Thule Society. Its official insignia:

"consisted of the swastika traversed by two lances." [360]

Manly P. Hall in his book entitled LECTURES ON ANCIENT PHILOSOPHY advised his readers just what the swastika represented:

"The swastika ... is the whirling cross that represents the centralizing motion of the Eternal ALL." [361]

One of the original founders of the Thule Society, Rudolf von Sebottendorf, linked the swastika with another symbol, the sun, when he made this statement in November of 1918:

"I intend to commit the Thule Society to this combat .... I swear it on this swastika, on this sign which for us is sacred, in order that you hear it, O magnificent Sun!" [362]

So the swastika was a symbol of the Thule Society; it was a symbol of the Nazi Party; it was somehow connected to a symbol of the Sun-god; and the Sun-god was a symbol of Lucifer.

And those who resisted the symbol of the swastika and all it represented had to pay for it with the supreme sacrifice on the bloody altar of war.

50 million people died in World War II.

50 million people sacrificed to the religion of Lucifer.

All because the historians who write the "accidental view of history" somehow were unable to determine that Adolf Hitler had joined a Luciferic cult named The Thule Society some 16 years before the war started.

But, remember, those who write the Accidental View of History do not believe that conspirators plan wars inside secret societies.

And they certainly do not believe that Lucifer is a being that is worshipped by secret societies.

Chapter 18
The Great Seal

"For more than three thousand years, secret
societies have labored to create the background of
knowledge necessary to the establishment of an
enlightened democracy among the nations of the world.
... all have continued ... and they still exist, as the
Order of the Quest." [363]

Thus wrote Manly P. Hall, the 33rd degree Mason, and
perhaps the most prolific writer on this type of subject in a
book entitled THE SECRET DESTINY OF AMERICA.

The title of his book is rather alarming.

The thought that America has a "secret destiny" will
probably startle those not familiar with secret societies and
their plans for America and the world. But that is the claim
made by Mr. Hall in his book.

He informed his readers that he saw this Order coming to
America:

"Men bound by a secret oath to labor in the cause of world democracy decided that in the American colonies they would plant the roots of a new way of life." [364]

He then told his readers when these conspirators came to America. He wrote that the Order of the Quest:

"... was set up in America before the middle of the 17th century," [meaning sometime between 1625 to 1675.] [365]

That means that Mr. Hall felt that the members of this Order came to America about the same time that the first settlers arrived. American history records that the first visitors from Europe to the American shore were the English settlers who came in 1607, to be followed by the Pilgrims in 1620. But Mr. Hall says that amongst those early settlers was a group committed by a secret oath.

But the only name he mentioned as being involved in the Order of the Quest was that of Benjamin Franklin, one of America's founding fathers:

"[Benjamin] Franklin spoke for the Order of the Quest, and most of the men who worked with him in the early days of the American Revolution were also members." [366]

He further identified most of those men as being, not only members of the Order, but also Freemasons as well:

"Not only were many of the founders of the United States Government Masons, but they received aid from a secret and august body existing in Europe [the Illuminati?] which helped them to establish this country for a particular purpose known only to the initiated few." [367]

So a secret society, or several secret societies, decided that America would be fertile ground for the establishment of a new society, or as Mr. Hall called it, a "particular purpose."

It can be known that those who created the Constitution of the United States and its resulting government were not connected to the Order of the Quest. Those who created the Declaration of Independence and the Constitution of the United States created perhaps the finest documents ever penned by men. The Constitutional Republic they created was the greatest form of government ever devised by man. They created some problems inside the document, (for example it permitted slavery,) but overall, they created the most magnificent form of government in the history of the world.

It is obvious that these men, even though Hall stated that they were men who "labored in the cause of world democracy," could not have been the original Founding Fathers, because their purpose inside the Order was known only to the "initiated few."

The creation of America's Republic was certainly a public act, made known, it is certain, to every freedom seeking nation in the world.

People do not keep freedom quiet! They let the world know that it has been officially recognized by the American Constitution.

Even in nations under totalitarian Communism, where freedom of the press is either non-existent, or in nearly total control of the government, people know that America did something that only a few other societies in the past had ever done: they had created a truly free Republic!

Even today, people still swim shark infested waters, climb over barbed wire fences, and dodge army patrols in the dark of night to come to America, because they seek freedom!

Free people do not conspire!

They make their activities known to the freedom seeking peoples of the world:

IT IS POSSIBLE TO CREATE A FREE GOVERNMENT!

Only those with evil purposes create "secret societies," with "secret oaths," with "particular purposes" known only to an "initiated few."

So the purpose of the Order of the Quest was not beneficial to freedom loving peoples, no matter that Mr. Hall says they "labored in the cause of world democracy."

They must know something that the rest of America does not know: their cause is evil!

Mr. Hall then instructed the reader that the Order of the Quest concealed their purpose inside the symbols of the Great Seal of the United States. This seal is the one that appears on the back side of the American dollar bill, and consists of two sides, what are called the Obverse side, the one with the eagle, and the Reverse side, the one with the pyramid.

Mr. Hall tells his reader:

"... if the design on the obverse side of the seal [the eagle] is stamped with the signature of the Order of the Quest, the design on the reverse, [the pyramid] is even more definitely related to the Old Mysteries." [368]

Here Mr. Hall connects the reverse side of the Great Seal with the ancient mysteries, the worship of Lucifer as a sun-god.

The Great Seal was designed and accepted in 1782, but not until several committees appointed by Congress had failed to design one.

The first committee was asked by the Continental Congress on July 4, 1776, to "prepare a device for a seal of the United States of America," and consisted of three men: Benjamin Franklin, John Adams, and Thomas Jefferson. This committee of three was not able to decide on a design, so Congress appointed a second committee. This committee also had difficulty in deciding, so Congress appointed a third committee. They referred the problem to Charles Thomson, the Secretary of Congress, and his designs were adopted on June 20, 1782.

Max Toth wrote a book about the history of the Egyptian pyramids, and including a brief review of the pyramid on the back of the dollar bill. This is what he wrote:

"All three committees appointed in succession by Congress between 1776 and 1782 included members holding various positions in Freemasonry." [369]

So, those who were deciding the design of the Great Seals were not only Masons, but were quite possibly members of the Order of the Quest. Mr. Hall said that the Order placed "their signature" on both sides of the Seal. So, there is reason to believe that at the very least, some of the Masons were also members of the Order.

Mr. Hall then commented:

"European mysticism was not dead at the time the United States of America was founded. The hand of the Mysteries controlled in the establishment of the new government, for the signature of the Mysteries may still be seen on the Great Seal of the United States of America." [370]

"The Great Seal is the signature of this exalted body -- unseen and for the most part unknown -- and the unfinished pyramid upon its reverse side is a trestleboard setting forth symbolically the task to the accomplishment of which the United States Government was dedicated from the day of its inception." [371]

He elaborated further:

"There is only one possible origin for these symbols, and that is the secret societies which came to this country 150 years before the Revolutionary war [about 1620, the date that the Pilgrims came to America.]

There can be no question that the great seal was directly inspired by these orders of the human quest, and that it set forth the purpose for this nation as that purpose was seen and known to the Founding Fathers." [372]

So America has a "secret destiny." And that secret purpose was being kept from the majority of America's citizens. But for the curious, there are ways of determining just what that secret destiny is.

The symbols of the Great Seals can be deciphered. Americans can know what that future is.

"Careful analysis of the seal discloses a mass of occult and Masonic symbols ...." [373]

Mr. Hall tells us that some of these symbols have Masonic interpretations. The Masons also have symbols, and have, on occasion, revealed what those symbols mean. So, it becomes possible to know what those Masonic symbols on the Great Seal mean.

137

James H. Billington has been the Director of the Woodrow Wilson International Center for Scholars at the Smithsonian Institute in Washington D.C. since 1973. He received a doctorate as a Rhodes Scholar at Oxford University in England, and taught history at Harvard and at Princeton. He has written a book entitled FIRE IN THE MINDS OF MEN, ORIGINS OF THE REVOLUTIONARY FAITH. He has written about the Great Seal as well:

"The ideal was ... the occult simplicity of its [meaning America's] great seal: an all-seeing eye and a pyramid over the words Novus Ordo Seclorum." [374]

So, the search for the "secret destiny" of America ends in the meaning of two symbols and a Latin phrase. Therefore, it would be possible to determine the future of America if these symbols could be deciphered.

But first, it would be helpful to decipher as many of the remaining symbols on both sides of the Great Seal as possible.

The words "Annuit Coeptis" have been traditionally interpreted as meaning "He, [presumably the God of the Bible] has prospered our undertakings." But, a far more acceptable interpretation would be that the words mean "announcing the birth of."

What the symbols are announcing is new. It was still in its infant stage in 1782, and what it is will be explored in some of the following paragraphs.

The eagle in the obverse side has very definite mystic meanings. Manly P. Hall gives us one:

"In mysticism the eagle is a symbol of initiation ...." [375]

Rex Hutchens gives another:

"The eagle: ... this emblem is of great antiquity figuring in the symbolic inventory of the Egyptians, as the sun; as wisdom is attained through reason, the eagle is also symbolic of reason."

"Among the Egyptians the eagle was the emblem of a wise man because his wings bore him above the clouds into the purer atmosphere and nearer to the source of light, and his eyes were not dazzled by that light. Since the eagle also represented the great Egyptian Sun god Amun Ra, it is a symbol of the infinite Supreme Reason of Intelligence." [376]

Another Mason who connected the eagle with the sun was Kenneth Mackenzie:

"With the Egyptians, the Greeks and the Persians, the eagle was sacred to the sun." [377]

Albert Pike also confirmed this connection when he wrote these comments about the eagle:

"a bird consecrated to the Sun in Egypt."
"The Eagle was the Living Symbol of Mendes, a representative of the Sun." [378]

Perhaps the reason that the eagle was considered to be sacred to the Egyptians was offered by Robert Hieronimus in his book entitled THE TWO GREAT SEALS OF AMERICA:

"... the eagle has been linked to the Sun [the word has been capitalized, apparently referring to the sun as a deity, rather than to the daytime sun] for it can fly nearer to the Sun than any other bird, and is the only bird that is said to symbolically look directly into the Sun's rays." [379]

Another writer who wrote a book on the Great Seal was E. Raymond Capt, and he added this confirmation in his book entitled OUR GREAT SEAL:

"The Eagle ... is also supposed to be the only creature that can look directly into the sun." [380]

It is revealing that some of the authors appear to understand the symbology of the Sun, and others think it is just the gaseous orb that lights the earth.

The drawing of the eagle conceals other secrets and it will assist the student to examine these as well. The eagle in the seal has nine tail feathers, and either 32 or 33 feathers on each of the two wings. These are symbols that have to be interpreted:

"The nine tail feathers of the eagle represent the nine beings in the innermost circle of enlightenment in the 'Great White Brotherhood -- or the Illuminati.'" [381]

There is another explanation, one more acceptable than the one offered above by Stan Deyo in his book entitled THE COSMIC CONSPIRACY. There are nine degrees in the York Rite of Freemasonry, and connecting the York Rite to the tail feathers appears to be the more plausible explanation.

The feathers on the two wings also conceal a secret. There are 32 on the right side, symbolic of the 32 degrees inside the Scottish Rite of Freemasonry, and 33 on the left side, symbolic of the honorary 33rd degree.

The "all-seeing eye" above the pyramid has two meanings, both related to the Masonic Order. One explanation was provided by the Masons themselves in an article that was inside a Masonic Bible. It said :

"The ubiquity of Masonic law was symbolized by the All-Seeing Eye." [382]

The word ubiquity is defined as the capacity of being everywhere at the same time. The Masons are saying that their law, the one that will punish the Mason should he reveal their secrets, is everywhere and that he cannot hide from it.

The second interpretation of the symbol of the eye has been offered by many Masons, including Albert Mackey:

"An important symbol of the Supreme Being, borrowed by the Freemasons from the nations of antiquity.
... the open eye was selected as the symbol of watchfulness, and the eye of God as the symbol of Divine watchfulness and care of the universe."
"The All-Seeing-Eye may then be considered as a symbol of God manifested in his omnipresence ...." [383]

So, the simplest explanation of the symbol is that it is the symbol of a deity. And some of the Masons in their writings have told the student who that deity is.

One of the Masons who took the next step in explaining what the symbol stood for was Kenneth Mackenzie who wrote this:

"The eye was also the symbol of Osiris." [384]

This was confirmed by another Mason, Carl Claudy:

"This [the All-Seeing Eye] is one of the oldest and most widespread symbols denoting God. The Open Eye of Egypt represented Osiris." [385]

Mr. Mackey also confirmed that the All Seeing Eye was a symbol of Osiris:

"... the Egyptians represented Osiris, their chief deity, by the symbol of an open eye ...." [386]

Albert Pike connected Osiris with the Sun with this comment from his book MORALS AND DOGMA:

"... Osiris, the Sun, Source of Light and Principle of Good ...." [387]

Manly P. Hall connected the symbol of the eye with the symbol of the sun with this statement:

"His symbol, therefore, was an opened eye, in honor of the Great Eye of the universe, the sun." [388]

Rex Hutchens, one of the most recent Masons to write a major book supporting the Masonic Order, also wrote that the all-seeing eye was a symbol of the sun. He wrote:

"On the right side [of a sash worn by a Member of the Masons inside the Temple] is painted an eye of gold, a symbol of the sun or of the Deity." [389]

Albert Pike however revealed the exact meaning of the symbol in his book MORALS AND DOGMA:

"The All-Seeing Eye ... which to the Ancients was the Sun." [390]

So, the all-seeing eye is a symbol concealing the Masonic belief that Osiris, a representative of the sun, was a god. And some of these writers have reported that the sun-god was Lucifer.

So, the all-seeing eye is a symbol of Lucifer, the all-seeing god of the universe. And it was placed on the American seal by those who knew what it meant.

The unfinished pyramid under the All-Seeing Eye also has a symbolic meaning, as described by the Treasury Department of the United States government in 1935:

"The pyramid is the symbol of strength and its un-finished condition denoted the belief of the designers of the Great Seal that there was still work to be done." [391]

(Notice that the Treasury Department reported that the pyramid was "unfinished |it had no capstone]" because "there was still work to be done" in the United States. The common explanation that the "New World Order" in the Great Seal was the creation of the Republic under the American Consti-tution simply isn't true. That work was finished by the time that the seal was approved in 1782. That means that the "work still to be done" had to be completed in the future. The work of creating a "New World Order" was, in 1782, "still in the future.")

But, the all-seeing eye has a far more symbolic meaning to the Masons, as was described by E. Raymond Capt:

"The triangle, in connection with the All-Seeing Eye, is the Masonic symbol of the 'Grand Architect of the Universe.'" [392]

Manly P. Hall told his readers who the Great Architect of the Universe was: he was the Master of the Masonic Lodges:

"The Mason believes in the Great Architect ....
Let him never forget that the Master is near. The All-seeing Eye is upon him." [393]

The Great Architect of the Universe is the title of the god of the Masonic order. But there are some who feel that this god is not the God of the Bible, but Lucifer, considered by these to be the god of some of the Masons. One who has pointed out why he considers this to be true is Edward Ronayne, a former member of the Masons, who wrote this in his book entitled THE MASTER'S CARPET:

"An Architect is a man who furnishes plans for, and superintends the erection of a building made from material already prepared; but God created of nothing the heavens and the earth, and all the host of them, and hence he cannot be a mere Architect, and it would be a direct insult to call him such a nickname." [394]

(The author is one of those who believe that Lucifer is the god of some of the Masons. It has been my purpose to prove that that conclusion is true with evidence from the Masons themselves. Some of that evidence has been presented in the material in earlier chapters of this study. Other evidence will follow in the remaining chapters of this book.)

Other Masonic symbols on the dollar bill, as told to the student by the Masons themselves in their magazine entitled The New Age are the:

13 leaves in the olive branches;
13 bars and stripes in the shield;
13 arrows;
13 letters in "E Pluribus Unum" on the ribbon;
13 stars in the green crest above;
13 granite stones in the Pyramid;
13 letters in "Annuit Coeptis";
On the front of the dollar bill is the seal of the United States, made up of a key, square, and the Scales of Justice, as well as a compass, which, of course, is an important symbol in Masonry. [395]

It is quite certain that the student of history will argue that the number 13 used in all of these symbols simply refers to the thirteen states that ratified the Constitution. This would be a reasonable explanation, were it not for the fact that the Masons claim the number as one of their own. It appears as if they decided that it was time to form the United States when the number of states that could be united in the Union reached 13. As was just illustrated, the Masons consider the number to have Masonic significance.

143

They apparently waited for just that time when there were exactly 13 states to form the union, and not 12 or 14.

One who has assigned an esoteric interpretation to the number 13 is Stan Deyo, the author who said this in his book entitled THE COSMIC CONSPIRACY:

"13 is the value assigned to Satan." [396]

But the key phrase on the back of the dollar bill and inside the Great Seal is the Latin phrase NOVUS ORDO SECLORUM. It means:

NOVUS: New
ORDO: Order
SECLORUM: World

The New World Order!

The New World Order on the American dollar bill is not the "republic" of thirteen states created by the founding fathers. It is the future one thousand year reign of Lord Maitreya, the New Age "messiah." Lord Maitreya is the earth's representative of the sun-god, Lucifer. And the future period is symbolized by the unfinished pyramid, signifying that the future work is yet to be done.

It is an easy task to show that the New World Order is not the republican form of government the founding fathers created, because the pyramid is unfinished. Whatever the New World Order is, it was not completed in 1782. And it is not in place yet.

America is to bring the New Age to the world of the future!

Some of this nation's founding fathers said so!

There is no question but that the Great Seal has great significance to both the Masonic Order and the "Order of the Quest" described by Manly P. Hall, a member of the Masons.

There is one final piece to be placed into the puzzle of the entire scenario, and that is to determine why these symbols appear on the dollar bill at all. Why should the great seal of the United States contain any symbols that conceal secrets from the overwhelming majority of the American people? Especially if those secrets are symbolic of a religion that few in America subscribe to.

Arthur M. Schlesinger Jr., in his book entitled THE COMING OF THE NEW DEAL, told how Henry A. Wallace, the Vice President in President Franklin Roosevelt's first administration, asked the President to put the two Seals on the back of the American dollar bill. Mr. Schlesinger wrote:

"The occult fascinated him [Wallace.] He saw special significance in the Great Seal of the United States ... even more in the reverse of the Seal ....

... Wallace did induce the Secretary of the Treasury [after he had talked to President Roosevelt] to put the Great Pyramid on the new dollar bill in 1935.

His susceptibility to the occult had drawn Wallace in the late twenties into the orbit of a White Russian mystic in the tradition of [Helena Petrovna] Blavatsky, Dr. Nicholas Roerich ...." [397]

Mr. Wallace himself put his recollections of the events in a letter that has been recorded several places, as well as in the book entitled OUR GREAT SEAL:

"The Latin phrase NOVUS ORDO SECLORUM impressed me as meaning the New Deal [the term applied to President Roosevelt's administrations] of the Ages. Therefore I took the publication [a copy of a book entitled THE HISTORY OF THE SEAL OF THE UNITED STATES] to President Roosevelt ....

[He] was first struck with the representation of the 'All-Seeing Eye,' a Masonic representation of the Great Architect of the Universe.

Roosevelt like myself was a 32nd degree Mason. He suggested that the Seal be put on the dollar bill rather than a coin and took the matter up with the Secretary of the Treasury." [398]

Some Masons created the Great Seal in 1782, and other Masons put it on the back of the American dollar bill in 1935. And it appears that all involved knew the meaning of the concealed symbols portrayed therein.

There is an abundance of evidence that the Masons were heavily involved in the founding of the United States and the design of the Great Seal.

The Supreme Council of the 33rd Degree of the Scottish Rite of Freemasonry has told the student that 13 of the 39 original signers of the Constitution were Masons. [399] Another Mason, Past Sovereign Grand Commander Henry Clausen, put the figure at 23 of the 39. [400] It is also interesting to note that there were 39 signers, exactly three times the Masonic number 13.

Other Masons assumed responsible positions inside the Army fighting for freedom against the English government. 33 Generals in George Washington's army and six of his aides were Freemasons. [401]

The Masons then and the Masons now are looking forward to the "NOVUS ORDO SECLORUM," the Latin phrase on the bottom of the reverse side of the Great Seal.

Manly P. Hall told the world about the return of Osiris, someday, when he wrote this:

"Osiris will rise in splendor from the dead and rule the world through those sages and philosophers in whom wisdom has become incarnate." [402]

The return to a worship of Osiris and what he represents as the sun-god, the worship of Lucifer, is still in the future. One who told the world that was C. William Smith of New Orleans, Louisiana, in the September, 1950 copy of the New Age Magazine, the official publication of the Supreme Council, 33rd Degree Scottish Rite of Freemasonry.

What Mr. Smith wrote is extremely revealing. After the student has learned that Lucifer is the god of some of the Masons, it appears that the way to truly understand what he wrote is to substitute the name Lucifer whenever he refers to God. He wrote:

"God's plan is dedicated to the unification of all races, religions and creeds. This plan, dedicated to the new order of things, is to make all things new -- a new nation, a new race, a new civilization and a new religion, a nonsectarian religion that has already been called the religion of 'The Great Light.'

Looking back into history, we can easily see that the Guiding Hand of Providence has chosen the Nordic people to bring in and unfold the new order of the world. Records clearly show that 95 per cent of the colonists were Nordics -- Anglo-Saxons.

Providence has chosen the Nordic race to unfold the 'New Age' of the world -- a 'Novus Ordo Seclorum.'

... God's great plan in America for the dawn of the New Age of the world." [403]

Yes, some Masons truly expect Osiris to rise from the dead and rule the world.

The New Age, the New World Order is near!

Some are expecting Osiris to rise!

Chapter 19
The Freemasons

An article in the November, 1946 issue of The New Age Magazine, published by the Scottish Rite of Freemasonry, called attention to the following comment made by Andre Tardieu, a former French Premier:

> "Freemasonry does not explain everything; yet, if we leave it out of account, the history of our times is unintelligible." [404]

Perhaps the reason Mr. Tardieu said that is because of what Manly P. Hall has said about Freemasonry. He called it:

> "the most powerful organization in the land." [405]

Alice Bailey, the New Age leader, has written this about the Masonic Fraternity:

"It is a far more occult organization than can be realised, and is intended to be the training school for the coming advanced occultists." [406]

The word occult is defined as hidden, concealed, secret, and esoteric. And an occultist is one who believes in concealing secrets from others.

The Masons, it is to be assumed, would rush in to defend themselves against such charges. Any secret, hidden or concealed organization would have to, especially if it was discovered that their purposes were not what the average citizen believed. And that appears to be exactly what this Order has done.

The traditional explanation offered by Freemasonry as to its purpose is this one offered by Henry Clausen, a former Sovereign Grand Commander of the Masonic Order. He said it was:

"a particular system of morality, veiled in allegory, and illustrated by symbols." [407]

The Masons will only admit certain individuals into their initiation ceremonies. Those qualifications are:

"A candidate for initiation must be a man, free-born, unmutilated and of mature age." [408]

There is one more requirement: they must profess a belief in a supreme being.

W.F. Brainard, a Mason in New London, Connecticut, gave a speech in 1825 describing the Order he was a member of. He said:

"What is Masonry now? It is powerful. It comprises men of rank, wealth, office and talent, in power and out of power; and that, in almost every place where Power is of any importance; and it comprises among other classes of the community, to the lowest, in large numbers, active men, united together, and capable of being directed by the efforts of others, so as to have the Force of Concert throughout the civilized world.

They are distributed too, with the means of knowing one another, and the means of keeping secret, and the means of cooperating, in the desk -- in the Legislative Hall -- on the Bench -- in every gathering of business -- in peace and war -- among enemies and friends -- in one place as well as in another!

So powerful indeed, is it at this time that it fears nothing from violence, either public or private, for it has every means to learn it in season, to counteract, defeat and punish it." [409]

As has been discussed, members of this powerful organization have access to a secret. Included in that secret are plans for the future of the world. And whatever those plans are, they are kept from the average citizen.

"Very early in our Masonic career, we are taught that Freemasonry is a system of morality, the peculiarities of which are veiled from [the] uninstructed and popular world by allegorical treaching [sic: teaching?] and symbolic illustration." [410]

It appears to be a logical conclusion that if the Masons had another morality, and if that morality was sound and would be of benefit to all the people of the world, you would think that they would make it public, instead of concealing it inside mysteries and allegories. One can only wonder if the reason their morality is kept secret is because their morality is not sound and of benefit to the general public. That would certainly explain why they want to keep it buried, away from the gaze of the citizens of the world.

Another Mason, George Steinmetz in his book entitled FREEMASONRY, ITS HIDDEN MEANING, says:

"It is in the ancient symbols of Freemasonry that its real secrets lie concealed and these are densely veiled to the Mason as to any other.

The most profound secrets of Masonry are not revealed in the Lodge at all. They belong only to the few." [411]

So the secrets of the Masons do not even belong to all of the Masons. Some Masons know and some other Masons do not know the meanings of the secrets. But the interesting thing is that the Masons who do not know are being lied to by those who do. Albert Pike confirmed that this statement was true by writing this in the book that used to be read by all Masons inside the Scottish Rite, Southern Jurisdiction, Masonic Order, entitled MORALS AND DOGMA:

"The Blue degrees [the first three degrees of the 32] are but the outer court or portico [a covered walk] of the Temple.

Part of the symbols are displayed there to the Initiate, but he is intentionally misled by false interpretations.

It is not intended that he shall understand them; but it is intended that he shall imagine that he shall understand them.

Their true explication is reserved for the Adepts, the Princes of Masonry." [412]

The initiate is being lied to by his own fellow Masons! One brother is lying to another! Some of the Masons are concealing the true meaning of the secrets from other Masons. And this is the way that the powerful Masons operate, the organization that men of rank, wealth, office and talent are joining?

Pike repeated that position inside the same book, but on another page:

"Masonry conceals its secrets from all except the Adepts and Sages, or the elect, and uses false explanations and misinterpretations of its symbols to mislead those who deserve only to be misled; to conceal the Truth, which it calls Light, from them, and to draw them away from it." [413]

It might be informative at this juncture to identify just what an "adept" believed in. Kenneth Mackenzie, a member of the Masons, wrote this in his book entitled THE ROYAL MASONIC CYCLOPAEDIA:

"Adept -- a name given to the Order of Illuminati." [414]

Was Mr. Pike admitting that only the Adepts, the
"illuminated Masons," or those who belonged to both organizations, knew the secret of the Masonic Lodges: that Lucifer
was a god?
It would certainly seem so.
Manly P. Hall also revealed the truth that not all Masons
understand the meaning of the secrets inside the Temple. He
wrote this in his book entitled LECTURES ON ANCIENT
PHILOSOPHY:

"Freemasonry is a fraternity within a fraternity --
an outer organization concealing an inner brotherhood
of the elect.
    ... it is necessary to establish the existence of
these two separate yet interdependent orders, the one
visible and the other invisible.
    The visible society is a splendid camaraderie of
'free and accepted' men enjoined to devote themselves
to ethical, educational, fraternal, patriotic, and hu-
manitarian concerns.
    The invisible society is a secret and most august
fraternity whose members are dedicated to the service
of a mysterious arcanum arcandrum |defined as a se-
cret; a mystery.|
    Those brethren who have essayed to write the
history of their craft have not included in their dis-
quisitions |a formal discourse or treatise| the story of
that truly secret inner society which is to the body
Freemasonic what the heart is to the body human.
    In each generation only a few are accepted into
the inner sanctuary of the work ....
    ... the great initiate-philosophers of Freemasonry
are ... masters of that secret doctrine which forms the
invisible foundation of every great theological and rational institution." [415]

He further amplified this thought when he wrote these
comments in another of his books, this one entitled THE
LOST KEYS OF FREEMASONRY:

"The initiated brother realizes that his so-called symbols and rituals are merely blinds, fabricated by the wise to perpetuate ideas incomprehensible to the average individual.

He also realizes that few Masons of today know or appreciate the mystic meaning concealed within these rituals." [416]

Other Masonic writers have confirmed that there are two classes of Masons. Kenneth Mackenzie added this confirmation:

"At the present day there are many secrets not usually given, and indeed the condition of Masonic education, except among a certain class, is very low.

There are many good Masons well acquainted with the ritual, and even the lectures, but they fail from want of taste and opportunity to grasp the subtler philosophy of Freemasonry." [417]

The Masons are quick to point out that they do not tell even their more intelligent fellow Masons what the secrets are; they ask them to figure it out for themselves. But, Pike says, they start the process by hinting that the Masons "worship" something other than the God of the Bible in the first degree.

Apparently, if the Mason can figure it out for himself just who the other Masons worship, he gets to be one of them.

This is what Pike wrote in MORALS AND DOGMA:

"It is for each individual Mason to discover the secret of Masonry ....

Masonry does not inculcate her truths. She states them, once and briefly; or hints them, perhaps, darkly; or interposes a cloud between them and eyes that would be dazzled by them.

That rite [the Scottish Rite] raises a corner of the veil, even in the Degree of Apprentice [the first degree of the Blue lodge] for it there declares that Masonry is a worship." [418]

Other clues that Masonry is not a fraternity of philanthropic gentlemen who meet on a regular basis for fellowship and works of charity are contained in other parts of Pike's book MORALS AND DOGMA, or in the writings of Manly P. Hall:

> "Every Lodge is a Temple ...." [419]
> "Masonry is a worship." [420]
> [421] "... Masonry is a religious and philosophic body."

> "Every Masonic Lodge is a temple of religion; and its teachings are instructions in religion." [422]

Since Masonry claims that it is a religion, it would be helpful to the student to define the term and see if Masonry meets the requirements.

A religion is defined as being either of these definitions:

1. A belief in a divine power to be obeyed and worshipped as the creator and ruler of the universe.
2. Any system of beliefs, practices, ethical values resembling, suggestive of or likened to such a system.

By the second definition, the Masons certainly qualify as a religion. But the Masons themselves deny that this is so. This view was presented in 1986 by Bill Mankin, a 32nd degree member of the Masonic Lodge, on a series of television programs concerning the Masons. The discussions were part of a television program called The John Ankerberg Show. Mr. Mankin said:

> "We [the Masons] have no creed, no confession of faith in a doctrinal statement. We have no theology; we have no ritual of worship. We have no symbols that are religious in the sense of symbols found in a church or a synagogue.
> Our symbols are related to the development of character of the relationship of man to men. They are working tools to be used in the building of life." [423]

The word religion is defined in another dictionary as:

1. A belief in a divine or superhuman power to be obeyed and worshiped as the creator and ruler of the universe.
2. Any specific system of belief in conduct and ritual, often involving a code of ethics and a philosophy.

So, by the definition of a religion contained in either dictionary, the Masons are a religion. That can be determined by a brief review of what the Masons do inside their temple.

1. The Masons worship a god, (they call him the Great Architect of the Universe);
2. They pray to this god inside their temples. For instance, during the Entered Apprentice degree, the first of the three inside the Blue Lodge, the Worshipful Master, the equivalent of the President of the lodge, prays:

    "Vouchsafe thine aid, Almighty Father of the Universe ...." [424]

3. They believe that this god in their temples hears prayer. The same prayer in the Entered Apprentice degree continues:

    "... and grant that this Candidate for Masonry may dedicate his life to thy service." [425]

4. They believe that their worship inside the temple will grant them immortal life. In the pamphlet prepared by the John Ankerberg Show, they quoted the Masonic manual which describes what the white apron worn by the Mason stands for:

    "He who wears the lambskin as a badge of a Mason is thereby continually reminded of purity of life and conduct which is essentially necessary to his gaining admission into the Celestial Lodge Above." [426]

5. They believe in the one god who is common to all religions. The same statement of the Grand Lodge of Maryland continues:

"Thus, Masonry is a great fellowship of men of all countries and ages who are capable of discovering in the religious teachings of all humanity, some of them crude indeed, the fundamental truth COMMON TO THEM ALL: that God is the Father of all mankind ...." [427] [emphasis by author]

Any student of worldwide religions is inevitably drawn to this conclusion: every religion has a different view of God. Every religion conceives the duties and functions of their deity to be different; and some religions do not even believe in one God, (some have many gods). But there is one thing that is probably common to all religions: all possess a belief that there is a force of evil in the world.

The Bible calls this force Lucifer, Satan, or the devil.

Henry Clausen, the Past Sovereign Grand Commander of the Scottish Rite, told his readers in his book entitled CLAUSEN'S COMMENTARIES ON MORALS AND DOGMA that there was only one god, and that one of the purposes of Masonry is to teach its initiates just who that one god is:

"The true knowledge of the One Supreme Deity is given." [428]

So the Masons openly state that there is only one god, and that this god is somehow different than the one that is worshipped by the religions of the world.

If the student of Masonry will read the statement of the Grand Lodge of Maryland again, with the thought that the religions of the world do not agree on the definition of their god, but do agree that there is a force of evil, the statement starts to make some sense.

As has already been illustrated in this study, the Masons consider Lucifer to be a god.

6. The Masons believe in a life after death. They believe in a "celestial lodge above."

7.   The Masons believe in a place where that life
continues after death. During the initiation
ceremony into the first degree of the Blue Lodge,
the initiate is told:

> "I'd like to present you, Brother (name), with
> this lambskin, or white leather apron, which is
> an emblem of innocence .... He therefore who
> wears a lambskin as a badge of a Mason is con-
> tinually reminded of that purity of life and
> conduct which is essentially necessary to his
> gaining ADMISSION INTO THE CELESTIAL
> LODGE ABOVE." [emphasis by author.] [429]

But, even with all of this contrary evidence, the Masons
continue to deny that Masonry is a religion separate from
any other.

And, to further compound the problem, the Masons
continue to teach that their religion is a continuation of
another ancient worship. Albert Pike stated in his book
MORALS AND DOGMA:

> "... the Sun, Moon and Mercury ... are still the
> three Great Lights of a Masonic Lodge."

And then he told the reader just what (or who) these
lights represent:

> "The three lights represent the Sun, the Moon
> and Mercury; Osiris, Isis, and Horus." [430]

So one of the lights inside the Masonic temple represents
Osiris, the sun-god. There are other connections inside the
Masonic religion back to the god of the Egyptians:

> "Osiris, Adoni, Adonis, Atys, and the other Sun-
> Gods -- had also a tomb, and a religious initiation; one
> of the principal ceremonies of which consisted in
> clothing the Initiate with the skin of a white lamb.
> And in this we see the origin of the apron of white
> sheep-skin used in Masonry." [431]

157

It is to be remembered that the Masons teach "the true knowledge of the One Supreme Deity." Is it possible to infer from their own words that they know just who that "Supreme Deity" is? Pike admitted that his writings concealed a secret mystery. He wrote this about the words in his book entitled MORALS AND DOGMA:

"If you reflect, my Brother, ... you will no doubt suspect that some secret meaning was concealed in these words." [432]

The evidence that Mr. Pike was concealing the truth about this secret from his fellow Masons has been presented in previous chapters of this study. And the fact that the Masons do not want the general public to know the truth about this hidden god is confirmed by at least two circumstances.

1.   Mr. Pike stated that his book was not "intended for the world at large," [433] and
2.   A copy of the book that turned up in a used book store had the following phrase stamped on the inside cover: "esoteric book, for Scottish Rite use only; to be returned upon withdrawal or death of recipient."

So, whatever secret is contained inside his book, Pike does not want it to be known by either the public or by his fellow Masons.

Albert Pike taught his readers a simple, but very profound Masonic truth on the bottom of page 324 in his book MORALS AND DOGMA:

"What is Superior is as that which is Inferior, and what is Below is as that which is Above, to form the Marvels of Unity." [434]

Notice that Pike capitalizes the words "Superior," "Inferior," "Above," and "Below," just as one would do when capitalizing the name of a deity. It appears that one of the things that is reversed is the understanding of the nature of the deity.

That teaching was just a few paragraphs after another statement of Pike's:

"The conviction of all men that God is good led to a belief in a Devil, the fallen Lucifer or lightbearer ...." [435]

Applying the principle that was taught in the last paragraph to the sentence contained above it, it is possible to see that Pike considers Lucifer to be the God that is good, and that the God of the Bible is the devil, the god of evil. That is what that statement about "that which is Below is as that which is Above" means. That means that the God in the heavens is the god that is below, and the god who is below is the god in the heavens.

So the Masons do believe in a god: it is in the fallen lightbearer, Lucifer. There can be no other reasonable explanation of what Mr. Pike just wrote.

And that thought will continue to be developed as this study continues.

Even though the Masons continue to publicly deny that their Order is a religion, they say it is in some of their writings. One example that this is so comes from the pen of Albert Mackey, a Mason, in his ENCYCLOPAEDIA OF FREEMASONRY:

"Look at its ancient landmarks, its sublime ceremonies, its profound symbols and allegories -- all inculcating religious observance, and who can deny that it is eminently a religious institution; and on this ground mainly, if not alone, should the religious Masons defend it." [436]

He repeats that claim in another book he wrote entitled TEXTBOOK OF MASONIC JURISPRUDENCE:

"The truth is, that Masonry is undoubtedly a religious institution, its religion being of that universal kind in which all men agree." [437]

Another writer, apparently not a Mason, shed a little light on the nature of the worship of the Masons. He wrote that they worshipped the Egyptian trinity of Isis, Horus, and Osiris:

> "... God has seventy-two known names and one ineffable name, unknown to man ....
>
> The supreme isiac initiation ... has as its sole purpose the transmission of this name, which constituted the Word.
>
> Freemasonry in its first three degrees is certainly very close to the Isaic rites.
>
> Few Masons are aware that their work within the temple is carried out under the aegis of the Egyptian trinity ." [438]

But Albert Pike apparently was one of those Masons who did know. He wrote:

> "Masonry is:
> identical with the Ancient Mysteries." [439]
> a successor of the Mysteries." [440]

Manly P. Hall repeated the claim:

> "... in Masonry, the ancient religious and philosophic principles still survive." [441]

Another writer, but in this case apparently not a member of the Masons, wrote this in his book entitled SERPENT IN THE SKY:

> "Now, the wisdom of the Egyptian Temple did not survive Egypt intact, or in its original form, but percolated down to our day through more or less underground groups without any apparent central organization -- ... Freemasons ... and others." [442]

And Henry Clausen, the Past Sovereign Grand Commander, also confirmed that Masonry is connected to the ancient mysteries:

> "We look toward a transformation into a New Age using, however, the insight and wisdom of the ancient mystics." [443]

It appears that the evidence presented so far has allowed the student of Masonry to draw the following conclusions:

1. The Ancient Mysteries, carried down to some of the worships of today, worshipped a sun-god, a veiled reference to Lucifer, the fallen angel of the Bible. This worship of the devil was concealed throughout the generations by giving him a different name.

2. There were two worships inside each sun-god temple: one for the average citizen, and another for those who had been initiated into the true meanings of the worship: that their god was in truth Lucifer.

3. By the Masons own admissions, they too worship the god of the ancients: the sun-god, Lucifer, known as the devil of the Bible.

4. The Masons of today conceal the truth of whom they are worshipping from their brothers inside the lodge by intentionally lying to them.

5. And probably the overwhelming majority of Masons today do not know this truth, which can be inferred from the fact that the Adept Masons admit that they conceal this truth from their fellow Masons.

And men of rank, wealth, office and power continue to join.

Chapter 20
Those Who Object

But are there others who know that certain Masons worship Lucifer? Are there others who know that the Masons want to bring about the New World Order? Are there warnings being issued for any one who will listen?

Captain William Morgan, A Mason who exposed the secrets of the Masonic Lodge in 1826 in his book entitled FREEMASONRY EXPOSED, wrote this:

> "The bane [defined as the ruin] of our civil institutions is to be found in Masonry, already powerful and daily becoming more so. I owe my country an exposure of its dangers." [444]

The publication of this book was not looked upon with favor by the Masons after it was made public. The Captain paid with his life for his attempts to warn America. The introduction to the original edition identified his murderers as being the Masons themselves. It said:

"... the author ... was kidnapped and carried away ... by a number of Freemasons ...." [445]

The Masons, however, do not believe that Captain Morgan was murdered. Albert G. Mackey in his ENCYCLOPAEDIA says this:

"There are various myths of his disappearance and subsequent residence in other countries.
... it is certain that there is no evidence of his death that would be admitted in a Court of Probate." [446]

Even though the Masons deny that the Captain was murdered, the newspapers of the day reported that his murder was fact, and it was widely accepted in America that members of the Masons were responsible for his death. As a result of the national furor over the killing, this nation's first third political party, called the Anti-Masons Party, sprang up as a protest to the activities of the Masonic Order.

A former Mason and Minister from New York, William Preston Vaughn, also attempted to warn America in 1830:

"If the lodge went unchecked, the United States would have a Masonic monarchy for its government, a Masonic church, a Masonic way to a Masonic heaven, and blood and massacre and destruction to all who subscribe not to the support of the Monarch." [447]

John Quincy Adams, the sixth President of the United States, also had strong feelings about the Masonic Order. He wrote this in 1833:

"I do conscientiously and sincerely believe that the Order of Freemasonry, if not the greatest, is one of the greatest moral and political evils under which the Union is now laboring." [448]

He continued by saying that Masonry was:

"a conspiracy of the few against the equal rights of the many; anti-Republican [here he was not refer-

163

ring to the Republican Party, but to the concept of a republic as a form of government] in its sap [meaning vitality.]" [449]

"I am prepared to complete the demonstration before God and man, that the Masonic oath, obligations and penalties cannot by any possibility be reconciled to the laws of morality, of Christianity, or of the land." [450]

Millard Fillmore, the thirteenth President of the United States, made this statement:

"The Masonic fraternity tramples upon our rights, defeats the administration of justice. and bids defiance to every government which it cannot control." [451]

Another who spoke out against the Masons was Ulysses S. Grant, the eighteenth President, who said this:

"All secret oath-bound political parties are dangerous to any nation, no matter how pure or how patriotic the motives and principles which first bring them together." [452]

John Marshall, the Chief Justice of the Supreme Court in the early days of this nation, was a member of the Masonic Lodge. Apparently he changed his mind and later recanted. He made this charge:

"The institution of Masonry ought to be abandoned as one capable of much evil, and incapable of producing any good which might not be effected by safe and open means." [453]

Another warning came from John G. Stevens, a Baptist clergyman, who denounced his Masonic ties by publishing his views in AN INQUIRY INTO THE NATURE AND TENDENCY OF SPECULATIVE MASONRY. Included in his writings were these conclusions:

"Masonry was a state within a state and that one day Masons would overthrow the democratic government of the United States and would crown one of their 'grand kings' as ruler of this nation." [454]

Another minister who came out of Masonic Order was Charles G. Finney, who left the Order when Captain Morgan was murdered. He wrote a little pamphlet entitled "WHY I LEFT FREEMASONRY," in which he made these observations:

"... in taking these oaths I had been grossly deceived and imposed upon. Indeed I came to the deliberate conclusion that my oaths had been procured by fraud and misrepresentations; that the institution was in no respect what I had been informed it was; and ... it has become more and more irresistibly plain to me that Masonry is highly dangerous to the State, and in every way injurious to the Church of Christ." [455]

But perhaps the most ringing criticism of the Masons came from Pope Leo XIII, the Catholic Pope from 1878 to 1903. He wrote these words in an encyclical entitled HUMANUS GENUS:

"Their ultimate purpose: namely, the overthrow of that whole religious and political order of the world which the Christian teaching has produced, and the substitution of a new state of things in accordance with their ideas, of which the foundations and laws shall be drawn from mere naturalism." [456]

The Pope went on later in his Encyclical to explain what he meant by the term Naturalism:

"... the fundamental doctrine of the naturalists ... is that human nature and human reason ought in all things to be the mistress and guide." [457]
"... the naturalists teach ... that marriage belongs to the genus of commercial contracts, which can rightly be revoked by the will of those who made them, and that the civil rulers of the State have power over the matrimonial bond." [458]

So the Pope correctly noted that the Masons were committed to creating a New World Order: they wanted to create a "new state of things" by overthrowing the "whole religious and political order." Then he identified the new world they wanted to replace it with: one based upon reason.

He continued his discussion of why he was concerned about the Masons:

"... their endeavor to obtain equality and community of all goods by the destruction of every distinction of rank and property." [459]

Here the Pope states that the Masons share the vision of Karl Marx, the Communist, who wanted to "abolish private property." The Pope said that the Masons wanted to destroy "the distinctions of property."

The Pope's fate after he wrote these warnings to the world was perhaps revealed in a Time magazine article on June 18, 1984. The article said this was what might have happened to him:

"... there were the whispers about how poison killed Leo XIII in 1903 ...." [460]

Another who attempted to warn the world about the Masonic Order was Bernard Fay, who wrote a book entitled REVOLUTION AND FREEMASONRY. This is why he shared his concern:

"The New Masonry did not aim to destroy churches, but, with the aid of the progress of ideas, it prepared to replace them." [461]

According to Mr. Fay, the Masonic religion wanted to replace the Christian religion!

Another writer on the subject of the Masons is Arthur Edward Waite, who wrote this in his book entitled THE ENCYCLOPAEDIA OF FREEMASONRY:

"The Latin Church |apparently meaning the Catholic Church] has agreed to regard Freemasonry ... as ... those forces which are at work in the world against the Church in that world." [462]

But more current examples of Christian churches warning its members, as well as the world, can be located. It is not just the Catholic Church which is concerned about membership in the Masonic Order.

The Orthodox Presbyterian Church met at Rochester, New York, on June 2-5, 1942, and they issued a report on the Ancient Order of Free and Accepted Masons. The following was part of their conclusions:

"... Masonry is a religious institution and as such is definitely anti-Christian. ... membership in the Masonic fraternity is inconsistent with Christianity." [463]

Furthermore, another church body, this time the Lutheran Church-Missouri Synod, passed a resolution in 1975 calling for "specialized literature for persons who belong to anti-Christian sects and cults." One of the six booklets that resulted from the call was one on the Freemasons called "HOW TO RESPOND TO THE LODGE."

But one of the more dramatic studies of the Masons occurred a short time ago in England, when the Church of England released a report on them after a summer session examined the Order. The article that appeared in the Arizona Daily Star, released by the Associated Press on July 14, 1987, said that:

"'Church of England leaders overwhelmingly endorsed a report yesterday that called Freemason rituals blasphemous ....'

The report: Freemasonry and Christianity: Are They Compatible?" said some Christians found Masonic rituals disturbing and 'positively evil.'" [464]

Perhaps the best summary of the whole concern about the Masonic Order came from an ex-Mason, Edward Ronayne, in his book entitled THE MASTER'S CARPET. Mr. Ronayne said this:

"Masonry ... is a system which has not the least shadow of support, either from history, from scripture, from reason, or from common sense, but, in fact, is diametrically opposed to them all." [465]

But, men of rank, wealth, office and power still join it.

Chapter 21
Albert Pike

One of the Masonic writers frequently cited in this study as being an expert on Masonic affairs has been Albert Pike, the Sovereign Grand Commander of the Southern Jurisdiction of the Scottish Rite of Freemasonry from 1859 to his death in 1891. So it might be helpful to know a little about his past.

He has been described by fellow Masons in a rather flattering manner. Carl Claudy has written this:

> "Pike was ... one of the greatest geniuses Freemasonry has ever known. He was ... a teacher of the hidden truths of Freemasonry. [466]

Manly P. Hall has written:

> "Albert Pike, who has gathered ample evidence of the excellence of the doctrines promulgated by the mysteries ...." [467]

And Dr. Robert Watts, a fellow 33rd degree Mason, made some very complimentary comments about him as well. He said that he was:

"... the world's greatest Masonic scholar."

And he praised:

" ... the tremendous genius of Albert Pike." [468]

Perhaps Pike's finest accomplishment for the Masonic cause was his book entitled MORALS AND DOGMA, published in 1871 by the Supreme Council of the Thirty-Third Degree for the Southern Jurisdiction of the United States. There is some disagreement as to whether or not this book is to be read by all Masons seeking higher degrees inside the Masonic Order. This author was told by members of the Masons in Tucson in 1985 that the book was still given to all Masons for their perusal. However, Rex Hutchens, a 32nd degree Mason, and the author who wrote a new book entitled A BRIDGE TO LIGHT for the Masons in 1988, said this in his book:

"MORALS AND DOGMA was traditionally given to the candidate as a gift upon his receipt of the 14th Degree." [469]

His use of the word "was" implies that it is no longer given to the Masonic candidate.

However, Mr. Hutchens had words of praise for it. He wrote:

"Contained within its pages are some of the most profound teachings of the Rite." [470]

Henry Clausen, one of Mr. Pike's successors as Sovereign Grand Commander of the Masons, also praised his book :

"... an inspired and classical compilation of Pike's own research ...." [471]

Other Masonic scholars who have come after him have revered his name. This comment came from Albert Mackey:

"His standing as a Masonic author and historian ... was most distinguished, and his untiring zeal was without a parallel." [472]

The Masonic Order as a body must have thought highly of Mr. Pike as well because they permitted him to rewrite the Scottish Rite rituals.

But perhaps the greatest example of the influence of this man was reported by General Gordon Granger, who had an occasion to meet with both Mr. Pike and then President Andrew Johnson, a fellow Mason. This event occurred in March of 1867, and was later testified to by General Granger in front of the House Judiciary Committee. They were investigating charges that President Johnson should be impeached, and they felt that the General's recollections of that meeting might be helpful.

The General told the committee:

"They talked a great deal about Masonry. More about that than anything else. And from what they talked about between them, I gathered that he [meaning Pike] was the superior of the President in Masonry. I understood from the conversation that the President was his subordinate in Masonry. That was all there was to it ...." [473]

But that wasn't all there was to it. On June 20, 1867, the President received a delegation of Scottish Rite officials in his bedroom at the White House where he received the 4th through the 32nd Degrees of the Scottish Rite.

But the important revelation is that the General had testified that the President of the United States was the subordinate to Albert Pike in Masonry!

And the importance of that fact can be gathered from the oath the initiate takes during the third degree, called the Master Mason's degree, inside the Blue Lodge. The initiate takes the following oath: (emphasis by author)

"Furthermore, I DO PROMISE and swear THAT I WILL OBEY ALL regular signs, SUMMONSES, or tokens GIVEN, handed out, sent, or thrown TO ME FROM THE HAND OF A BROTHER MASTER MA-

SON or from the body of a just and lawfully constituted lodge of such ...." [474]

The capitalized words when taken together read: "I do promise that I will obey all summonses given to me from the hand of a brother Master Mason."

That means that the President of the United States had to take orders from Albert Pike should he order him to do so!

The significance of that startling proposition will become more evident as additional evidence of just what Mr. Pike believed in is presented in further chapters of this study.

There is a hierarchy in the United States!

And Presidents who are Masons take orders from other Masons!

Chapter 22
Hiram Abif

The Masons have wrapped their initiation ceremony around a legend involving an individual named Hiram Abif. The Masons have constructed this legend themselves from two brief references to him in the Bible.

This information on Hiram comes from Mackey's ENCY-CLOPAEDIA:

> "When King Solomon was about to build a temple to Jehovah [called Solomon's temple,] the difficulty of obtaining skillful workmen to superintend and to execute the architectural part of the undertaking was such, that he found it necessary to request of his friend and ally, Hiram, King of Tyre, the use of some of his most able builders. Hiram [the King] willingly complied with his request [and dispatched] Hiram out of Tyre." [475]

The Bible, in the 1st Book of Kings 7:13, says that Hiram Abif was:

"... a widow's son, ... and was filled with wisdom and understanding."

The Masons claim that Hiram Abif was a Master Mason, and possessed the secrets of the degree, secrets that he could not share with his fellow workers. The reason for that was because the other workers at the Temple were "apprentice Masons," not entitled to a share of the secrets of the Master Mason.

"Fifteen Fellow Crafts [masons but not possessors of the secrets] seeing the temple about to be completed and being desirous of obtaining the secrets of a Master Mason ... whereby they might travel into foreign countries, work and receive Masters' wages, entered into a horrid conspiracy to extort [the secrets] from [the Master] or take his life.
 ... twelve of them recanted, the other three, however persisted in their murderous design." [476]

According to the legend, Hiram Abif was slain by these three "ruffians" at "high twelve," because he refused to share the secrets. The three ruffians were named Jubela, Jubelo, and Jubelum.

The Masons admit that the death of Hiram is "a purely symbolic event ...." Therefore, the student must look elsewhere for an explanation of what his symbolic death means.

In addition, they further admit that the story is not based completely on the two brief mentions of Hiram in the Bible:

"Thus the Biblical account of the story of Hiram is occasionally at variance with the legend as told in Masonic literature." [477]

The remaining parts of the legend of Hiram Abif are not pertinent to this study, so they will not be discussed here.

However, it will be helpful for further discussion in a later chapter of this book for the following comments to be added at this juncture.

Rex Hutchens, a 32nd degree Mason, has placed an important piece into the puzzle in his book entitled A BRIDGE TO LIGHT. He gives his readers this explanation as to what the symbolic death of Hiram means:

"What are the symbolic meanings of the attacks upon Hiram?

Hiram is first accosted at the south gate of the Temple where the instrument of the attack is the rule. In Greek, the word for a 'rule' whether a measuring instrument or a code of conduct, is canon. Thus we see the bureaucracy of the early Church establishing the Canon Law to regulate conduct.

This law was to be obeyed with unquestioned loyalty, hence it is an apt symbol of the suppression of freedom of speech which might question the divinity and justice of these laws; therefore Hiram, with the rule, is struck where the organs of speech are.

The instrument of attack at the west gate of the Temple was the square ...; it represents the merger of civil and religious power intending to control man's emotions, telling him not only what he can do but also what he can believe.

Thus Hiram is struck near the heart, the traditional seat of the affections.

The setting maul, an instrument of brute force, is a fitting symbol of the blind, unreasoning mob. It fears the force of the intellect and seeks the destruction of the products of the mind.

Hiram is killed at the east gate by a blow to the head, the seat of the intellect." [478]

So Mr. Hutchens is telling his reader that the "ruffians" that killed Hiram Abif were not individuals seeking the secrets of Masonry from Hiram, the Master Mason, but were concealed symbols of "the Church," the "church and the state," and the forces fearing the power of man's "reason."

This is an amazing revelation! It is rare that the Masons share the exact interpretation of their secrets as they have done in this instance. Remember that the contents of Mr. Hutchens' book have been approved by the Supreme Council of the 33rd degree of the Scottish Rite of Freemasonry. This explanation has official sanction! They want us to know that the enemies of the Masons are the Church, the State, and opposition to "man's reason."

In another part of his book, Mr. Hutchens provides the reader with another explanation of the symbols. This additional explanation of the true meaning of the symbols is strikingly similar to the first.

> "... the Master Hiram is the symbol of intelligence, liberty and truth and the assassins are the symbols of tyranny, ignorance and intolerance or fanaticism." [479]

So he equates the church and the state with tyranny, ignorance, intolerance and fanaticism. As will be shown in another part of this study, the Masons have pledged themselves to avenge the death of Hiram! They have pledged themselves to destroy the state and the church!

So, the real purpose of the Masons has been discovered. The Masons are not a philanthropic organization out to assist men to better themselves.

They have a hidden purpose.

And it takes but a little fortitude to discover what that purpose is.

Their purpose is to destroy organized religion, and the state, just like the Illuminati and the Communist Party!

They have said so in their own literature!

There can be no doubt!

Additional evidence that the above interpretation of Mr. Hutchens' comments is correct will follow.

Chapter 23
The Hierarchy

Alice Bailey, one of the leaders of the New Age Movement, reported that she was aware that a group existed that she called the Hierarchy that possessed enormous power. She wrote that she actually visited this group during one of their meetings:

> "... as one of the Masters, unknown to you, re-marked at a meeting of Members of the Hierarchy a few weeks ago ...." [480]

She further amplified her thoughts on what these individuals did:

> "The Hierarchy directs world events ... so that the unfolding consciousness may express itself through developing and adequate social, political, religious and economic world forms. They give direction; They throw

a light; They definitely influence the tide of human affairs." [481]

"The Hierarchy receives that esoteric 'Fire of God' which brings to an end cycles, ideologies, organisations and civilisations when the due and right time comes."
[482]

According to Miss Bailey, these "Masters" have been working for the good of man for:

"millions of years.
... the Hierarchy has stood in silence behind world events, occupied with the following work -- a work which will eventually be carried on exoterically [meaning in the open] instead of esoterically [meaning hidden.]" [483]

She wrote an answer to the question of what her supporters could do to "facilitate their work." She admitted that they could:

"... teach the law of evolution and its inevitable corollary, perfected men.
Men must be taught that such Great Souls exist, and exist entirely to serve Their fellow men. The public must be familiarized with Their names and attributes, with Their work and purpose, and men must be told that They are coming forth for the salvation of the world." [484]

Another hint that the world is not run by the people that the public thinks was provided by Manly P. Hall in his book entitled THE SECRET TEACHINGS OF ALL AGES:

"... the sanctuary of wisdom wherein dwell the real rulers of the world -- the initiated philosophers." [485]

It appears as if Mr. Hall is indicating that those who have been initiated into Lucifer worship are the real rulers of the world.

That is certainly not what the people of the world believe.

But Mr. Hall has actually gone further and identified those who truly rule the world. He added this revealing thought in his book entitled THE LOST KEYS OF FREE-MASONRY:

"Masonry is an ordainer of kings. Its hand has shaped the destinies of worlds." [486]

But, even if the people do not know that their rulers are not the visible heads of their governments, Albert Pike pointed out that they will soon demand that they be led by these people. He wrote in his book entitled MORALS AND DOGMA:

"The World will soon come to us for its Sovereigns [apparently meaning its governmental leaders] and Pontiffs [apparently meaning its religious leaders.]
We shall constitute the equilibrium of the Universe, and be rulers over the Masters of the World." [487]

And Manly P. Hall repeated the thought: the people will be soon asking that the illuminated ones rule the world:

"The criers of the Mysteries speak again, bidding all men welcome to the House of Light.
The great institution of materiality has failed.
Religion wanders aimlessly in the maze of theological speculation.
Only the illumined reason can carry the understanding part of man upward to the light." [488]

Private property (called "materiality" by Mr. Hall) has failed. Religion has not succeeded in solving man's problems. The people will soon demand that someone else with a new set of solutions step forward.
And those with the Light of Lucifer are waiting to step forward to rule.
There is no adequate explanation as to why some people want to rule others. But history is replete with individuals, groups, organizations, nations, and conspiracies, etc., all of whom have wanted to rule over others. One satisfactory

179

answer as to why this is so comes from a book written by B.F. Skinner entitled WALDEN TWO. Mr. Skinner has his alter ego declare:

> "I've had only one idea in my life -- the idea of having my own way. 'Control' expresses it -- the control of human behavior.
> ... it was a frenzied, selfish desire to dominate.
> I remember the rage I used to feel when a certain prediction went awry. I could have shouted at the subjects of my experiments, 'Behave! Behave as you ought!'" [189]

The world knows that there are people who have desired power over the lives of others. History is strewn with the carnage of those who wanted to rule the world.

Masons, believers in the New Age Movement, the Communists, the Illuminati and others want to control human behavior. The moral mind of the population in general cannot comprehend this desire for power; all that the citizens of the world can do is become aware of that strong compulsion, and to try to prevent those who desire power over others from gaining control.

The New Age appears to be on schedule! And those who are anxious to lead the world of the future are preparing themselves for the task.

Chapter 24
Masonic Obligations

The Scottish Rite of the Freemasons has a total of 33 initiation ceremonies, one for each of the first 32 earned degrees, and one for the honorary degree, called the 33rd degree.

Students of the Masons can know just what the initiation rites of the various degrees consist of. Many individuals, such as Masons, ex-Masons, and historians who have researched the Masonic Lodges, have described the exact content of the ceremonies in a variety of books and articles.

For instance, it is possible to know how Masons protect themselves from harm by reading part of the oath the Mason takes during the initiation ceremony of the Third degree, called the Master Mason degree. The initiate binds himself to this oath:

> "Further, I will keep a worthy brother Master Mason's secrets inviolable, when communicated to and received by me as such, murder and treason excepted.

Further, I will not cheat, wrong or defraud a Master Mason's Lodge, nor a brother of this Degree, knowingly, nor supplant him in any of his laudable undertakings, but will give him due and timely notice, that he may ward off all danger." [490]

That means that any Mason who determines that a fellow Mason has committed, or is about to commit, a crime, "murder and treason excepted," will be oath-bound not to report him to the proper authorities. A Mason who tells a fellow Mason that he is going to blackmail a non-Mason, can know that the hearer will not report him.

And, if the first Mason learns that the blackmailing Mason is about to be arrested for his crime, the first Mason must report his discovery to the other Mason.

But these examples of Masonic oaths are but a part of the evidence. The student can learn about the other commitments that the initiated Mason obligates himself to.

Another book that explains the obligations that Masons assume is one entitled the MASONIC HANDBOOK, and it further explains what these commitments are. This written manual explains what the Mason should do if he is selected on a jury and observes the defendant identifying himself as being a member of the Fraternity:

"If you're on a jury, and the defendant is a Mason, and makes the Grand Hailing sign [a secret sign that identifies one Mason to another,] you must be sure not to bring the Mason guilty, for that would bring disgrace upon our order.

It may be perjury, to be sure, to do this, but then you're fulfilling your obligation, and you know if you live up to your obligations you'll be free from sin."

And the HANDBOOK advises the member that it is permissible to cheat or swindle certain people:

"If you cheat, wrong, or defraud any other society or individual, it is entirely your own business.

If you cheat the Government even, Masonry cannot and will not touch you, but be very careful not to cheat, wrong or defraud a brother Mason or a lodge, whoever you may defraud; live up to your obligation and you'll be free from sin."

And this advice to the Mason further extends to the crimes of murder and treason:

"You must conceal all the crimes of your brother Masons, except murder and treason, and these only at your own option, and should you be summoned as a witness against a brother Mason be always sure to shield him, prevaricate, don't always tell the whole truth in this case, keep his secrets, forget the most important points.

It may be perjury to do this, it is true, but you're keeping your obligations, and remember if you live up to your obligation strictly, you'll be free from sin." [491]

The Mason also redefines the two words adultery and chastity:

"Furthermore do I promise and swear that I will not violate the chastity of a Master Mason's wife, mother, sister, or daughter, I knowing them to be such, nor suffer it to be done by others, if in my power to prevent it." [492]

Critics of this part of the initiation ceremony observe that this restriction, in essence, allows the Master Mason to engage in adultery with any other wife, mother, sister, or daughter, just as long as that woman is not connected to another Master Mason. It would appear that a better reading of that oath would be something like this:

"Furthermore do I promise and swear that I will not violate the chastity of anyone's wife, mother, sister or daughter ... especially be they connected to a fellow Master Mason."

But that is not what the oath taken by the Third Degree Mason says. That oath implies that permission is given to violate any other woman, just as long as they are not connected to another Master Mason.

A brief summary of this advice was offered by Carl Claudy in his book entitled INTRODUCTION TO FREE-MASONRY. He wrote:

> "We keep our brother's secrets, guilty or innocent. It makes no difference in what way our brother stumbles. We are not told to stretch forth the hand in aid if, and perhaps and but!
> Not for us to judge, to condemn, to admonish ... for us only to put forth our strength unto our failing brother at his need without question and without stint." [493]

So, the Mason protects his fellow Masons, even if they commit murder or treason. And the Masons teach their fellow Masons that certain forms of adultery are acceptable.

As has already been explained, the Mason takes oaths to obey orders from his superiors inside the Masonic Order. Albert Mackey told all Masons this truth in his book entitled THE ENCYCLOPAEDIA OF FREEMASONRY under the title of "Obedience:"

> "The first duty of every Mason is to obey the mandate of the Master. The Masonic rule of obedience is like the nautical imperative: 'Obey orders, even if you break owners.'" [494]

So, the Masons obey orders, protect criminal activities, lie if necessary, and are free to commit adultery with anyone other than a fellow Mason's wife, child, mother or sister.

And the Masons claim that their Order is a moral one.

And the average citizen continues to believe that it teaches its members good values.

And worldwide, men of rank, wealth, office and talent continue to join it.

Chapter 25
The 33rd Degree

As has been previously discussed, some of the most respected Masonic writers have been awarded the honorary 33rd Degree. That includes the three most quoted writers in this study: Albert Pike, Albert Mackey and Manly P. Hall.

Mr. Hall has instructed his readers just how important the 33rd degree is:

> "Philosophically, the Thirty-third degree of the Ancient and Accepted Scottish Rite represents the innermost sanctuary of Masonic mysticism." [495]

The 33rd degree is reportedly the smallest circle of the entire Masonic Lodge, having the least number of members of any degree inside the Lodge. It is believed by many that this is where the ultimate power resides. In fact, the 33rd Degree Council, the one that resides in Washington D.C., claims to be The Mother Council of the World, and The Mother Jurisdiction of the World.

One of the reasons why this degree is so important is because it appears that it possesses the knowledge of the final secret of the Masons. In fact, the candidate receiving the 32nd Degree is told that "he still has not reached the light." [496]

One of the symbols explaining this truth to the 33rd degree Mason is the symbol of this degree: the Phoenix bird. The dictionary defines the Phoenix bird as an Egyptian myth, a beautiful, lone bird which lived in the Arabian desert for 500 years and then consumed itself in fire, rising renewed from the ashes to start another long life.

The Phoenix bird is dramatically depicted on the cover of Albert Pike's book entitled MORALS AND DOGMA. It shows up as well on the covers of pamphlets circulated by the 33rd degree Masons. It is an object of jewelry worn around the neck by 33rd degree Masons.

The Masons know what the symbol means.

Manly P. Hall tells his readers that:

"the Phoenix |bird| is the symbol of the Reborn in Wisdom." [497]

And that:

"the phoenix |bird| was regarded as sacred to the sun ...." [498]

So the Phoenix bird is a symbol of the sun, and of the rebirth of man into a new religion: the religion where wisdom and reason become god.

Others in their writings have indicated that they also understand the symbology of the Phoenix. Fred Gittings, in his book entitled SECRET SYMBOLISM IN OCCULT ART, wrote this:

"the phoenix bird will live for a period of five hundred years, at the end of which it builds itself a nest of precious spices. The nest completed, the phoenix sings a doleful song and then flaps its wings to set the nest on fire.

The bird is soon burned to ashes, and from this mass of carbon there miraculously springs to life a new phoenix.

... we may see in it [this myth] certain ideas
which must have appealed to them [the occultists.]
From the ashes of burned material forms there
could spring forth new life."
... the phoenix ... is linked with the Sun ...." [499]

The phoenix bird symbolizes a rebirth, not only of an individual inside the Masonic religion but also of a new civilization arising out of the ashes of the ruined one. According to
this symbol, the world has been destroyed by the religious
teachings of God, and as soon as these beliefs are eliminated
from the world, a new civilization will be built upon a new
religion. That religion will be constructed on a belief in the
unrestricted use of man's reason.

This appears to be the true meaning of the Phoenix bird
utilized as a symbol by the 33rd degree Masons.

But it appears that there is one more secret of the Masonic Order and it is taught to the initiates of the 33rd degree. This explanation of the final secret is one that is not
available to any of the other 32 degrees. It appears that this
secret is only hinted at in these other degrees, but is actually
described to at least some of the initiates of the 33rd degree.

Evidence has been presented in previous chapters that the
Masons conceal the fact that they are out to avenge the murder of their legendary hero, Hiram Abif. Their writers have
told their readers that the three assassins of this Master
Mason are described as being actual individuals in the actual
rituals, but are in truth symbols of the real assassins, the
institutions of the church and the state. So the real goal of
the Masons is the actual destruction of organized religion and
national governments.

Rex Hutchens, a 32nd Degree Mason, has written simply
to make that point clear in his book entitled A BRIDGE TO
LIGHT. He explained that these statements were true:

"The axe [used as a symbol in the 22nd degree]
should remind the Mason of the march of civilization
and progress which required him to hew the poisonous
trees of intolerance, bigotry, superstition, uncharitable-
ness and idleness to let in the light of truth and
reason upon the human mind." [500]

According to this position, mankind's problem is that he has not been allowed free exercise of his "reason" by a God who restricts man with a series of "Thou shalts" and "Thou shalt nots." If religion were out of the way, the "illuminated mind" of the super-intelligent could build a paradise here on earth. The unrestricted use of man's mind is the solution to the problems of the earth.

According to this view, religion has been the source of all of man's problems. All that must be done is to abolish religion and the world will be a paradise. That is the true meaning of Mr. Hutchens' writings.

He then explains what the ebony crucifix utilized in the 18th Degree means:

"The ebony crucifix (black, meaning evil, dark-ness) represents the world's treatment of those who strive to make known the truth.

The Lost Word, one recalls, is a representative of many things -- the loss of reason, intellect and the moral sense and the loss of a true conception of Deity. In the world represented in this apartment, Man has made not only God, but the Devil, in his own image." [501]

According to this theory, God is a figment of man's mind. He doesn't exist. If God doesn't exist, what mankind calls religion is fictional. Man does not need religion; in fact, religion has caused immense problems all over the world. When religion disappears, man can use his mind to solve man's problems. Reason will discover man's morality, and all of the problems of the past will disappear.

Mr. Hutchens then went on to explain what the axe displayed in the 30th degree meant:

"The Great Order (Templars) naturally revolted against a Church which demanded of its members an absolute surrender of the reason as well as of the will." [502]

Once again, the church restricts mankind by not allowing him to obey his instincts or base passions. Religion teaches that these must be kept in check by a moral code, one that is given to him through the Bible. For instance, religion teaches

that man is truly free if he does not take the life of his
fellow man, steal his neighbor's property, take his neighbor's
wife, and if he conducts himself in all of his dealings with
honesty and integrity.

According to the Masons, this teaching of God restricts
mankind's "reason as well as his will." They feel that this is
an intolerable situation and remedies must be sought. But
since many in the world would not wish to willingly give up
their religious views, and would rebel if they discovered that
others are seeking to destroy their religion, the conspirators
have to meet in secret. Those with these plans must surround
themselves with others who are not aware of their goals so
that they can deny that their activities are what they truly
are. So the conspirators work inside secret organizations,
keeping the truth from their fellow members, and only teaching a few individuals the true goals of their secret society.

This is the true meaning of what Mr. Hutchens is writing.

He went on to explain what the additional symbols of the
"skull, tiara and crown" meant. These objects are displayed as
well as the axe in this 30th degree ceremony. Mr. Hutchens
explained what these objects represent:

> "The crown represents all those kings and em-
> perors who have usurped or abused power, reigned for
> themselves and not for the people and robbed a free
> people of their liberty ....
>
> The tiara is not a symbol of any particular re-
> ligion or creed [This is not true. On a previous page,
> he states that the tiara is a "Pope's tiara," meaning
> that it is a symbol of the authority of the head of the
> Catholic Church] but of the patron of ignorance and
> ally of despotism [obviously the Pope] which in every
> age has made dupes of men and enslaved humanity
> through fear and superstition." [503]

This thought was continued in another section of his book:

> "... a grave voice announced [during the 30th
> degree initiation ceremony] the duties of a philosopher
> and a Knight Kadosh [the name of the 30th degree.]
> The candidate learns that the Knight Kadosh 'now
> pursues with feet that never tire and eyes that never

sleep, the personifications of the three assassins of Hiram, the Incarnations of Evil which these three were but the tools;" [504]

And Mr. Hutchens amplifies these thoughts with this comment in his explanation of the 32nd degree:

"To be a Soldier of the True Religion [the "True Religion" is a knowledge that Lucifer is the true god of the world] is to recognize the corruption of the true religion given to man. Thus, we may combat, with reason and truth, all spiritual tyranny over the souls and consciences of men." [505]

These words contain some real truth in a concealed form. With this understanding of what Mr. Hutchens just wrote, it is now possible to summarize the truth contained in his writings. The following is a fair interpretation of what this author is saying in his explanation of the symbols utilized in the 30th degree.

1. The crucifix used in this degree is black, meaning that it is evil and darkness. The crucifix is the symbol of Christianity, and has been for nearly 2,000 years. But here, Mr. Hutchens tells the reader that the crucifix is a symbol of evil and darkness. The Christian Church is considered by this Masonic writer to be darkness and evil.

2. The Church has treated the Masons, those who are secretly preaching a new religion, with contempt. This claim of the Masons has been discussed in previous chapters.

3. The Masons feel that the Church has deprived man of his ability to utilize his reason by asking that mankind obey God's Moral Absolutes. Mr. Hutchens apparently wants man to "know good and evil," the exact knowledge that the devil offered man in the Garden of Eden.

4. The Bible claims that God made man in His own image. It is the contention of the Mason that the exact opposite is the truth: man has made God in his image. Since God is the product of an active imagination, there is no God.

Mr. Hutchens then quotes from a book written by Albert Pike called LEGENDA:

"Men are good. Evil institutions alone have made them bad; and it is the duty of Masonry and every Knight to aid in leading them back to the truth." [506]

The Christian position is that all men are sinners, and that they must improve themselves by freely choosing moral alternatives; but here Mr. Hutchens quotes Mr. Pike who takes the opposite position: it is the environment that has made man evil. In fact, man is good. Man is not at fault; if only man could change the environment, man would be perfect. The two positions are diametrically opposed to each other.

But the Masons will set the record straight when they establish their control over all of mankind.

The 33rd degree of the Masons has been described as representing "the innermost sanctuary of Masonic mysticism." So this degree is the innermost center of the entire Masonic Order. Here must reside the final mystery. And it appears that the public can know what that final mystery is.

The motto of the 33rd degree is ORDO AB CHAO, translated by the Masons as meaning: Order out of Chaos. [507]

According to the Masons, the present world is in chaos because of organized religion. but it will soon be made right. And the 33rd degree Masons apparently are volunteering for that task.

Adam Weishaupt, the founder of the Illuminati, put the problem into the same perspective:

"Liberty and Equality are the essential rights that man in his original and primitive perfection received from nature.

Property struck the first blow at Equality; political society or Governments were the first dispossessors of Liberty: the supporters of Governments and Property are the religions and civil laws; therefore to reinstate man in his primitive rights of Equality and Liberty, we must begin by destroying all Religion, all civil society and finish by the destruction of all property." [508]

But there is evidence that not all 33rd degree Masons receive the remaining "light" when they go through the initiation ceremony.

One who can testify to that evidence is Jim Shaw, a 33rd degree Mason who apparently became a Christian between the 32nd and 33rd degrees. But Mr. Shaw went to Washington D.C., the site of the initiation ceremony into the 33rd degree anyway. He told what happened to him during the three days of the ceremony in his book entitled THE DEADLY DECEPTION:

> "The first day:
> We |all of the candidates for the 33rd degree] were called into one of the offices, one at a time, and interviewed by three members of the Supreme Council.
>
> I was ushered into the office and seated. The very first question I was asked was 'Of what religion are you?'
>
> Not long before this I would have answered with something like 'I believe the Ancient Mysteries, the 'Old Religion,' and I believe in reincarnation.
>
> However, ... I found myself saying, 'I am a Christian.'
>
> After they sent me back out, I sat down and thought about it. When the next man came out, I asked him, 'Did they ask you if you are a Christian?' He said, 'Yes, they did.'
>
> 'What did you tell them?' I asked, and he replied, 'I told them 'No, and I never intend to be!'
>
> Then he said a strange thing to me, 'They said I'm going higher,' and he left through a different door, looking pleased." [509]

So according to this 33rd degree Mason, there are two layers inside that degree exactly as there are throughout the rest of the Masonic Lodge. Apparently, the one who states that he is a Christian does not proceed further.

Mr. Shaw, now a Christian minister, reported that nothing special happened during the other two days, so he returned to his home.

But there was an interesting comment that he made about who else was present during those three days of ceremonies:

"There were some extremely prominent men there that day, including a Scandinavian King, two former Presidents of the United States, an internationally prominent evangelist, two other internationally prominent clergymen, and a very high official of the federal government ...." [510]

Unfortunately for the student of the Masonic Order, Reverend Shaw did not identify who these gentlemen were.

However, he did state the reasons why he has left Masonry:

"Having left Freemasonry after 19 years and attained the 33rd degree, I feel ... a duty to warn others to avoid the satanic trap of Freemasonry." [511]

The Reverend shares the view of this writer: Masonry is satanic! They worship Lucifer, also known as Satan, the devil!

Someone has published part of the initiation ceremony of the 33rd degree. That part of the ritual is included on pages 363 and 364 of a book entitled OCCULT THEOCRASY, written by Edith Starr Miller. This book was not published until after her death in 1933.

The following is what takes place inside the 33rd degree initiation ceremony:

"For the Sovereign Grand Inspector General the 33rd is the last degree of the Rite. The Order is the Great Avenger of the assassinated Grand Master [the 33rd degree is the avenger of the death of Hiram Abif] and the grand champion of humanity, for the innocent Grand Master is man, man who is Master, King of Nature, man who is born innocent and unconscious. [Hiram is a symbol of all men.]

But he has fallen under the blows of three assassins, three scoundrels have thwarted his happiness and rights and have annihilated him.

The three infamous assassins are Law, Property and Religion. [Here is the true explanation of the three assassins of Hiram: they are Law, meaning government; Property, meaning the right to own private property; and Religion, the concept that man is to live by God's moral absolutes.]

Law, because it is not in harmony with the rights of the individual man and the duties of social man in society, rights which belong to all. Duties are but the immediate consequence of the rights inherent in all, for the enjoyment of all rights.

Property, because the earth belongs to nobody and its fruits belong to all in proportion as they are required by each for the needs of his own well being.

Religion, because religion is but philosophies evolved by men of genius and adopted by the people in the belief that they would increase their well being.

Neither law, property nor religion can be imposed on man as they annihilate him by depriving him of his most precious rights. They are assassins on whom we have sworn to wreck vengeance, enemies against whom we have declared war to the death and without quarter.

Of these three infamous enemies it is on religion that we must concentrate our most deadly attacks, because no people has ever survived its religion. Once Religion is dead, Law and Property will fall to our mercy, and we shall be able to regenerate society by founding on the corpses of the assassins of man, Masonic Religion, Masonic Law, and Masonic Property." [512]

So, the final secret of the Masonic Order has been made public! The student of the Masons can now know what their goals are.

The Masons are out to destroy the right to private property; the right to worship a God in an organized religion; and the right to set up a government based upon a concept that government exists to protect man's God given rights to life, liberty and property.

The Masons teach:

"You are here to think, if you can think;
And to learn, if you can learn." [513]

Those who wish to expose the Masons can think!
And they can learn!

And what they can learn after thinking is simple:

Some of the Masons worship Lucifer!

And some of the 33rd degree Masons want to destroy the right to private property, the right to orderly government, and the right to worship the God of the Bible!

And the student can know because some of the Masons have told them!

They stand convicted by their own words!

Chapter 26
The Humanists

There is a religion in America today that embodies many of the beliefs of the Masons, the New Age Movement, and the Communists.

It is called the Humanist Religion.

This religion even has a dictionary definition:

> Humanism: a modern, nontheistic, rationalist movement that holds that man is capable of self-fulfillment, ethical conduct, without recourse to super-naturalism.

Some call this religion Secular Humanism, and the word Secular is defined as "of relating to worldly things as distinguished from things relating to church and religion." The word is connected to the Latin word saecularis, meaning worldly.

The English word "Secular" is connected to the translation of the Latin phrase found on the back of the dollar bill, "Novus Ordo Seclorum," meaning the New World Order.

Some powerful people have identified themselves with this religion. One of these was former Vice President Walter Mondale, later an unsuccessful candidate for the Presidency in 1984 as a Democrat. He made his support known during a speech to the 5th Congress of the International Humanist and Ethical Union held at the Massachusetts Institute of Technology in August of 1970. Mr. Mondale said:

> "Although I have never formally joined a humanist society, I think I am a member by inheritance. My preacher father was a humanist ... and I grew up on a very rich diet of humanism from him.
> All of our family has been deeply influenced by this tradition including my brother Lester ...." [514]

The former Vice-President has been so moved by his religious views that he has been a contributor to a magazine called The Humanist.

Jimmy Carter, then the President of the United States, sent the American Humanist Association a telegram in April of 1978, in which he praised them for their activities:

> "Those who participate in the Annual Meeting of the American Humanist Association are furthering a movement that greatly enhances our way of life.
> The work of your organization in this area is, therefore, especially gratifying to me, and I welcome this opportunity to applaud your important accomplishments." [515]

The Humanists have issued two manifestos in which they have stated what their religion believes in, and any student can determine just what those positions are.

The first one was issued in 1933, and has been called simply THE HUMANIST MANIFESTO I. The introduction to that document reads, in part, as follows:

"The time has come for widespread recognition of the radical beliefs throughout the modern world. The time is past for mere revision of traditional attitudes.

Science [apparently meaning Evolution] and economic change [meaning Communism] have disrupted the old beliefs. Religions the world over are under the necessity of coming to terms with new conditions created by a vastly increased knowledge and experience.

In every field of human activity, the vital movement is now in the direction of a candid and explicit HUMANISM.

In order that religious Humanism may be better understood, we, the undersigned, desire to make certain affirmations which we believe the facts of our contemporary life demonstrate.

There is a great danger of a final, and we believe fatal, identification of the word RELIGION with doctrines and methods that have lost their significance and which are powerless to solve the problems of human living in the 20th century.

While this age does owe a vast debt to the traditional religions, it is none the less obvious that any religion that can hope to be a synthesizing and dynamic force for today must be shaped for the needs of this age. To establish such a religion is a major necessity of the present. It is the responsibility which rests upon this generation." [516]

What was just expressed in those paragraphs of the introduction can be summarized in a few short sentences:

1.   Science and economic changes have shown the world that religion no longer has the answers to man's problems,

2.   Humanism has the new answers.

3.   We can thank "religion" for what it has done in the past, but it is time to move on to new beliefs.

4.   And humanism is the new religion that can
      replace the old.

This Humanist Manifesto contains fifteen planks of their
beliefs, but only five are pertinent to this study. The First of
these states:

"First: Religious humanists regard the universe as
self-existing and not created."

Since the universe has always been, and was not created,
there is no reason to believe in a creator. So the humanist
religion is an atheist one, believing that there is no god.

"Second: Man has emerged as the result of a continuous process."

The Biblical view is that man and animals were all created within a period of six days. The Humanists believe that
evolution is a more satisfactory explanation of the origins of
both the universe and of man. And that the process has tak-
en billions of years. The Humanists have stated that evolution is part of their religious view of man.

"Fifth: ... the nature of the universe ... makes
unacceptable any supernatural or cosmic guarantees of
human values."

There is no prayer answering god in the universe, and
there are no God created moral absolutes.

"Sixth: We are convinced that the time has
passed for theism [a belief in one God,] deism [a belief
in the existence of a God on purely rational grounds
without reliance on revelation or authority] ...."

Once again, the Humanists profess their belief that God
does not exist. Obviously, modern man is too sophisticated to
believe in a god whose existence cannot be proven.

"Fourteenth: The humanists are firmly convinced
that existing acquisitive and profit-motivated society
has shown itself to be inadequate and that a radical

change in methods, controls and motives must be instituted.

A socialized and cooperative economic order must be established to the end that the equitable distribution of the means of life be possible." [517]

It will be remembered that Karl Marx, the so-called "father of Communism", supported the concept of a "socialized and cooperative economic order." He stated that position in his writings. He wrote:

"From each according to his ability, to each according to his need."

And he added this additional comment, which many consider the very essence of Communism:

"In one word, you reproach us with intending to do away with your property. Precisely so: that is just what we intend." [518]

That is what the Humanists believe!

The Humanists, just like Karl Marx, do not approve of an economic system that encourages the right to own private property. They believe in the economic system known as socialism, just like Karl Marx.

The beliefs of the Humanists can be summarized by stating that the religion stands on a stool with three major legs: evolution, atheism, and communism. There should be not doubt as to what they believe in. Any student can read it in the two Manifestos.

This 1933 edition of the HUMANIST MANIFESTO was signed by thirty-four men, only two of whom have any bearing on this study. One was Professor John Dewey of Columbia University, the father of so-called "progressive education," and the other was Lester Mondale, the brother of the Vice-President.

Professor Dewey's religious views on life have had a dramatic effect on education in America.

In 1974, Saturday Review magazine published their "golden anniversary issue," and as a part of their commemoration of those 50 years, they asked various American leaders to name the "most influential figure" in their respective fields of endeavor. [519]

The individual that they named as the "most influential figure in American education" during the period of 1924 to 1974 was:

John Dewey!

One dean of a major university in California was quoted as saying:

"It has to be Dewey .... I'd allege that he is the only great educator in our history."

Another educator said that Dewey:

"towers above everyone else."

And another educator said:

"No individual has influenced the thinking of American educators more ...."

John Dewey was a Socialist/Communist, an atheist, and believed in the fraud known as evolution. He believed that there were "no moral absolutes," and that man should develop his own set of "moral" values. He believed that Christianity was "powerless to solve" man's problems.

Yet this is the individual who "has influenced the thinking of American educators" the most.

To further illustrate the convoluted thinking of this man, one only needs to examine a quote attributed to him:

"There is no God, and there is no soul. There are no needs for the props of traditional religion.

With dogma and creed excluded, then immutable truth is also dead and buried.

There is no room for fixed, natural law or permanent moral absolutes."

These opinions are absolutely incredible, and reveal just how shallow and confused Professor Dewey's thoughts were.

He claimed that when religion was removed from the environment, "immutable truth" would be "dead and buried."

This is impossible!

The word "immutable" is defined as being unchangeable.

The professor was admitting that truth was "immutable."

He was saying that "unchangeable truth" could be changed!

That which is unchangeable cannot be changed! By its own definition!

Yet Professor Dewey said it could be!

He also said that there was "no room for ... permanent moral absolutes." That which is permanent cannot be done away with. It can only be ignored. But if they are permanent, they will still remain.

Professor Dewey believed that that which is unchangeable can be changed. He believed that that which is permanent can be done away with.

Professor Dewey was out of touch with reality.

Those who are out of touch with reality are defined as being insane. Those who believe that that which is unchangeable can be changed are insane!

Yet Professor Dewey has "influenced the thinking of American educators more than any other educator."

And his religious beliefs are becoming the official religion of America.

In 1973, on the fortieth anniversary of the issuance of the first Manifesto, the Humanists issued the second Manifesto. This one basically reaffirmed what the first Manifesto said:

> "As in 1933, humanists still believe that traditional theism, especially faith in the prayer-hearing God, assumed to love and care for persons, to hear and understand prayers, and to be able to do something about them, is an unproved and outmoded faith.
>
> No deity will save us; we must save ourselves." [520]

Once again, the Humanists stated their belief that God does not exist. Since there is no God, man is on his own. Since man is on his own, man needs to create his own religion, and the Humanists have done just that.

The Second Principle of the Humanist Manifesto II states:

"Promises of immortal salvation or fear of eternal damnation are both illusory and harmful. Rather, science affirms that the human species is an emergence from natural evolutionary forms ...."

Here the Humanists restate their conviction that man is nothing more than a highly evolved animal. It is a fact of modern reality that this position is no longer the sole theory of origins being offered to the world by the scientific community. The Theory of Evolution is currently being challenged by what is known as Creation Science. This approach is rapidly proving, using scientific data, that evolution is a fraud and a hoax. Scientists of world renown are deserting their long held evolutionary beliefs after being exposed to this competing theory. The scientist who has the integrity to compare the two theories side by side is discovering that evolution is not scientific. Debates between the evolutionists and the creationists on college campuses all over the world are being won by the creationists. As a result, science is slowly returning to the position held by the scientific world before Charles Darwin revolutionized it with his unprovable and unsound theories known as Evolution.

In spite of this, Evolution is an official part of the Humanist religion.

The Third Principle reads:

"Ethics is autonomous and situational, needing no theological or ideological sanction. To deny this distorts the whole basis of life."

There is no God, therefore there are no God-given Moral Absolutes. The words of these Absolutes, such as "Thou shalt not," have no relevance to today's societies, and because this is true, man does not have to obey these teachings. He is therefore free to decide these matters for himself. It follows, therefore, that Religion will shortly pass away. All that needs to be done is for it to be officially buried by the Humanists, New Agers, Masons and Communists.

This new "moral" philosophy has an official name, Situational Ethics, and will be examined more in detail in a subsequent chapter of this study.

The Fourth Principle states:

"Reason and intelligence are the most effective instruments that humankind possesses. There is no substitute: neither faith nor passion suffices in itself."

Here the Humanists side with the Masons who have deified reason. As was just discussed, this view holds that man's mind is the ultimate savior of mankind. Humanists strive to create an environment where man can utilize his mind to save humanity. That means that religions must be removed from that environment so that man will be free to utilize his mind so that he can solve man's problems without religious interference.

The Sixth Principle reads:

"In the areas of sexuality, we believe that intolerant attitudes, often cultivated by orthodox religions and puritanical cultures, unduly repress sexual conduct. The right to birth control, abortion and divorce should be recognized."

According to this Principle, religions in America have been "unduly repressive" in their teaching about mankind's sexuality. They have taught the world that abortion is murder (believing that abortion is a violation of the Moral Absolute "Thou shalt not kill.") The Humanists believe that birth control must be available, and abortion on demand permitted.

The Eighth Principle reads:

"We must extend participatory democracy in its true sense to the economy, the school, the family, the workplace and voluntary associations."

The Christian and Jewish religions for centuries have taught that the husband is the head of the household. But the humanists would change that, by allowing the entire family to decide the direction that the family is going to take. If the family is having difficulty in making a decision, such as whether to take a vacation in the mountains or at the seashore, the family is to decide democratically: each person is to have one vote. And if there are three children and their choice is the seashore, and the majority rules, the two parents, and the family, will visit the seashore. The fact that the parents know that they cannot afford the vacation at the ocean is to have no bearing on the decision. The majority rules!

It is almost inconceivable that a "rational" mind could conceive of such a program for a family unit, but that is what the new Humanists propose.

And not only must the family experience the joys of participatory democracy, so must the workplace. Imagine the experience of having a work force of 5,000 deciding how much the production will be that day, and at what price they will be offered, and to whom they will be sold.

This is what the Humanists want.

And the Humanists want the students to have a say as to what will be taught that day in school. Allowing five year olds to determine the subjects to be discussed will practically eliminate education as an instructional tool.

The Eleventh Principle reads:

"We believe in the right to universal education."

Karl Marx, who declared himself a "humanist," in the Communist Manifesto, wrote this in the Tenth Plank:

521 "Free education for all children in public schools."

The education of the children used to be the direct responsibility of the family. Parents were originally the teachers of this nation's children, and later were thought able to pay for the educational needs of their own children once this nation went to a system of public education. But here the Humanists side with the Communists who believe that education should be the concern of the entire society. In other words, those couples who have either decided against having children of their own, or elderly parents, who have already raised their children, were to be made to support the educational costs of the parents who produce children.

The concept that parents without children should pay for the education of the parents with children came directly from the writings of Karl Marx, the communist. He wrote "From each according to his ability, to each according to his need."

Marx taught that parents without children had to pay for those parents with children.

The Twelfth Principle reads:

> "We deplore the division of humankind on nation-
> alistic grounds. ... the best option is to transcend the
> limits of national sovereignty and move toward the
> building of a world community ....
>   We thus reaffirm a commitment to the building of
> world community ...."

The world government is coming, and the Humanists are
proud to announce their support for it.

The Fourteenth Principle reads:

> "... excessive population growth must be checked
> by international concord."

The thought that some held the position that there was a
"population explosion" was discussed in my book entitled THE
UNSEEN HAND, and was shown to be a fraud. This is what
I wrote:

> "Oregon, a rather small state by comparison to
> others in the United States, has a total of 95,607
> square miles inside its borders. The world has
> approximately four billion (4,000,000,000) inhabitants.
>   If the entire population of the world moved to
> Oregon, and left the remainder of the world completely
> devoid of human life, a family of four would have a
> piece of Oregon approximately 50' by 53'. This is about
> half the size of a typical residential lot in a sub-
> division." [522]

The idea that the world is exploding because there are
simply too many people on the earth is a fraud, but the
Humanists believe it. In fact, that belief in a lie is a part of
their official belief structure. And, not only do they
acknowledge the non-existent "problem," they wish to involve
government in solving it. Governments deciding to "control
populations" is the thing that makes dictators exceedingly
happy.

So the population explosion was not an explosion at all,
but was being offered for other purposes. Those who were
frightening the population of the world into believing that

government had to intercede to control a non-existent problem had a hidden agenda. The operative word is the word "control," and would have gladdened the heart of any dictator. The type of government necessary to coerce people into controlling the non-existent "population explosion" is one that should frighten any thinking person.

But this thought has apparently not occurred to those who ascribe to the Humanist religion.

The last paragraph of their Manifesto contains a summation of their basic beliefs:

> "We further urge the use of reason and compassion to produce the kind of world we want ...."

So the Humanists have linked themselves with the others who look to man's reason as the solution to all of the problems caused, in their way of thinking, by the religions of the world.

This second Manifesto was signed by 102 individuals including some very familiar names:

Isaac Asimov, author,
Alan F. Guttmacher, Planned Parenthood Federation,
Lester Mondale, brother of the former Vice-President,
Andre Sakharov, Academy of Sciences, Moscow, USSR, and
Joseph Fletcher, Visiting Prof., School of Medicine, University of Virginia.

Each year, the Humanists honor the "Humanist of the Year" with an award and those honored in the past have been some of the most influential people in the world:

1969: Dr. Benjamin Spock
1972: B.F. Skinner
1975: Betty Friedan
1980: Andre Sakharov
1981: Carl Sagan, the noted astronomer
1984: Isaac Asimov
1985: John Kenneth Galbraith, economist
1986: Faye Wattleton, president of Planned Parenthood

But one of the most well known Humanists is Madalyn Murray O'Hair, the woman who in 1963 was successful in her attempts to eliminate prayer and Bible reading in America's public schools.

Mrs. O'Hair has had an interest in the religious views of Humanism for many years. She was once the editor of the magazine entitled THE FREE HUMANIST, and was elected to the Board of the American Humanist Association in 1965, and was elected in 1973 for a second four year term.

In public statements. she has been quoted as saying that "there's absolutely no conclusive evidence" that Jesus ever lived and that Christianity has never "contributed anything to anybody, anyplace, at any time." She has called religion "the mental excrement of primitive man," and has said that:

> "religion is the wildest form of insanity. I would turn every church into a home for the aged or out-patient clinic, etc. Christianity, which is anti-science, anti-life, anti-sex, anti-woman, anti-freedom, anti-peace, is detrimental to the United States."

She has not confined her activity to just the prayer-in-school issue, either. Her attack on Christianity has gotten her involved in other issues.

In December of 1974, she supported the Lansman-Milam petition (RM 2493) to the Federal Communications Commission (the FCC.) This petition asked them to impose an immediate freeze on all:

> "applications for reserved educational FM and TV channels ... by any and all 'Christian,' Bible, 'Religious,' and other sectarian colleges and institutions." [523]

In September of 1977, she filed suit in the federal court to remove the motto "In God We Trust," from all U.S. currency. She asked the court to declare the motto unconstitutional, and then order the Secretary of the Treasury to no longer place it on any American money. [524]

In November of 1977, she involved herself in a demand that the Governor of Texas prohibit the display of a nativity scene in the State Capitol during the Christmas holidays. She also objected to a monument inscribed with the Ten Commandments on Capitol grounds. However, she went on to say that she found no objection to the Christmas tree placed inside the Capitol building, because that was "a pagan thing which has nothing to do with religion."

Earlier that month she was arrested and charged with disrupting a public meeting for loudly protesting the opening of a city council meeting with a prayer. The article that reported her activity quoted her as saying:

> "I'm going to try to have the mayor and the minister who leads the prayers arrested. They're interjecting religious activity into a governmental meeting." [525]

Two years later, in 1979, the Supreme Court unanimously rejected her suit about the removal of the "In God We Trust" motto from all American currency. The judge who ruled against her in the District Court was quoted as saying that the motto:

> "has nothing whatsoever to do with the establishment of religion. Its use is of a patriotic or ceremonial character and bears no true resemblance to a governmental sponsorship of a religious exercise. Moreover, it would be ludicrous to argue that the use of the national motto fosters any excessive governmental entanglement with religion." [526]

One of her more recent cases involved a group that she was the founder and the President Emeritus of, called the Society of Separationists. They sued the state of Texas, claiming that they had been systematically excluded from jury duty because of their refusal to swear an oath to God. They claimed that the oath that all prospective jurors must take before they are sworn in as members of a panel that requires them to be sworn in "so help me God," was a violation of "the constitutional separation of church an state. [527]

That was an interesting, but not persuasive, argument because the Constitution of the United States contains no such statement in its wording. There is no required "separation of church and state." Those are the words of Thomas Jefferson and not of the Constitution.

The First Amendment to the Constitution of the United States reads:

"Congress shall make no law respecting an establishment of religion, or prohibiting the free exercise thereof; [the remainder of the Amendment protects other rights and does not concern itself with the right to religious freedom.]

Notice that Congress is prohibited from establishing a national religion. Notice furthermore that the states may do so if they so choose. That is because of the Tenth Amendment to the Constitution that reads:

"The powers not delegated to the United States by the Constitution, nor prohibited by it to the States, are reserved to the States respectively, or to the people."

So, Congress has no authority to require anyone to believe in any particular religion. There is no reason why the national government may not print a motto such as "In God We Trust" on its currency.

Mrs. O'Hair's string of failures has affected her family as well. All of her activity for the cause of atheism has failed to induce one of her two sons to believe in the theory.

Her son, William Murray, the child she filed the suit to restrict prayer in public schools for, later became a Christian. He said in a letter in May, 1980, that he was publicly apologizing to the American people because:

"the part I played as a teenager in removing prayer from public schools was criminal. I removed from our future generations that short time each day which should rightly be reserved for God. Inasmuch as the suit to destroy the tradition of prayer in school was brought in my name, I feel gravely responsible for the resulting destruction of the moral fiber of our youth that it has caused." [528]

In June of 1988, he told us a little about what his mother believed in. He told the world in an interview that:

"My mother was always a Marxist. She was the manager of the New Era Bookstore in Baltimore, which was and is today an official Communist Party bookstore."

Mr. Murray further amplified his thoughts about his mother in a book he wrote about Nicaragua. He said:

"Many people identify me as being the son of atheist leader Madlyn Murray O'Hair. Granted, she is my mother, but her identification as an atheist 'leader' is not quite true. It was never her intent to be an atheist leader, but a Marxist leader."

He reminisced about his childhood with his mother when he added these thoughts:

"... I'm able to reflect upon the change in my own life [Mr. Murray, as mentioned previously, has since become a Christian] from being raised in a home where there was hatred toward freedom; hatred toward free enterprise; and hatred toward God."

It wasn't until 1988, however, when some of the truth about Mrs. O'Hair's lawsuit came out. The Houston Chronicle told the world in its June 18, 1988 newspaper, that:

"Madalyn Murray O'Hair ... said she invented a non-existent public interest group so it would not appear that she was fighting the battle alone.
'I lied like **** [expletive deleted] during the whole thing. The public wasn't willing to listen to just one single woman alone with two kids tugging at her ... so what I did was invent the Maryland Committee for the Separation of Church and State, which really didn't exist."

Others of national and international renown have embraced the Humanist religion as well.
Another who publicly did was Karl Marx, the Communist. He also claimed Humanism as his own. He wrote:

"Communism as a fully developed naturalism is humanism ...." [529]

And in 1970, the New Program of the Communist Party, U.S.A., stated:

"Marxism is not only rational; it is humanist in the best and most profound meaning of the term." [530]

But Humanism is not just a word in a dictionary. It is becoming the official religion of the United States. The proof that Humanism has received official sanction as the religion of the United States starts with a Supreme Court decision in a 1961 case called Torcaso versus Watkins. The Court ruled that Humanism was to be officially sanctioned as a religion when they declared:

"Among religions in this country which do not teach what would generally be considered a belief in the existence of God are Buddhism, Taoism, Ethical Culture, Secular Humanism and others." [531]

The Court ruled that the First Amendment to the Constitution granted the same protection and imposed the same limitations on the "religion of Secular Humanism" as are applicable to other religions.

And in 1965, the Supreme Court in another case wrote that:

"... a humanistic belief that is sincerely professed as a religion shall be entitled to recognition as religious under the Selective Service Law. [532]

The result of this decision is to exempt anyone from the draft who professes that his religion is called Humanism.

So the Supreme Court has correctly identified Humanism as a "religion." And even the Humanists declare that their religion is a religion. The President of the American Humanist Association wrote this:

"Humanism is a religion without a God, divine revelation or sacred scriptures." [533]

And Sir Julian Huxley, a signer of the Humanist Manifest II, wrote this in a Humanist Association promotional brochure:

"I use the word 'humanist' to mean someone who believes that man is just as much a natural phenomenon as an animal or plant; that his body, mind and soul were not supernaturally created but were products of evolution." [534]

And to show that the government of the United States has officially recognized the Humanists as a religion, the American Humanist Association has been granted a religious tax exemption.

So, as has been illustrated, Humanism is based upon a belief in three major philosophies:

Communism, evolution and atheism.

And it is being taught in the schools of America (this will be explored in a later chapter of this study.)

In 1987, some parents with young children in the Alabama public school system found the teaching of this religion in their tax-supported schools to be objectionable. They filed suit to prevent their children from being taught a religious view in violation of their own personal religious views. An article that appeared in the Arizona Daily Star reported what happened:

"A federal judge ordered Alabama officials yesterday to remove 36 textbooks from public schools, saying they furthered a belief in humanism and denied the role of religion in American society.

The sweeping ruling, a victory for 624 conservative Christians who pressed the lawsuit, found for the first time that secular humanism is a religion that is unconstitutionally advanced in the nation's public schools.

[U.S. District Judge W. Brevard Hand] found that five home economics textbooks, published by such giants as McGraw Hill Book Co., advance religious tenets in violation of the First Amendment's prohibition against governmental establishment of a religion.

In addition, Hand found that 31 history and social studies textbooks, also published by major houses,
were 'not merely bad history, but lack so many facts
as to equal ideological promotion.'" [535]

The Alabama Civil Liberties Union was not pleased with
the decision. The article quoted their executive director Mary
Weidler as saying:

"This decision confirms our worst fears of federal
censorship over local public school matters. It severely
threatens non-sectarian public education in Alabama
and around the nation."

This concern about "federal censorship" by the Alabama
Civil Liberties Union is very puzzling. Their position that the
removal of textbooks from the public schools by the federal
government constituted "censorship" revealed a blatant hypocrisy. Because in the "Creationism Science versus Evolution
Science" court case also in Alabama a few years later, the
American Civil Liberties Union, presumably the parent of the
Alabama organization, took the opposite position. In that
case, they argued that Creationism science textbooks should
be removed from the students in Alabama's science classrooms. It was their position that the Creationism Science
could not be taught side by side with the theory of Evolution
in science classes in the state. They argued that only Evolution could be taught.
In other words, they argued in favor of the censorship of
Creationism textbooks from the classroom.
Their objection in that case was basically that the Creationism textbooks taught a religious view of science in opposition to the traditional Evolutionist view. In other words, those
who claim to protect America's "Civil Liberties" wanted the
books removed in one case, but not in the other.
They claimed that the Creationists wanted to teach a religious view in the science classes, and they urged that the
court to remove the textbooks. The Christians claimed that
the Humanists were teaching a religious view in other classrooms in the school districts, and the Civil Liberties Union
objected when the judge removed the books.

This doesn't make sense, unless those claiming to protect America's "civil liberties" wanted only the Humanist religion taught in the public schools. That conclusion fits the facts.

If they were concerned about "federal censorship of school matters," they should have been consistent. They should have allowed the state to utilize Creationism science textbooks because they "feared federal censorship."

But they didn't. The "civil libertarians" are not consistent.

Censorship is not called censorship if your side does the censoring.

And the American Civil Liberties Union wants to be the censor.

Chapter 27
Situation Ethics

"If we are gods, we can develop our own truth."

But if Humanism succeeds and religion is removed from the American lifestyle, the Christian style of morality will be done away with as well. That means that the Humanists must have a moral view to offer in its place.

And they do: it is called Situation Ethics.

The dictionary defines "situation ethics" as:

> "A system of ethics according to which moral rules are not absolutely binding but may be modified in the light of specific situations."

The Humanists have declared their support of this concept. They have included it in their Humanist Manifesto II:

> "Third: We affirm that moral values derive their source from human experience.

Ethics is autonomous and situational." [536]

Douglas Grothuis, author of UNMASKING THE NEW AGE, wrote:

"Once you've deified yourself [made yourself into a god,] which is what the New Age is all about, there is no higher moral absolute. It's a recipe for ethical anarchy." [537]

In essence, the New Agers are saying: All moral values are situational. The situation determines what's right or wrong, and since situations constantly change, what's right today may be wrong tomorrow.

The New Age Movement, the Humanist Religion, and the Communists have made a god out of man; they have deified mankind. The new morality for a man-god is whatever he decides it is, and that is what the New Age-Humanists-Communists have done. Their new morality is called Situation Ethics.

Dr. Arthur E. Gravatt, M.D., defined the term for a scientific journal:

"... moral behavior may differ from situation to situation. Behavior might be moral for one person and not another. Whether an act is moral or immoral is determined by the 'law of love;' that is the extent of which love and concern for others is a factor in the relationship." [538]

But it was another who coined the phrase "Situation Ethics." That honor belongs to Joseph Fletcher, who first used the word in a speech to Harvard alumni in 1964. He was a professor at the Cambridge Episcopal Theological Seminary.

This is what he believes:

"... for me there are no rules -- none at all ....
... anything and everything is right or wrong according to the situation -- what is wrong in some cases is right in others ....

> ... a situationist would discard all absolutes except the one absolute: always to act with loving concern." [539]

By this definition, mass murderers would not be in error if they professed that their acts were based on a love for humanity, and that they had committed their murders with "a loving concern." If, for example, one of these murderers killed people in an area polluted with radioactive wastes, and said that these acts were being committed because the murderer did not want them to be affected by the pollution, and that he loved them, the act would be acceptable according to those who believed in Situation Ethics.

This "morality" known as "Situation Ethics" is the underlying philosophy of the Communists/Socialists who murder a percentage of a nation's population in a quest for their goal of Communism or Socialism. The advocates of these "-isms" claim that their goal is so desirable that those who they murder must give way for the good of all humanity. The corollary of this position is "The end justifies the means."

The Communists in Russia murdered up to 42 million people in the Communist Revolution of 1917 because the Communist society was deemed to be worth all of the carnage by the murderers.

It is certain that Adolf Hitler felt that his murders of some 50 million people during World War II were not wrong because the "Third Reich" that would result after the war was over would be worth it.

Chou En-Lai and Mao Tse Tung murdered as many as 64 million people in their Communist Revolution that started in 1923 and ended in 1949 and one can know that they felt that the price the dead people had to pay for the rest of the Chinese was worth the end result.

It will be remembered that Adam Weishaupt, the founder of the Illuminati, wrote that "the ends justified the means."

Weishuapt wrote further that "no man [would be] fit for our Order who [was] not ready to go to every length." [540]

Only one with no moral values, in other words, one who believed in Situation Ethics, would be "willing to go to every length."

John Robison, the exposer of the Illuminati, wrote:

> "Nothing was so frequently discoursed of as the propriety of employing, for the good purpose, the means

which the wicked employed for evil purposes; and it was taught, that the preponderancy of good in the ultimate result consecrated every mean employed." [541]

A modern day exponent of the Situation Ethics philosophy is actress Shirley MacLaine. She has written:

"There is no such thing as evil. Evil is fear and uncertainty. Evil is what you think it is.
This business of 'evil' and 'satan' was a ridiculous concept to me." [542]

And the Masons also believe in Situation Ethics. Mason H. L. Haywood wrote in his book entitled GREAT TEACHINGS OF MASONRY:

"Human experience ... is the one final authority in morals.
Wrong is whatever hurts human life or destroys human happiness ....
Acts are not right or wrong intrinsically but according as their effects are hurtful or helpful." [543]

And he repeated the thought in another of his books, THE MEANING OF MASONRY:

"What is good for me may be evil for you; what is right to do at one moment may be wrong the next." [544]

And Albert Pike agreed with this comment in his book MORALS AND DOGMA:

"... all truths are truths of Period, and not truth for eternity." [545]

Mr Pike held that there were no absolutes. All truths were only for the period. This view is called Situation Ethics.
Mr. Pike called his book MORALS AND DOGMA. Situation Ethics is a particular view of morality. Judging from Mr. Pike's comments, it would be fair to conclude that this was the moral view of the book. Mr. Pike was instructing every

Mason who read the book that the Masonic religion believed in Situation Ethics.

Fellow Mason Manly P. Hall took a little different tack, but said basically the same thing:

> "It has always been a serious question to me whether Jesus ever actually spoke the words: 'If ye love me, keep my commandments,' for the statement is clearly out of accord with both divine and human reason." [546]

Jesus taught his followers that they were to obey his commandments. Those commandments were called Moral Absolutes. Mr. Hall was saying that Jesus never taught that, and that human reason would not accept the principle that there were moral absolutes. Human reason has concluded that keeping a divine commandment is not "reasonable."

Friedrich Nietzsche, whose powerful dissertation on THE GENEALOGY OF MORALS sought to make "a revaluation of all values," wrote that "so-called evil was good, and what was habitually believed to be good was evil." [547]

The Communists are also taught that there are no absolutes in life. Nikolai Lenin, the Russian Communist, certainly believed in Situation Ethics. His revolution in 1917 murdered, as has been discussed before, nearly 42 million people, to achieve the goal of Communism for the Russian people. He wrote:

> "Communism is power based upon force and limited to nothing, by no kind of law and by absolutely no set rule." [548]

> "The dictatorship of the proletariat is nothing else than power based upon force and limited by nothing -- by no kind of law and by absolutely no rule." [549]

> "We must combat religion. This is the ABC of all materialism and consequently of Marxism.

> Down with religion. Long live atheism. The spread of atheism is our chief task.

> Communism abolishes eternal truths. It abolishes all religion and morality." [550]

Lenin showed that his thinking was just as illogical as that exhibited by John Dewey. He stated that "Communism abolished eternal truths."

This is impossible!

The word "eternal" is defined as being of infinite duration, or perpetual.

That which is eternal has no end. It will continue to exist throughout all of time.

Lenin admitted that in his view, these "truths" were eternal. Yet he admitted that Communism would "abolish" these "eternal truths."

That which is eternal cannot be abolished.

Unless your thinking is as convoluted as that of Nikolai Lenin!

Lenin was just as insane as John Dewey!

He continued with other similar thoughts:

"We, of course, say that we do not believe in God. We do not believe in eternal morality.

We repudiate all morality that is taken outside of human, class concepts. We say that our morality is entirely subordinated to the interests of the class struggle.

Communists must regard themselves as free, indeed morally obligated to violate the truthfulness, respect for life, etc., when it is absolutely clear that a great deal more harm [to Communist objectives] would be done by adhering to such principles than by violating them.

That is moral, that serves the destruction of the old society." [551]

"We must repudiate all morality which proceeds from supernatural ideas, or ideals which are outside class conceptions. Everything is moral which is necessary for the annihilation of the old exploiting social order and for uniting the proletariat.

In what sense do we repudiate ethics and morality?

In the sense that they were preached by the bourgeoisie [meaning the rich?] who declared that these were god's commandments." [552]

Frederick Engels, a co-worker in the world of Communism with Karl Marx, wrote:

> "leaving aside the problem of morality ... for a revolutionist any means are right which lead to the purpose, the violent, as the seemingly tame." [553]

Feodor Mikhailovich Dostoevski, the Russian novelist, wrote this in one of his writings:

> "If there is no god, everything is permitted." [554]

What happens to the individual's mind after he accepts the philosophy of situation ethics can be best illustrated by studying the writings of Sergei Nechayev, the Russian Revolutionary. This young man had an enormous influence on the outcome of the Russian Bolshevik Communist Revolution of 1917, and the resulting deaths of approximately 42 million people, because his writings had an enormous influence on Nikolai Lenin. Nechayev wrote:

> "Our cause is terrible, complete, universal and pitiless destruction .... Let us unite with the savage, criminal world, these true and only revolutionists of Russia." [555]

Only a believer in Situation Ethics could ever say such a thing. There are no moral absolutes when complete destruction is your goal. And that was the goal of this revolutionary. He continued:

> "The revolutionary is a doomed man. He has no personal interests, no business affairs, no emotions, no attachments, no property and no name.
> Everything in him is wholly absorbed in the single thought and the single passion for revolution.
> The revolutionary knows ... he has broken all bonds which tie him to social order and the civilized world with all its laws, moralities and customs and with its generally accepted conventions.
> The object is perpetually the same: the surest and quickest way of destroying the whole filthy order.

The revolutionary ... despises and hates the existing social morality ....

For him, morality is everything which contributes to the triumph of the revolution. Immoral and criminal is everything that stands in his way.

[The revolutionary] must be tyrannical toward others. All the gentle and enervating sentiments of kinship, love, friendship, gratitude, and even honor must be suppressed in him and give place to the cold and single-minded passion for revolution."

"Do not pity .... Kill in public places if these base rascals dare to enter them, kill in houses, kill in villages.

Remember, those who will not side with us will be against us.

Whoever is against us is our enemy. And we must destroy enemies by all means." [556]

What this young revolutionary wrote about was unrestricted Situation Ethics, where there absolutely is no right and wrong. Nechayev's thoughts are the logical result of this type of thinking. Once the revolutionary accepts this ethical code, anything is permitted. Murder, looting, pillaging, and torture become acceptable behavior.

And this is the ethical code of the Humanist.

Situation Ethics leads some into a position of hating the entire society, and of wishing to destroy the whole social fabric, the "old world order." Then those who wish to fill the void can remake the world. And the new world that will be created will be called The New World Order.

Remember that Nechayev wrote that the revolutionary intended to "destroy the whole filthy order." The goal of the revolutionary was to destroy the "old world order" and replace it with the "New World Order."

Perhaps the major purpose of Situation Ethics was made clear in a book written by Aldous Huxley entitled BRAVE NEW WORLD REVISITED. He identified the destruction of the individual as the primary goal of this new ethical teaching. He wrote:

"... a new Social Ethic is replacing our traditional ethical system -- the system in which the individual is primary.

... the social whole has greater worth and significance than its individual parts, ... that the rights of the collectivity take precedence over ... the Rights of Man." [557]

But Situation Ethics is not new. It is as old as the Bible. Isaiah the prophet was moved to write about the system in about 740 B.C. He wrote this in Isaiah 5:20-21 in the Old Testament of the Bible:

"Woe unto them that call evil good, and good evil, that put bitter for sweet, and sweet for bitter."

Situation Ethics calls evil good and good evil.

And it is the philosophy of the Humanists, the Communists and some of the Masons.

And it is rapidly becoming the morality of America.

Chapter 28
The Attack on Religion

The New World Order is already here.

There are already people and organizations attacking the family, nationalism, the right to private property, the right to worship, and the right to practice a decent morality, among other things.

One of the first areas of "The Old World Order" to come to the attention of the destroyers was the Christian Church.

And one of the first to be attacked in recent history was Pastor Everett Sileven of Louisville, Nebraska. He is the pastor of a fundamentalist church in that community and he taught his congregation that they had the scriptural obligation to teach their children themselves. And, to accomplish this end, the church voted to open a Christian school in the summer of 1977.

The church felt that educating the children of the congregation was a ministry of the church, just like Sunday school, or preaching. And, since the church felt the need to do this as a part of their religion, they chose not to register their school, nor license their teachers, through the state of Nebraska. They also believed that the First Amendment to the Constitution of the United States protected their right to freedom of religion.

That First Amendment reads in part:

"Congress shall make no law respecting an establishment of religion, OR PROHIBITING THE FREE EXERCISE THEREOF ...."

Since government was prohibited from passing a law abridging the free exercise of their religious rights, the church felt that they would not be interfered with.

This church was the first in Nebraska to open a Christian school without licensing their teachers. So, they were the first to be challenged by the state government of Nebraska.

Later, in August, the Nebraska Department of Education entered the school and told the Pastor that the school was breaking state law because they had not certified their instructors. They cited Rules numbered 14 and 21, which they said were procedures for getting the school licensed, and for licensing their faculty.

The Pastor explained their position, but his arguments were not listened to. Later, The sheriff came and arrested the Pastor, and the case went to a county court. The Pastor also used as his defense Article 1, Section 4 of the Nebraska State Constitution which read:

"All persons have a natural and indefeasible [defined as that which cannot be undone or made void] right to worship Almighty God according to the dictates of their own consciences ... nor shall any interference with the rights of conscience be permitted.

Religion, morality and knowledge, however, being essential to good government, it shall be the duty of the legislature to pass suitable laws to protect every denomination in the peaceable enjoyment of its own mode of public worship, and to encourage schools and the means of instruction."

The Pastor then testified:

"... the primary objection of the Faith Baptist Church to accepting licensure from the State is the violation of Ephesians 1:22 which reads:

'The God of our Lord Jesus Christ gave him [Jesus] to be the head over all things of the church.'"

And Colossians 1:18:

'... and he [Jesus] is the head of the body, the church ....'

The Pastor continued to resist, and the judge rewarded that resistance with several terms in prison.

Pastor Sileven wrote an explanation as to why he refused to allow the state to control his school in his book entitled THE PADLOCKED CHURCH:

"We came to the firm conclusion, unanimously, that Christ could not be submitted to the authority of the state, leaving the state the right to determine the philosophy of the curriculum or the qualifications of the teachers." [558]

In addition, the Pastor looked at the activities of the judge who ruled in this case:

"The judge who presided in our case admitted that he did not look at the First Amendment [to the U.S. Constitution] before deciding our case. He also admitted that he defines education as non-religious; therefore, he defines away our religious beliefs and rights." [559]

The Pastor and the members of the Faith Baptist Church continued to believe that the operation of a school to teach the children of the church's members was a part of the church's ministry. The state countered with the argument that they were not qualified to determine what their children were to be taught, nor capable of determining who should teach them.

And, since the Pastor refused to neither shut his school down, nor allow the state to license his teachers, the judge ordered the sheriff to enter the church during a service, arrest the Pastor, and anyone else who resisted, and then padlock the church doors.

The final outcome of the whole case occurred in January of 1985 when the State Supreme Court overturned the Pastor's final eight month jail conviction, and it appeared that there would be no further court action on the case.

The state had used its powers without legal support, and the Christian school of the Faith Baptist Church continued operating. The Christian Church, at least in Nebraska, did not have to allow the state to set the policy of the school, determine the curriculum, nor license the teachers of their children.

But the battle is not over.

It has only begun.

This was just one of the early skirmishes.

Chapter 29
The Attack on the Family

The family unit has been called the cornerstone of civilization. The concept that the parents are responsible for the upbringing of the children produced during the marriage is the cornerstone of American life. Yet, there are efforts in America today to undermine, if not to destroy, the family unit altogether.

The desire to destroy the family unit is, as has been briefly alluded to in previous sections of this study, one of the goals of the New Age-Humanist-Communist movement.

Marilyn Ferguson, the New Age writer, has written this about the family unit in her book entitled THE AQUARIAN CONSPIRACY:

> "Many sociologists anticipate the 'evolution' of monogamy. Marriage, they say, must be transformed as an institution if it is to survive at all.

If monogamy is tied inextricably with the restriction of all sexual expression to the spouse, they
said, it will ultimately be monogamy that suffers." [560]

The word "monogamy" has two meanings, both of which
are applicable to this study. The word is defined as:

1. The practice or state of being married to only
    one person at a time.
2. The practice of marrying only once during
    life.

The dictionary added an appendage to the second
definition: it said that that definition was "rare."
And indeed it is.
The tradition in America that the husband takes himself
a wife, and then remains faithful to that spouse for the remainder of their life together is a Judeo-Christian one. In
other words, it comes from the beliefs and teachings of two
religious faiths.
Since this is not something that is written instinctively
into the hearts of all men, and since man is given free choice,
man is free to accept or reject the created institution of the
family. The married man does not have to have but one wife
and to remain faithful to her. It is only religion that has
taught him that the monogamous marriage is the preferable
lifestyle.
Marilyn Ferguson, a New Age writer, writes further:

"Traditional monogamy contravenes the growing
sense that the greatest good of human existence is
deep interpersonal relationships, as many of these as
is compatible with depth.
... younger people are trying to devise and invent
a form of marriage appropriate to a new era." [561]

As has been previously illustrated, the New Age
Movement and the Communist Movement want to destroy the
family. Here, one of the major New Age writers says that it
is the young people who are attempting to devise a new
marriage institution. The children are being taught to change
the marriage contract by those in the New Age Movement

who have written the textbooks, or encouraged a dialogue with the intent of changing their attitudes.

Even the definition of a family, meaning a male husband, a female wife, a child or children, has to be redefined for the New Age. Marilyn Ferguson has told us that this has already taken place:

> "The American Home Economics Association redefined the family in 1979 as 'two or more persons [meaning two men, or two women as well as one man and one woman] who share resources, share responsibility to one another over time.
>
> The family is that climate that 'one comes home to;' and it is this network of sharing and commitments that most accurately describes the family unit, regardless of blood, legal ties, adoption, or marriage.'"

The American concept of marriage is that of a male husband, and a female wife. Homosexual or lesbian marriages are not legal. But that can change anytime those who make the laws decide to change it. The New Agers apparently want to change the laws to allow the marriage of two men or two women.

A major step in changing the traditional definition of the family just occurred in the state of New York. The headline of the July 6, 1989 article that discussed the change, reads:

> "Court rules gay couple a 'family.'"

The article reported:

> "New York's highest court ruled today that a partner in a long-term homosexual relationship may take over the couple's rent-controlled apartment when the lover who signed the lease dies.
>
> ... the Court of Appeals ordered a lower court to reconsider its decision to evict a New York City man from a rent-controlled apartment he shared ... with his now-dead lover.
>
> ... the court expanded the definition of a 'family'....

The word is crucial because state law says only 'family members' may take over rent-controlled apartments when the tenant of record dies.

The court said that the definition should include adults who show long-term financial and emotional commitment to each other, even if they don't fit the traditional meaning of a 'family.'" [562]

So, even the definition of a family is under attack. It will have to be changed if the family is to be destroyed.

As discussed, there are some who want the family unit to be destroyed altogether. The destruction of the family unit has been the goal of the Communists and Socialists for over 140 years. Karl Marx, the so-called father of Communism, wrote that that was the goal of the Party:

"Abolition of the family!
Even the most radical flare up at this infamous proposal of the Communists." [563]

And Robert Owen, the so-called father of Socialism, wrote:

"In the new moral world, the irrational names of husband and wife, parent and child, will be heard no more. All connection will the result of affection; the child will undoubtedly be the property of the whole community." [564]

And the process of the change from the idea that the raising of the child should be the responsibility of the family to that where the child will be raised by the state has already started in some of the Communist countries.

One of those countries is Cuba.

The Cuban people were once basically a religious people, with the overwhelming majority belonging to the Catholic Church. But much of that has changed since Fidel Castro, the Communist, converted that nation into a Communist country. These comments are from a 1988 article in the New American magazine:

"Heterosexual relations in Cuba are characterized by rampant promiscuity and widespread prostitution.

The abject poverty to which Castro has reduced the island encourages prostitution.

The institution of marriage has almost lost its meaning in Cuba. Many persons marry and divorce frequently.

... the Castro regime has worked to destroy family ties and to break the control of parents over their children. The Communists in Cuba have baited children with the offer by setting up live-in schools in the countryside. At these schools students study half a day and then must work in the fields for the other half.

While attendance at these 'escuelas en el campo' [meaning camp schools] is not mandatory, students of junior high and high school levels are encouraged to attend. Even students who do not attend the live-in school must participate yearly in a six-week work period deep in the rural areas of Cuba.

The Castro regime relies heavily upon the use of hundreds of thousands of unpaid school children to work in the fields each year. Under the cover of educational programs, the Castro regime exploits child labor and disrupts parental authority." [565]

It is interesting that the leader of Cuba, Fidel Castro, sets the example for infidelity and promiscuity in the marriage union. He has five known children born out of wedlock to different mothers. [566]

Other Communist nations have shown their commitment to the destruction of the family. The Communists in China have also been at least partially successful in their drive to destroy the family unit. Those who have studied that nation's past know that the family unit had been the cornerstone of their civilization for centuries.

One Chinese citizen who was able to flee his country after the Communists took control in 1949 was Reverend Shih-ping Wang, the East Asia director of the Baptist Evangelization Society. He testified before the House Committee on Un-American Activities about what happened to the family when Communism seized control of China:

"The family unit is broken up. Husbands and wives are separated in different barracks. The children are taken away from the parents and placed in government-run nurseries.

Husbands and wives meet only once a week for two hours -- they have no other contact ....

The parents may see their children once a week and when they see them they can show no affection toward their children. Names are taken away from children and they are given numbers.

There is no individual identity." [567]

Some of the measures to control the family unit in China are rather subtle, while others are not. For instance, any couple wishing to get married must have permission of the Communist Party. Political dissidents, for one, are not permitted to marry. Once any couple is granted that permission, even the decision as to how many children the couple can have in these so called "marriages" is a decision of others.

One who testified to that fact was another Chinese refugee, Dr. Han Suyin, a native of Peking, who reported in an address to the Swiss Society of Surgeons in 1975 that the:

"residents of each neighborhood in the People's Republic of China meet annually to decide how many babies will be born during the next year and to which families.

Priority is given to newly married women without children. As a guarantee against chance or mistakes, contraceptive pills are distributed on each street every morning." [568]

This policy of allowing the "people" to decide just how many children each couple can have in China has led to the practice of infanticide, meaning the intentional killing of babies. The government does not allow any couple to have more than one child, and this edict has caused the following problem:

"a leading newspaper of Southern China [has] reported that during 1980, eight female infants were found dead, abandoned in front of the local party headquarters ....

Most had been suffocated." [569]

The article continued by explaining why only female children were being killed by distraught parents:

"Should a couple's first [and only] child be a girl, many parents fear that they will be left without an heir or source of support in their declining years. Thus, in certain areas some parents have begun murdering their first-born female offspring."

Other options are available for those parents who do not have the courage to murder their children. A recent report, in March of 1989, reported that some parents have developed another method of allowing their children a way to survive:

"An estimated 25 million 'illegals' are living in Red China. They are unregistered children who are not immigrants or aliens, but native-born Chinese whose parents hide them and keep them unregistered by the government because of its official 'one family-child' policy.
The unregistered children cannot attend government schools, receive government aid of any kind, or work for the government in any capacity." [570]

This decision to allow only one child to a couple in China is enforced by other practices:

"If a couple persists in having a second child, one of the parents is forced to buy all grain rations at twice the regulation prices for the next seven years. The third child does not get the identity card that entitles him to food rations." [571]

But if the Communist Party discovers that a Chinese woman got pregnant without their permission, they force her to have an abortion. Jonathan Mirsky, in an article for The Nation, wrote that women who got pregnant without permission had been kidnapped on Communist Party orders and forced to have an abortion, even if she was in the third trimester of her pregnancy.
This "one-child per family" concept poses another problem: what does the Communist Party do if the woman gives birth

to twins? That question was answered by an American who visited Red China.

Stephen Mosher was a graduate student at Stanford University working on his doctorate when he was asked to do research for his thesis in China. He consented, and went to live in a small village in the southern part. His discoveries of life in that nation astounded him. These are his comments about what happens when a Chinese woman gave birth to twins:

"... an official ... demanded that she specify which of the two she wished to raise. The mother could not answer him, so the official made the decision for her, disposing of one of the newborn babies." [572]

The practice of abortion has become so widespread that the United States government has estimated that more than 78 million were performed in Red China between the years 1971 and 1982.

But the Chinese Communists place other obstacles in the way of a Chinese couple. These obstacles hinder the ability of the couple to enjoy married life.

"It is now mandatory for women to work in the fields. They do, and they still do all the housework."

Obviously, a Chinese woman forced to work in a field does not have time to be involved in the full-time raising of a family.

The utter despair of some of the women in China because of these Communist imposed conditions has led to a new problem:

"Peasant girls in the remote southern region of China are taking their lives in unprecedented numbers." [573]

Girls are committing suicide in record numbers in Red China because of the pressure on the marriage, the abortion problem, and the requirement that they can give birth to only one child.

But the problem in China is not too many Chinese.

It is simply to much Communism.

The Communists have imposed Communism, also called the New World Order, on the Chinese people, and it has failed, just as could have been predicted by anyone who had studied the history of Communism.

The Communist system does not work; it has never worked; and it is not working in China.

And there is an easy way to prove that that statement is correct.

Off the shore of Communist China lies the islands known as Formosa or Taiwan. This separate Chinese nation has not bought the fraud known as Communism. It is basically allowing its citizens to enjoy the right to private property. The Taiwanese government is supporting the economic system known as the Free Enterprise System.

Former Congressman Eldon Rudd of Arizona illustrated the difference between Communism and Freedom:

"With 270 times the land area and 58 times the population, the Gross National Product [the G.N.P.] of Mainland China [Communist China] is only 10 times the G.N.P. of Taiwan.

The figures I have cited illustrate beyond contradiction the material abundance created by freedom's climate.

In my view, this is the smallest and least important of the remarkable differences between the People's Republic of China [meaning Communist China] and the free government of Taiwan. The true difference is spirit -- the human condition, the absence of compulsion and regimentation, the presence of individual opportunity." [574]

So the problem in China is not too much population.

It is too much Communism.

It is too much "New World Order."

So the family unit in China, the cornerstone of their civilization for centuries, has essentially been destroyed by the Communist Party.

And it was not destroyed by mistake. It was planned that way.

And the Bolshevik Communists in the Soviet Union have nearly duplicated the "success" of the Chinese Communists.

The September, 1988 Reader's Digest magazine carried an article called Should We Bail Out Gorbachev? in which they discussed life in the Soviet Union. This is one of the comments made in that article:

"At least 13 million urban families still must live in communal apartments or dormitories, sharing bath, kitchen and even bedrooms with other families. In Moscow, newly constructed apartment complexes are crumbling." [575]

So a great percentage of the Russian families do not have a place to live separate from other people. Married life does not seem exceptionally attractive to a young couple contemplating marriage. So, if the Communists are trying to destroy the family in Russia, one of the ways to do it would be to not construct enough government owned apartments or houses. And that is exactly what they have done.

Also, the Soviet Union is utilizing the same infanticide that is occurring in Red China.

"Topping the world in legal abortions is the Soviet Union -- where there are an estimated eight million annually of the 30 million worldwide.

According to the Moscow News, an astounding nine of 10 of the first pregnancies in the U.S.S.R. end in the legal killing of the unborn child.

The corresponding figures in the United States, reports the Alan Guttmacher Institute in New York City, is one of three of the first pregnancies terminating in abortion and 1.6 million abortions annually." [576]

Those who support the concept of legal abortions often claim that those who charge that life begins at conception are wrong.

Their position is that life begins at birth. But there are others who are claiming that even that date is not adequate, and that life should start at some later date.

One of these is Sir Francis Crick, a British medical doctor, a socialist and, by the way, a signer of the HU-

MANIST MANIFEST II. He has been quoted as saying that he foresees the day when:

"no newborn infant will be declared human unless it has passed certain tests regarding its genetic endowment. If it fails these tests, it forfeits its right to live." [577]

Picture the anguish of the parents who have given life to a newborn child, deemed to be "defective" by Dr. Crick, when they discover that the good doctor has decided to "take its right to life." Imagine what this concept does to those planning a family.

And now the reader can understand what some of the Humanists think of the value of human life. Once an individual denies the existence of God, he becomes god himself, and he can decide all of those things that other people feel God used to decide. Such things as: the right to life, the right to property, etc.

But the attacks on the family in America are a little more subtle. But they are real, none the less.

In 1988, the Supreme Court decided that a husband has no right to stop his wife from having an abortion. The appeals court, which passed the decision onto the Supreme Court, had stated that the husband "has no right to veto [his wife's] decision [to have the abortion] as such [a] decision concerns only her." [578]

This decision certainly had a long-lasting effect upon the marriage where both parties to the marriage contract are supposed to have a say in any decision that affects both parties.

But the latest attack on the family is a new phenomenon called "child abuse." The National Committee for the Prevention of Child Abuse advises there were 1.2 million reports of child abuse in 1984. Those who have paid attention to this or more current figures are suitably outraged, having been conditioned to believe that this abuse is rampant inside the American society.

However, the reason that the response to these statistics can be called hysteria, is this comment from Douglas Besharov, the first director of the National Center on Child Abuse and Neglect, who has charged that over 60 percent of these complaints are totally unfounded. And others have said that that figure might be as high as 80 percent.

And in most of the remaining cases, the injury actually involved neglect -- failure to provide what some social worker deemed to be adequate food, clothing or shelter -- a far cry from the sordid crimes widely publicized in the press.

One foreign nation which responded to the hysteria was Sweden, which passed a law in 1979 punishing parents who spank their children. The Parade magazine article that reported on the law mentioned the case where a father told his son not to take his younger brother out on a bicycle ride. The son disobeyed his father, and the father gave him a spanking on the buttocks.

The son marched down to the local police station and reported his dad for spanking him. A jury later found the father guilty and fined him.

In America, this hysteria has led to a horrendous intrusion of the government into private family matters, much of which appears to be unwarranted and some of which is demonstrably harmful to the children involved.

The definitions of "child abuse" have basically made criminals out of nearly every parent in America. A federally funded study, sponsored by the National Institute of Mental Health, and released in November of 1985, defines the victims of "violence against children" as being those who have "slapped or spanked," or "pushed, grabbed, or shoved" their children. It would be difficult to find any parent in America that wouldn't be included in those categories.

The broad definition of "child abuse," which makes every parent in America into a criminal, makes sense if the observer remembers that there are people in America today who want to destroy the family. The way for them to achieve their goal is to convince the world that families abuse their children, and that "social workers" do not. Then, when the authorities come to take the children away from the parents of America, the overwhelming majority of the remainder of the citizens will accept the action as being required by the conditions.

And the traditional family, as was known in America for centuries, will exist no longer.

And some will be pleased.

Textbooks are beginning to teach that the family unit is a relic of the past. Arthur W. Calhoun wrote a book entitled A

SOCIAL HISTORY OF THE AMERICAN FAMILY. It was a social service textbook utilized as a vehicle to educate students that the society must assume traditional responsibilities assumed by the family. Mr. Calhoun wrote:

"The view is that the higher and more obligatory relation is to society rather than to the family; the family goes back to the age of savagery while the state belongs to the age of civilization. The modern individual is a world citizen served by the world, and home interests can no longer be supreme.

But as soon as the new family consisting only of the parents and the children stood forth, society saw how many were unfit for parenthood and began to realize the need for community care.

As familism of the wider sort ... weakens, society has to assume a larger parenthood.

In general, society is coming more and more to accept as a duty the task of guaranteeing wholesome upbringing of the young ... the child passes more and more into the custody of community experts [called teachers or social workers] who are qualified to perform the complexer functions of parenthood ... and which the parents have neither the time nor knowledge to perform." [579]

The family unit in America is decaying, and the thinking is that society must hire "experts" who are capable of the raising the children instead of the parents. So, suddenly "child abuse" articles started showing up in the newspapers of America. When the "experts" say that it is time to take the children away from all of the parents, the society will accept the decision because it appears to be the proper solution.

An organization known as Friends of Earth decided that the solution is to "license" parents:

"If the less stringent curbs on procreation fail, someday perhaps childbearing will be deemed a punishable crime against society unless the parents hold a government license.

Or perhaps all potential parents will be required to use contraceptive chemicals, the governments issuing antidotes to citizens chosen for childbearing." [580]

In addition to the family causing all of this harm to children, parents are also producing too many offspring. The contention is that the world is simply over-populated. Fortunately, for the planners, the same Friends of Earth has become aware of this problem and they are offering their solution:

> "... we should set a goal of reducing population to a level that the planet's resources can sustain indefinitely at a decent standard of living -- probably less than two billion." [581]

When one considers that the world has approximately five billion people on it now, one can only wonder how the Friends of Earth are going to eliminate 3 billion people. So far, the solutions do not include plans to simply poison or shoot billions of people, but one can only wonder what the Friends of Earth will offer the world if the people do not voluntarily solve this purported problem.

The organization does not rule out the use of force to stop the "population explosion," however. They continued:

> "Ultimately, those policies may have to embrace coercion by governments to curb breeding." [582]

It doesn't take much imagination to envision the size of a government that would have the ability to prevent every couple in the world from producing unwanted pregnancies.

Nor does it take superior intelligence to see what the next step would be should all of these "voluntary" methods fail. If the world population will not voluntarily stop producing too many children, then coercive measures must be employed.

But, it can be assumed that the Friends of the Earth believe that those 3 billion people will understand when they come to exterminate them. Don't forget, it is for the good of humanity!

But in the future, the parent who believes that he or she is capable of raising children will become a criminal. One organization that sees that situation occurring in the future is the World Future Society, which wrote this:

> "The adult criminal of the twenty-first century may be less common than his twentieth century coun-

terpart, in part because of the way society treats children from the moment they are born.

Parental care in the year 2000 may be different from today's, and better, since by then the movement to license or certify parents may well be under way."

In most cases, certified couples would be allowed to have their own natural children. In some instances, however, genetic scanning may find that some women and men can produce "super" babies but are not well suited to rear them. These couples would be licensed to breed, but will give up their children to other people licensed to rear them.

Child breeding and rearing may be considered too important to be left to chance.

"... wanted children will have fewer environmental reasons to turn to crime, and controlled breeding will result in fewer biological reasons for crime." [583]

The attack on the family in America has taken several clever and unique twists. The family destroyers have resorted to cleverness to disguise their original intent: they do not want the parents to know that the destruction of the family is their goal. So they conceal their purposes by quietly causing problems that create intense pressures on the family.

One of the methods utilized is that of inflation.

Inflation is simply defined by a dictionary as an increase in the money supply, causing prices to go up. That means that whoever controls the money supply controls the price level. Increase the money supply, and prices rise. Decrease the money supply and prices go down (called Deflation.) Once Inflation or Deflation has been documented, the government economists point with pride at the supposed perpetrators: the public. They never direct their attention at the real culprit in America: the privately owned Federal Reserve system.

This private banking establishment has complete control over the quantity of money in circulation. Therefore, they have the ability to create Inflation or Deflation whenever they choose to do so.

The rising price level without a corresponding increase in a family's income causes the wife in a family unit who has chosen to care for her own child at home to leave the nurturing of the children to others in order to seek gainful employment so that she can increase the family's earnings. The parents are forced to place their children in a government run school. This enables the planners to teach the children what they want taught at an earlier age. And it places the mother in a position where she sees less and less of her children, and the children see more and more of the government trained substitute "parents."

The planners have been extremely successful, as the number of working mothers has been steadily increasing. According to a report issued in 1987, more than 44 percent of women work outside the home, compared to only 32 percent in 1960. Of women with children under one year of age, close to 50 percent are currently employed, a figure that has doubled since 1970. [584]

But, what happens to the child when they are placed into day care centers? Are they better off? One group of individuals who feel that they are not are the doctors inside the American Academy of Pediatrics who have reported that the children placed in these centers are subject to all sorts of diseases caused by bacteria, viruses and parasites. They are more than 12 times as likely to catch flu viruses and 15 to 20 times more likely to catch other diseases than children under maternal care.

So the day care center has a negative impact on the health of a child placed there by a working mother. When the child gets sick, the mother must take time off from her job to care for the child, or to place the child in the hands of the medical fraternity. If the mother gets paid by the hour, and only gets paid when she is on the job, this frequent sickness costs the family additional revenue. And the only time that the mother sees her child, other than evenings or weekends, is when the child is sick and not feeling well. This does not tend to support warm mother-child feelings.

But there is another lesser known problem when the mother is not directly involved in the care of the child. Until fairly recently, the assumption that care by the mother was the best kind of child care went unchallenged. John Bowlby's widely acclaimed book entitled MATERNAL CARE AND MENTAL HEALTH, published in 1951, concluded that the "warm, intimate, and continuous" care of the mother or permanent mother substitute was essential to the "development of character and mental health." He called the absence of this mother-child relationship "maternal deprivation" and said that it was likely to result in "maladjustment of the child."

This was the consensus view of the vast majority of psychologists, psychiatrists, pediatricians, and the general public until the medical and professional organizations capitulated to the demands of the feminist movement in the 1970s.

The continuing debate over Dr. Jay Belsky's recent "heresy" is testimony to the power of the feminist/day care lobby in academic and professional circles. Belsky, a professor of child psychology at Pennsylvania State University, was, a decade ago, one of the influential voices that saw no harm in institutional child care. Now, he says, convincing research shows that non-maternal care for more than 20 hours per week for children under a year old is a "risk factor." Day care at that young age can impede secure parent/child relationships and lead to rebellious and aggressive behavior, or shy and withdrawn behavior in the preschool and early years. His views have caused him much grief, as colleagues and feminists have come down hard on him for his views. They have impugned his research, his credentials, and his motives. [585]

Even Dr. Benjamin Spock, certainly no "conservative" in other matters, has also resisted the push for group child care, especially before the age of three. He has taken a position that appears to be out of character for him. He has written:

> "It is stressful for children to have to cope with groups, with strangers, with people outside the family." [586]

And another "certified Harvard liberal," Professor Burton White, warns parents:

> "Unless you have a very good reason, I urge you not to delegate the primary child-rearing task to anyone else during your child's first three years of life." [587]

But the debate is certain to continue. Those who want to destroy the family will continue to urge mothers to leave the home and "become fulfilled in the workplace." When the mother goes into the workplace to "become fulfilled," or to increase the family's income, she leaves the care of the children to others.

Those who warn against such practices will continue to be scorned by the feminists and others who have a hidden agenda: they want to destroy the family.

Another subtle pressure against marriage was concealed inside a headline in a local newspaper that read: "New tax laws to increase 'marriage tax' for many." The article defined the term "marriage tax" as a term used to:

> "describe the extra tax burden paid by a married couple when compared with the tax paid by two single people with the same total income." [588]

So, those individuals smart enough to know how the tax laws work against them decide not to get married.

And in some cases, the destruction of the family has not gone unnoticed. Newsweek magazine of January 12, 1981, carried an article by Dr. Jonathan Kellerman, a psychologist, and author. He wrote this:

> "However, when one examines the role government has played in its relationship to the family, it is clear that not only has there been no support, on the contrary there has been a systematic erosion of the family, perpetuated by executive, legislative and judicial branches of government.
>
> The trend of the last two decades toward more government intervention and control has carried with it a clear message to families: you are not competent to decide how to live your life -- we know better." [589]

And some in America have discovered that the psychologist was correct. An article in the Arizona Republic reported that "Family life [was] harmed by government, poll says." The article quoted pollster George Gallup, who said that:

> "nearly half of those who responded to his organization's 1980 survey on the American family believe the federal government has an unfavorable influence on family life." [590]

And the government is once again using the tax laws to discriminate against families with full time mothers. The present tax code favors families whose mothers enter the work force over families with full-time mothers. Those parents who do not send the mother out into the work force must subsidize those who do.

Secondly, the tax laws are weighted heavily against parental choice in child care. Most surveys indicate that working parents generally prefer leaving their child with relatives, neighbors or friends. Current tax laws do not recognize these forms of child care as legitimate; thus, parents who choose to use them do not receive an income-tax credit for the costs of child care. So many parents choose to have the government assist them in the costs of their child care by providing a tax credit and give their children over to the government to raise them.

And lastly, current or proposed legislation concerning child care tax credits discriminate against the many church-related day care facilities. These laws prohibit funding for any child care facility "unless all religious symbols and artifacts are covered or have been removed."

A classic example of the unrestrained use of government force against a child care facility occurred in 1984, when the State of Texas attempted to completely shut down three children's homes run by Pastor Lester Roloff. He, like Pastor Silevin before him, refused to allow the state to license his homes for the children who had been voluntarily placed there by their parents. The state of Texas went to court, but in 1981 a state district judge denied its request for an injunction against the Pastor's homes, concluding that the licensing procedure as applied to the church running them would violate the constitutions of both the United States and Texas. The federal Court of Appeals affirmed the trial court's decision.

However, the state Supreme Court rejected the church's contention that licensing would interfere with religious freedom. The Chief Justice did not object to the quality of the care provided by the Roloff homes; his concern was the simple fact that they would not submit to licensing. He noted that the homes have "a good record of high quality service," and that they could "easily satisfy licensing requirements, but had chosen not to do so."

So the state wanted certain restrictions on the care provided children in Pastor Roloff's homes. Several of those restrictions were so incredible that they show that the major reason the state went after the child care facilities was simply that they were too successful.

The first of these restrictions was (not a complete list):

1. "You should not threaten a child with the displeasure of Deity."

In other words, you couldn't tell a child that he was a sinner. Remember that these children had been placed in these homes because they had become disciplinary problems to their parents. The parents, who had seen their children become involved in prostitution, drugs and criminal activity, had turned to the Pastor for help in turning their child around. They turned to him because he was a Christian Pastor, and because he had demonstrated success in hundreds of similar cases before. These parents loved their children and wanted them to stop their criminal and anti-social behavior. They cared for them enough to voluntarily place them in a program that had proven successful. Only a very small percentage of these children had been placed in these homes by the court system.

One of the reasons the Pastor was successful was because he turned the children to religion. But the state told him he could not use that as a method of correcting the child.

The second restriction was:

2. "The institution shall see that each child is supplied with personal clothing suitable to the child's age and size. It shall be comparable to the clothing of other children in the community."

The Pastor and his staff felt that much of the clothing the children were wearing was too suggestive and improper. So they attempted to provide the children with modest clothing less stimulating and provocative. They felt that this restriction would place the children back into the clothing that in many cases had caused them to have problems before their arrival at the Roloff homes.

The third restriction was:

3.   "Children should be encouraged to form friendships with persons outside the institution."

It would be fair to observe that such friendships were frequently what brought the children to the homes in the first place.

The fourth restriction was:

4.   "The opinions and recommendations of the children in care shall be considered in the development and evaluation of the program and activities. The procedure for this shall be documented."

Letting the inmates run the prison sounds like an excellent idea until the prisoners suggest that the restraining bars should be removed. Many of these children had become discipline problems mainly because they had decided that they could best run their own lives. When this determination had failed, the parents placed them into Pastor Roloff's homes so that they would learn some discipline. But the state wanted them to learn how to run their own lives again.

The purpose of all of this incredible pressure on the Roloff homes appeared to be the desire of the state to weaken the ability of the Roloff homes to be successful with these troubled children. A secondary purpose appeared to be the desire to weaken the family, and encourage the state to devise methods that would remove the control of the children from the parents and to give them over to the state.

Perhaps the role model that the family destroyers want to emulate is the Soviet Union, where enormous pressures are intentionally placed upon the Russian family.

Parade magazine carried an article about an American family which had returned to Russia in 1987 after having lived there in the late 1960's. The wife in the marriage has written a book about modern life in that nation, and these are some of her observations.

"... the average young married woman in the Soviet Union ... is a prisoner of the Soviet custom and doctrine, which calls for a wife, without her husband's help, to perform the tough, rough, rugged household chores -- the laundry, the cleaning, the cooking, the moving, the shopping, the child-caring -- all of these in addition to holding down her own job outside the home eight hours a day." [591]

In Russia, work is a duty of its citizens. That obligation has been written into their Constitution.

Article 12 reads as follows:

"Work in the U.S.S.R. is a duty and a matter of honour for every able-bodied citizen, in accordance with the principle: 'He who does not work, neither shall he eat.'

The principle applied in the U.S.S.R. is that of socialism: 'From each according to his ability, to each according to his work.'"

It would appear from a cursory examination of these sentences that work in Russia is for men only. The first paragraph refers to work being a male occupation: "HE who does not work ...," and the second says: "... according to HIS ability." However, the first paragraph says that "Work is a duty ... for every able-bodied citizen." Women are "able bodied citizens" just like men. Therefore, the Constitution makes it clear that this work requirement is for both sexes. Women must toil for the Russian economy as well as men.

This means that married women are obligated to work as well as single women. The fact that the married woman must work for the state obviously leaves the children free to be raised by the government. And that is the desired result of that provision in the Constitution.

And the fact that the married woman must work for the society means that she has less time to spend with her family.

The article continued with some of the obstacles that the Russian economy puts on the wife during the typical day:

"... the Soviet woman ... rises early, not much past 6, prepares breakfast for the family, gets the children off to school, goes to her own work. During lunch, it's hurry up and wait. Instead of enjoying her breather, she bolts down her food and races to the nearest store, where she waits and waits and waits to buy whatever approximates the needs of her family. Almost always there's a shortage of meat, fruit, vegetables, soap and quality products of anything."

The Soviet economic system, called Communism. has been proven to be a failure by 6000 years of experience. The Communist system destroys the incentive to produce and the population suffers from the lack of consumption goods. No Communist would be bold enough to admit that it is the system that has failed. So contrived explanations are offered to explain the shortages.

There is no food because a "drought" reduced farm yields. "Military equipment spending priorities" have replaced production quotas for consumption goods.

It is certainly conceivable that those in charge want the married family to suffer these pressures, so that few in the married population will be happy. The entire system is intentionally designed to be a failure, and no one would dare correct it.

It is clear that pressure on the family is the desired product of Communism.

The article confirmed this with this comment:

"No wonder so many Soviet men drink, sulk and accuse their wives of frigidity and indifference. No wonder the Soviet Union is so rife with divorce."

The married woman in Russia is obviously too tired to care for her husband, and the result becomes predictable: a rising divorce rate.

And no one blames those who have intentionally created an economic system that was certain to put those pressures on the family. The planners have experienced their desired result: marriage has become the least desired relationship in Russia.

Perhaps the entire scenario was placed into perspective on the side of the government "experts" by B. F. Skinner, the chairman of the Harvard Department of Psychology, who wrote this about his book entitled BEYOND FREEDOM AND DIGNITY:

"My book is an effort to demonstrate how things go bad when you make a fetish out of individual freedom and dignity.

If you insist that individual rights are the 'summum bonum,' [meaning the highest good,] then the whole structure of society falls down." [592]

So, those who want to destroy the family want the world to turn the society over to them.

And those running the society continue to destroy it.

The strategy is not new. In fact, it has been the strategy of this conspiracy for centuries.

They cause the problem.

Then they solve the problem with more government.

And the people are convinced that their solution is desirable, generally because that is the only solution offered.

And the end result is less freedom for the people.

And it works nearly every time.

Chapter 30
The Right of Association

One of the cornerstones of freedom is the right to negotiate a contract with another individual or a group of individuals. The free man or woman has the right to decide who they will enter into a contract with. It follows, therefore, that no one has the right to force another into a contract that the individual does not freely want to enter into.

Forcing one individual into a contract that that individual did not freely enter into is called slavery or involuntary servitude.

Allowing the government to choose an individual's associates and forcing them to join together is also wrong and is another form of involuntary servitude or slavery.

All men and women have the right to protect themselves from the coercive force of other individuals or groups. Men and women join together to form governments to protect their rights from the aggressive and coercive activities of others.

One of the functions of government is to protect people from contracts that were not freely entered into. These contracts are to be declared null and void, and are to have no legal force or effect.

One of the basic purposes of The New World Order is to restrict the right of the individual to be free from the coercive force of another.

These definitions of slavery and involuntary servitude are currently being challenged by those who wish to enslave mankind. Examples of how slavery is becoming fashionable are appearing in every segment of society, and courts are making slavery the law of the land.

A legal contract is defined as one in which two or more parties agree to certain terms in order to reach mutually acceptable goals. If one party is forced into any contract against his or her will, the contract is declared to be null and void and therefore unenforceable.

As was discussed, one of the functions of the courts of the United States is to enforce valid contracts between two consenting individuals. Once an individual enters into a contract, the other party has the right to have the terms of the contract met, even if the first party decides later not to perform as required. But, todays courts are enforcing contracts where one party was forced into the terms of the contract. Or, in other cases, where one party did not agree to the terms. In those cases, the courts have chosen to force that party to abide by the terms of a contract that they were unwilling to make.

This is simply called slavery.

A good case in point was a Supreme Court ruling in 1987 where they forced the Rotary Clubs, a group of men voluntarily joined together for friendship and acts of charity, to accept women as members. The article that reported on this ruling said:

"The Supreme Court, toppling another sex barrier, declared yesterday that state civil rights laws may force Rotary International and similar all-male private clubs within the state to admit women as members.

By a vote of 7-0, the justices concluded that a California anti-discrimination statute requiring women to be admitted to Rotary clubs within the state does not violate the right of members to choose their own associates." [593]

A review of the comments of the Supreme Court reveal exactly how words have lost their meaning, and are to mean exactly what the Court says they mean.

First of all, the Court agreed that these clubs were "private." That meant that the members were not publicly inviting others into their organization. They were exercising their right to associate with whomever they chose to associate with. These men, acting as free individuals, were choosing to associate in a voluntary manner with only those people they wished to associate with.

This is a right of free men.

The Court was forcing them into a contract with people that they freely chose not to associate with. After the court decision, one can only wonder what would have happened if the Rotary Clubs decided to disband because they wished to associate only with men. Would the Court have forced them to continue their meetings? And, then what would have happened if no one chose to attend? Would the court have jailed the missing members? How would they have known whether a person's failure to attend was the result of a legitimate illness or because he chose not to attend? Would the court have forced him to provide a doctor's excuse to explain his absence?

The Court said that this use of court ordered force did not violate the "right of members to choose their own associates." The Court admitted that the men had this right, and then ruled that they didn't have this right. This is double-talk of the highest order.

Freedom does not mean that certain people are free to force other people into associations that the first have deemed advisable.

Simply stated:

> Free men discriminate.
> Slaves do not.

Free men have the right to "choose their own associates." Slaves do not.

Therefore, when the Court ruled that the Rotary Clubs had not chosen correctly, and forced them to associate with individuals that they had freely chosen not to associate with, the men in the Clubs were no longer free to "choose their own associates."

The Court has decided that slavery was preferable to freedom.

In another flagrant violation of a free man's right of association, the U.S. Justice Department filed suit against a Christian conference center, claiming that it violated federal civil rights laws when it prohibited the Mormons from using the facilities to espouse their own teachings.

If one individual has the right to associate with whomever that individual chooses to associate with, a group of individuals also have that right.

In this case, the discrimination charges were levied by a Mormon group that was denied permission to rent the facilities to hold their own conference and teach Mormon religious beliefs. The director of the center stated that he had turned them down because the Mormon view of Christianity differed markedly from the beliefs of the owners of the center. Should a court determine that the Inn is a "public accommodation" on the basis of offering meals and overnight lodging, the decision could signal increased governmental control over other religious conference facilities, or, for that matter, any "public" facility.

Should a hotel be allowed to refuse the rental of a room to a group advocating the violent overthrow of the government?

Should a hotel be allowed to not rent to a group advocating violent animal sacrifice if they determine that when the group asks for facilities for the purpose of conducting their religious rites?

Just where does the right of one group to practice their religion end, and where does the right of the hotel to rent to anyone they choose to begin?

In another case, the Minnesota Court of Appeals also ruled against the right of free association. In 1986, they upheld a $300-a-day fine levied against a chain of health clubs for failing to bring a halt to employment practices involving religious discrimination. The owners of the health clubs argued that they could not comply with the order to cease discrimination against non-Christians because they felt that they had the right to employ only those who agreed with their religious views. In other words, they believed that they had the right to employ only fellow Christians if they had freely chosen to do so. [594]

The court ruled that they were wrong.

And even an organization as "all-American" as the Boy Scouts of America does not have the right to freely chose their associates. In 1983, the 2nd District Court of Appeals decided that the Boy Scouts did not have the right to refuse membership to those young people who were homosexual. [595]

It is not a stretch of this "logic" to imagine that the courts will soon decide that a church does not have the right to reject the application for church membership of an admitted "atheist." This would be "religious discrimination."

But, to further confound the problem, it appears that this nation's courts do not have a clear and definite policy about discrimination.

In 1987, a state court of appeals ruled that boys could be barred from playing on girls' high school teams to prevent them from dominating the game and displacing the girls. [596]

So, the result of these and similar decisions is to clearly say to the world:

> you will discriminate when ordered to do so, but
> you may not freely choose to discriminate.

The courts have now made it mandatory that you can "freely associate" only with whomever they decide that you can "freely associate with."

And if you do not choose to "freely associate" with someone they wish you to "freely associate" with, the courts will force you to "freely associate" with that person.

That is simply called court ordered slavery.

Obviously, "slavery" is no longer "slavery."

And "freedom" is no longer "freedom."

Furthermore, if the above cited examples were not enough, even certain Senators in the United States Senate have admitted that they no longer know what the two words mean.

In April of 1989, Senator John McCain, a Republican from Arizona, introduced Senate Bill 781, a bill called the National Service Act of 1989. This bill calls for the Administration to "develop a comprehensive, mandatory national service program."

The Senator offered the curious public a brief explanation of his bill in a news release dated April 13, 1989. In it, he explained that:

"This legislation will establish a program leading to a comprehensive, fair and mandatory system of community or military service to the nation." [597]

The bill stipulates:

"... that both men and women between 16 and 26 would be required to serve either in the community of in the military. They would serve 24 hours a month and two weeks during the year for two to four years." [598]

The Senator's news release stated that this bill would be "fair." Somehow, forcing someone to serve the nation is now deemed to be "fair."

Slavery used to be defined as forcing one individual to serve another.

Slavery used to be called "madness."

Now it is being called "fair."

But that is what the Senator says in his news release.

The news release further explained why the Senator had chosen to introduce the bill:

"This program will allow us to combine the responsibilities of citizenship with a concerted effort that addresses vital community and national defense needs that, otherwise, will be unmet in the years ahead."

So "mandatory service" to the government has now become a "responsibility of citizenship."

Man was created to be free!

Man was not created to be a slave of government!

In fact, government was created by men to be the servant of mankind!

Man was not to be the servant of government!

America used to be called "the land of the free and the home of the brave."

Now, one will be mandatorily obligated to serve the nation. That is the new "requirement of citizenship."

Freedom is not mandatory service!

To show that there is bi-partisan support of this concept of "fairness," Arizona's other Senator, Dennis DeConcini, a Democrat, also publicly announced his support of the idea.

Senator McCain had a somewhat revealing experience before he ran for this office. He was a pilot in the so-called Vietnamese "war" and was taken captive by the North Vietnamese after his airplane was shot down. He spent several years in a Vietnamese prisoner of war camp, prior to being released after the end of the "war."

The Senator was not "free" to leave the prisoner of war camp. He was a "slave" of the Vietnamese. He was there "involuntarily." He had to do as he was told.

One can only presume that if anyone should understand the words "slavery," "involuntary" and "mandatory," it should be the Senator. But, for some reason, he does not. And, apparently, neither does Senator DeConcini.

It is ironic that both of these men had taken the same oath when they became Senators. That oath reads:

"I do hereby swear or affirm that I will support and defend the Constitution of the United States against all enemies, foreign and domestic; that I will bear true faith and allegiance to the same; that I will take this obligation freely without any mental reservation or purpose of evasion; and that I will well and faithfully discharge the duties of the office on which I am about to enter, so help me God."

These two Senators took an oath to defend the Constitution of the United States when they became Senators. If either had taken the time to read the document in its entirety, they would have read the 13th Amendment which was passed after the Civil War of 1861-1865. There are some historians who claim that that war was fought to end slavery. That amendment reads:

"Neither slavery not involuntary servitude, except as a punishment for crime whereof the party shall have been duly convicted, shall exist within the United States."

If Senator McCain's bill makes all of America's young people "slaves" of the government, or requires "involuntary servitude," and the only "slavery" or "involuntary servitude" that is legal is as a "punishment for a crime," it follows that citizenship in America must be termed a "crime," the punishment for which is "involuntary servitude."

So "slavery" becomes "freedom," and "freedom" becomes "slavery," in the convoluted thinking of these two Senators. "Involuntary servitude" becomes "fair." "Mandatory service" becomes a "responsibility of citizenship."

America's founding fathers had no such problem with understanding the difference between the two words "freedom" and "slavery." They wrote this in the Declaration of Independence:

"We hold these truths to be self-evident that all men are created equal, that they are endowed by their creator with certain inalienable rights, that among these are life, liberty and the pursuit of happiness."

A "self-evident truth" is one that is not debatable. It is true simply because it is true. No one can say that a "self-evident truth" is false, because man's mind tells him that it is true. Man cannot debate whether these rights belong to mankind, because they are not debatable.

These rights were deemed to be "inalienable" by those who wrote the Declaration. That word is defined as:

"that which may not be taken away or transferred."

The Declaration went on to say that "liberty" was one of those inalienable, self-evident rights.

The word "liberty" is defined in a dictionary as:

"freedom or release from slavery, imprisonment, captivity, or any other form of arbitrary control."

Liberty is freedom. Freedom from government. Freedom from "mandatory service." Freedom from the slavery of Senators like McCain and DeConcini.

Man's inalienable right to "Liberty" is no longer a "self-evident" truth. Senators have now decided that "liberty" is "mandatory service."

Slavery is now "fair."

The New World Order is getting closer.

Chapter 31
The Attack on Education

On Thanksgiving Day in 1984, three brothers and their wives were all arrested in Idaho and jailed for 21 days.

About the same time, two others, a husband and wife, were arrested and imprisoned for 132 days.

These people all had one thing in common: they believed in religious freedom. They had all taken their children out of public school so that they could teach them at home.

The Constitution of the United States, in the First Amendment, guarantees to every American their God-given, inalienable right to the free exercise of their religious views. The pertinent part of that Amendment reads as follows:

"Congress shall make no law respecting an establishment of religion, or prohibiting the free exercise thereof ...."

These parents were exercising their God-given rights to religious freedom, but were denied, and even imprisoned, for attempting to exercise those rights.

The Masons/Communists/Humanists/Illuminists all want the government to train the children of the nation in government run schools.

Adam Weishaupt, the founder of the Illuminati, wrote:

"We must win the common people in every corner. This will be obtained chiefly by means of the schools." [599]

"We must acquire the direction of education -- of church -- management -- of the professorial chair, and of the pulpit." [600]

And Professor John Robison wrote in his book about the Illuminati entitled PROOFS OF A CONSPIRACY that:

"They [the Illuminati] contrived to place their Members as tutors to the youth of distinction." [601]

Karl Marx, the Communist, wrote this plank in his COMMUNIST MANIFESTO:

"Free education for all children in public schools." [602]

Matt Cvetic, who for nine years was an undercover agent in the Communist Party USA for the FBI, attended a secret meeting of top-level Communists in 1948, at which a Soviet Agent played a speech from Joseph Stalin, the head of the Communist Party in Russia. The Russian dictator had given directions to the American Communists to put new emphasis on the recruitment of youth. This is part of that speech:

"We Communists gained control of the Youth in Russia before we were able to wage a successful Communist Revolution in Russia, and Comrades, we must gain control of the Youth in the United States if we are to wage a successful Communist Revolution in that nation.

For this purpose, we are ordering our Comrades to set up a new Communist Youth group in the United States." [603]

Six years later, Pravda printed a Declaration of the Central Committee of the Communist Party. It was signed by Premier Nikita Khrushchev, the dictator of Russia. The declaration proclaimed:

"... scientific and atheistic propaganda is an integral part of the Communist education of the working people, and has as its aim the dissemination of scientific, materialist knowledge among the masses and liberation of believers from the influence of religious prejudices." [604]

But even more recently, Victor Mikronenko, the current head of the Young Communist League, called Komsomol, was interviewed by New York Times reporter Bill Keller in February, 1988. Mr. Keller reported that Mikronenko:

"said he sees no reason to change the policy banning believers [in God] from Komsomol. Atheist education is one of the primary tasks of the youth organization."' [605]

The Communists see education as a vehicle to re-educate young children away from religion and a belief in God. Similar attempts have occurred and are occurring in America.

The Masons have lent their support to public education. Henry C. Clausen, 33rd degree Mason, and the Sovereign Grand Commander for the Scottish Rite of Freemasonry until a short time ago, wrote a little pamphlet entitled DEVILISH DANGER. In this he makes the case for Masonic support of public education. He wrote:

"So, we [presumably he spoke for all Masonry] say again: Hands off our public schools! Keep church/state forever separated! Stay American!" [606]

The Supreme Commander of the Masons said he was concerned that the Supreme Court in 1983 had granted permission for the state of Minnesota to allow a tax deduction for undercollegiate private/church school tuition. He felt concern, apparently, that the private school parents were getting a religious exemption over those who were not religious. As far as could be seen in his pamphlet, he expressed no concern about why Christian parents, who wished to pay for a private education for their children in a private school, should be forced to pay for two educations, one of which the parents never utilized.

The issue involved the reasoning behind the requirement that parents who provide an alternative education for their children have to pay for two educations: the one they use, and the one they don't use. The issue is not about religion: it is about freedom!

But Mr. Clausen did not see it that way.

He apparently wants all children taught what the government wants taught in government schools.

And secondly, Mr. Clausen apparently did not recognize the fact that "non-religious" people have the same God-given right to take their children out of government schools and teach them at home as do "religious" people.

The Mason also did not answer the question posed by Sam Blumenfeld, an author of great merit who writes on the subject of education. He posed this question in his book entitled NEA: TROJAN HORSE IN AMERICA:

> "If the [states] can forbid the slightest hint of religion in its public schools on the grounds that it violates the separation of church and state, how can it then justify its massive intrusion into the life of a church school?" [607]

This is a legitimate question and one that the Humanists/Illuminati/Communists/New Agers appear to be unwilling to answer.

And Mr. Blumenfield makes this observation as well:

> "... the government does not have the right to compose a prayer for use in its own schools, but in Nebraska and elsewhere it claims the right to regulate the curriculum of a church school that doesn't even want government support and would be denied it even if it wanted it on the grounds that such support would violate the establishment clause [meaning the First Amendment prohibiting the "establishment of a religion."] [608]

The Humanists added their support for public education with this, the 11th Principle in the HUMANIST MANIFESTO II:

"We believe in the right to universal education." [609]

Some have told the world why they want the state to educate the children. Ashley Montague wrote this:

"Every child in America comes to school 'insane' at the age of six because of the American family structure." [610]

Others who saw the problem of children being brought up with what they consider to be the poisonous attitudes of religious parents was the National Training Laboratories, a program run by the National Education Association, the national teacher's union. They wrote:

"Although they [the children of religious parents] appear to behave appropriately and seem normal by most cultural standards, they may actually be in need of mental health care, in order to help them change, adapt, and conform to the planned society in which there will be no conflict of attitudes or beliefs." [611]

The humanists apparently see it as a problem when the parents control what their children are taught. The parents have complete control of their children for at least the first five or six years of their lives. Then the state begins the educational process when the child is placed into either kindergarten or the first grade.

One of the major concerns of the humanists is that the parents might instill some religious values in their child before the public school begins their formal training program. One who voiced that opinion was Paul Blanchard who said this in 1976:

"I think that the most important factor moving us toward a secular [meaning worldly] society has been the educational factor.

Our schools may not teach Johnny to read properly, but the fact that Johnny is in school until he is sixteen tends to lead toward the elimination of religious superstition.

The average American child now acquires a high school education, and this militates against Adam and Eve and all other myths of alleged history." [612]

Another who foresaw that the public schools were the solution to the problem of children being taught religious beliefs by their parents was John Dunphy, who wrote an essay entitled A RELIGION FOR THE NEW AGE for the Humanist magazine. This is part of what he wrote:

"I am convinced that the battle for humankind's future must be waged and won in the public school classrooms by teachers who correctly perceive their role as the new proselytizers of a new faith: a religion of humanity that recognizes and respects the spark of what theologians call divinity in every human being. [There is that thought again that man is god.]

These teachers must embody the same selfless dedication as the most rabid fundamentalist preachers.

The classroom must and will become an arena of conflict between the old and the new -- the rotting corpse of Christianity, together with all its adjacent evils and misery, and the new faith ... resplendent in its promise ...." [613]

One of the most celebrated educators of the past was Professor George S. Counts of Columbia University. He wrote that he saw the need to change the purpose of education in a 1932 monograph entitled DARE THE SCHOOLS BUILD A NEW SOCIAL ORDER? He made his views very clear as to what he thought the purpose of education was with these comments:

"Ignorance must be replaced by knowledge, competition by cooperation, trust in Providence [meaning a belief in God] by careful planning, and private capitalism by some form of socialized economy ...." [614]

With all of this discussion about what education should or should not be, one would think that all of the dialogue has caused education to become a science of precise definition. By now, the purposes of education should have been carefully thought out, so that there should be no further debate as to what it is. However, such is not the case.

In 1979, a newsletter called EDUCATION USA reported that at least one judge stated that no one knew what education was. That rather revealing conclusion was offered by a judge in a court case involving a mother who sued the San Francisco Unified School District in 1976 because her son, who was a high school graduate, could not read or write. She sought damages for remedial education and the wages her son would be unable to earn because of his lack of educational skills. The judge disagreed, according to the newsletter, saying:

> "Schools have no legal duty to educate. If there is no legal duty to educate, there can be no malpractice where education fails." [615]

The judge in the district court that heard the case reported that "schools have no legal duty to educate," because the purpose of education was not known. Not even the educators know what they are to do with the children forcibly brought to their schools.

The judge in the appeals court explained:

> "The science of pedagogy [defined as the art or science of teaching] itself is fraught with different and conflicting theories ...."

As a result, he said, there is no way to assess the school's negligence when they do not educate any child.

So the courts do not know what the purpose of education is.

But some of the educators know. It is to make certain that the child in the government schools no longer believes in what his parents have taught him. They certainly know that the purpose of education is to remove all religious values taught by parents. That is what they are clearly saying!

Some in America do know why they want the children in the government schools. The judge was wrong. Some know, and some want the parents to send them their children.

But the child still does not learn the three essentials of a good education: what used to be called the "3 R's: reading, 'riting and 'rithmetic." The pablum offered all of the children, and the holding back of the bright child to teach the slow child, has caused a nation of anxious, dull students.

The sight of children in school unable to learn has caused medical doctors and psychologists to create a whole new field of childhood diseases called either Attention Deficit Disorder or Minimal Brain Disfunction. Children are now termed to have Learning Disorders. Children are now called Learning Disabled.

The "bible" of the psychiatric industry, known as the Diagnostic and Statistical Manual of Mental Disorders, gives the symptoms of this new disease: (only a partial list):

A. Inattention: At least three of the following: exhibiting activity like: often failing to finish things he or she starts; often doesn't seem to listen; easily distracted; has difficulty concentrating on schoolwork or other tasks requiring sustained attention; etc.
B. Impulsivity: At last three of the following: exhibiting behavior like: often acts before thinking; shifts excessively from one activity to another; etc.
C. Hyperactivity: At least two of the following: exhibiting behavior like: running about or climbing on things excessively; has difficulty staying still or fidgets excessively; etc.

And quite often after the child has been diagnosed as having this disorder, he or she will be given Ritalin, a drug that is supposed to cause normal behavior. The drug also has another name: people on the streets call the drug "speed."

But the drug has negative reactions: it can cause nervousness, insomnia, skin rashes, dermatitis, nausea, dizziness, headaches, drowsiness, blood pressure and pulse changes, fast heart beat, and weight loss.

But the drug is still being prescribed.

Because of all of these concerns, parents all over the United States are withdrawing their children from the public schools and either teaching them at home or placing them in private or Christian schools that teach religious values. And all of this activity has not gone unnoticed by the Humanists/ New Agers/Communists.

Two researchers wrote a report in the February, 1980 PHI DELTA KAPPAN about this new challenge to the government school system. They concluded that the trend of removal will continue, and perhaps accelerate:

"as fundamentalists remain locked into rigid, theologically based positions on many issues while American society moves forward."

They say that the fundamentalists have a right to:

"march resolutely toward the values of their past, but one may question whether they should take a growing percentage of America's youth there with them." [616]

Obviously, declining public school attendance figures have caused some government school officials to become concerned, because the placing of children in a private school removes them from the indoctrination of the public school system. So, many states have taken steps to close many of these schools down.

One glaring example of the misuse of the power of the state government occurred on January 14, 1986, when thirty state and local government officials, including nearly a dozen uniformed and plain-clothes officers surrounded the church and school of the Santa Monica Foursquare Church in Southern California.

What had provoked this show of force? Were the teachers beating the children? Were they forcing them to take drugs? Were they teaching the children that cannibalism was a moral option?

No, the school was operating without a state issued license.

In another state, in this case North Dakota, a judge convicted a Baptist minister and his wife on charges of violating that state's compulsory school attendance law by sending their children to the fundamentalist school they operated. The pastor took the same position that other ministers in the nation have taken:

> "For us to submit ... is to admit that the state is lord over the church." [617]

Those who support public education must fear those parents who have opted to provide their children with a private education in America. They must be trembling because of the growth of both private schools and home schooling. Hundreds of thousands of children are not being taught what the Humanists/Masons/Communists/New Agers want taught in government schools.

Some children are being taught religious values.

And that is not acceptable to those who believe in The New World Order.

Chapter 32
Russian Laws

When George Washington, America's first president, left office in 1789, he delivered what has been called his Farewell Address. He spoke of many things, but part of that speech consisted of a warning directed to the people of America should they ever turn away from a basic religious view of mankind. He said:

> "Of all the dispositions and habits which lead to political prosperity, religion and morality are indispensable supports ....
> Let it simply be asked where is the security for prosperity, for reputation, for life if the sense of religious obligation desert?
> And let us with caution indulge the supposition that morality can be maintained without religion." [618]

The President attempted to warn the people that moved away from a concept that God was the father of all mankind, that He had endowed his creatures with rights, and that governments were created to protect those rights.

There are nations in the world today that have moved away from the religious concept of a Creator and those nations live under a totalitarian form of government. One such nation is the Union of Soviet Socialist Republics, the USSR. Article 124 of their constitution plainly states that move away from God:

> "In order to ensure to citizens freedom of conscience, the church in the U.S.S.R. is separated from the state, and the school from the church."

That provision in the Russian constitution is an exact expression of the philosophy of the New Agers/Communists/ Masons/Humanists, who are working for the same goals as the Russians Communists. In addition, Russian law adds some interesting restrictions on the religious rights of its citizens:

> "Religious associations must be registered with Government authorities ...."

This is the reason that private school administrators and fundamentalist preachers in America have objected to licensing their private schools.

Communist nations register their churches.

Communist nations control their churches through registration.

Free nations do not.

America is trying to register its churches.

The result will be the same.

Other Russian laws say:

> "Religious associations may not ... give material help to their members; organize for children, young people and women special prayer or other meetings, circles, groups, departments, for Biblical or literary study, sewing, working or the teaching of religion ....
>
> Surveillance over the activities of religious associations ... shall be exercised by the registration agencies."

It is almost as if the New Agers/Humanists/Communists/Masons had written the Russian Constitution and its supporting laws.

The net result of the Russian Constitution and similar laws is that there is no religious freedom. The Gulags, the Russian concentration camps, house about 6 million prisoners. It has been estimated that one half of those prisoners, over 3 million people, are there simply because they dared to worship a God in a nation that says it is illegal to worship.

So religion in America must be destroyed, just as it has been in Russia. The Russians have put their concerns in their writings, just as others in America have done so.

The Program of the Communist International, adopted at the Sixth World Congress in 1928, states:

"One of the most important tasks of the cultural revolution affecting the wide masses is the task of systematically and unswervingly combatting religion -- the opium of the people.

The proletarian government must withdraw all state support from the church, which is the agency of the former ruling class; it must prevent all church interference in state-organized educational affairs and ruthlessly suppress the counter-revolutionary activity of the ecclesiastical organizations." [619]

Lunarcharsky, the Russian Commissioner of Education, phrased it as clearly as possible when he said:

"We hate Christians and Christianity. Even the best of them must be considered our worst enemies.

Christian love is an obstacle to the development of the revolution.

Down with love of one's neighbor! What we want is HATE .... Only then can we conquer the universe." [620]

Karl Marx repeated the same thought. Religion had to be destroyed:

"Religion is the sign of the oppressed creature, the sentiment of a heartless world, as it is the spirit of spiritless conditions. It is the opium of the people." [621]

And the Communists have attempted to do exactly that in Russia. Alexander Solzhenitsyn, the Russian dissident now living in America, wrote this as a warning to the American people:

"In my country the communist powers took military steps against the Christian faith.

Millions of peasants were slaughtered in order to eradicate faith from the very roots of the people. Millions of hours of propaganda time were used in order to burn the faith from the hearts of the children.

Despite this, communism has not destroyed the Christian faith. Christianity went through a period of decline, but it is now growing.

The political atheist literature maintains that Marxism continues what Christianity began, that it makes possible what Christianity failed to achieve.

But this [is a] sleight of hand.

Socialism [meaning Communism in Russia] is, in fact, absolutely opposed to Christianity." [622]

One of the major tenets of basic Christianity is that each man has but one life, and that upon his death his spirit does not return to earth in the body of another individual. The New Agers believe in reincarnation. This view holds the opposite position: that the spirit of an individual comes back to earth in another body after death. Therefore, if it is deemed necessary that a Christian must die because Communism must succeed, those who share the belief in reincarnation have no problem with making certain that the Christian dies. And the reason for that is because it is their belief that his, or her, spirit will return and inhabit the body of another individual. This is why the Communists can slaughter millions of innocent people and show absolutely no remorse.

Constance Cumbey, a researcher into the New Age religion, has explained their views on reincarnation with these words:

"The movement teaches the Law of Rebirth or reincarnation. This is basically a teaching that man does not really die, but that he instead is endlessly reborn into new life cycles until such time as he perfects

himself sufficiently to qualify for endless rest (Nir-
vana.)" [623]

Another departure from the traditional Christian teaching
in America is the theory of Evolution. This non-scientific
"science" holds that man is nothing more than a higher form
of animal, that he has evolved from a simple one celled or-
ganism.

The New Agers have carried the theory of evolution one
step further. They believe that certain men have "evolved" to
a higher form of mankind. This evolutionary super-species is
one step above the rest of mankind.

> "... the New Agers claim they are a 'new species.'
> They have 'evolved' into 'Homo Noeticus' [the remain-
> der of the human species are Homo Sapiens.]
> They have 'evolved' by employing mind-expansion
> techniques such as meditation and the 'other tech-
> niques.'" [624]

So, those who have utilized "mind expansion techniques"
are better off than the rest of mankind. "Smarter" means
"better."

One who has written about the differences between Christianity and this new thought is the Masonic writer Manly P.
Hall. He wrote an explanation of the differences between
these opposing religious views:

> "The Christian theory of redemption is unique in
> that it emphasizes salvation as attainable in spite of
> vice rather than because of virtue; in fact, the prime
> saving virtue for the Christian is acceptance of the di-
> vinity of Jesus Christ.
> That a viewpoint so philosophically unsound could
> have gained so firm a foothold in the number and
> power of its adherents is more than passing strange.
> Like all external things, it will finally pass away
> and be remembered only for that which it contributed
> to the inner realization of its devotees." [625]

The Humanists have also stated that they believe that religion as an institution will pass away. The preface to the
HUMANIST MANIFESTO II states that position:

"As in 1933, humanists still believe that traditional theism, especially faith in the prayer-hearing
God, assumed to love and care for persons and understand their prayers, and to be able to do something
about them, is an unproved and outmoded faith." [626]

And this is the reason they believe that:

"We find insufficient evidence for belief in the existence of a supernatural ...." [627]

Since there is no God, man does not have to believe in religion anymore. In fact,

"We are convinced that the time has passed for
theism...." [628]

And to show that those who wish religion to perish are in
control of the situation, one has only to look at some of the
events occurring in contemporary America. The attack on religion in the United States has already started.

In fact, ministers are being attacked just as they were in
early America.

For instance, one of the earliest attacks on religion in
America occurred in 1771. Three Baptist ministers, all from
the same church in Ruther Glen, Virginia, were arrested and
imprisoned for preaching without a government license.
Through the able defense of Patrick Henry, the ministers
were acquitted, establishing for other ministers their right to
preach and conduct church ministries free of governmental
interference.

Yet, almost 200 years later, this same church was fined
$250 a day for once again refusing to obtain a license from
the state, this time for failure to obtain a license to operate
its educational ministries.

An organization formed to fight such cases for the cause
of religious freedom is the Coalition for Religious Freedom,
located in Washington D.C. They reported in 1987 that:

"the last 15 years have seen more religious
freedom cases than any time since the American Revolution." [629]

The battle lines are being drawn.

The Humanists/Masons/Communists/New Agers are waging war against the Christian religion.

The New World Order is getting closer.

Chapter 33
The Attack on Property

The right to private property is one of the cornerstones of freedom. Man must be free to acquire and then be allowed to possess property, the sustenance necessary to maintain his right to life.

Benjamin Disraeli, the Prime Minister of England between 1874 and 1880, reported that the secret societies wanted to destroy the right to own private property in the form of land. He wrote:

> "They do not want constitutional government ... they want to change the tenure of the land, to drive out the present owners of the soil and to put an end to ecclesiastical [meaning religious] establishments." [630]

Mr. Disraeli implied, quite correctly, that it was the religious establishments that taught that man had the right to

279

private property. It is the church that teaches support for this human right by teaching that one individual has no right to steal from another individual.

This teaching is found in both the Old and New Testaments of the Holy Bible.

The Commandment "Thou shalt not steal" is found in Exodus 20:15 in the Old Testament, and in Matthew 19:18 in the New. In fact, in the New Testament, it is a direct commandment of Jesus himself.

That means that no man has the right to take the property of another. The secret societies that the Prime Minister was referring to want to "change the tenure," meaning the ownership, "of the soil." This means that they want to abolish private property.

So it is the church that stands in the way of those who wish to abolish the right to private property.

And it is the church that must be destroyed to eliminate mankind's right to private property.

The Illuminati also saw the connection between the churches and the Biblical teaching. Adam Weishaupt wrote:

"The baneful [meaning one causing of distress] influence of accumulated property was declared an insurmountable obstacle to the happiness of any nation whose chief laws were framed for its protection and increase." [631]

Karl Marx, the Communist, echoed the concept that certain individuals did not possess the right to own private property. He wrote:

"The emancipation of labor demands ... an equitable distribution of the proceeds of labor." [632]

Marx envisioned a government large enough to divide the property accumulated after labor. He wrote this:

"From each according to his abilities, to each according to his needs." [633]

Those who have the ability to produce must have their property taken away and given to those who have the need for that property.

He then continued:

"... the theory of the Communists may be summed
up in the single sentence: Abolition of private property." [634]

And the Humanists want to participate in the debate
about the right to own private property. They also do not believe that man has the right to own and possess property.
They have verbalized it in the Fourteenth Principle in the
HUMANIST MANIFESTO II

"The humanists are firmly convinced that existing
acquisitive and profit motivated society has shown itself to be inadequate and that a radical change in
methods, controls and motives must be instituted.
A socialized and cooperative order must be established to the end that the equitable distribution of the
means of life be possible." [635]

A "socialized and cooperative order" would be one where
the government takes from those who have the ability and
gives it to those who have the need. That is precisely what
Karl Marx advocated.

So those who wish to abolish private property have included it in their religion.

In America, the attack on private property is very subtle:
those who wish to destroy man's right to possess property do
not directly identify that as their goal. They conceal their
purposes behind other issues, but the end result is the same.
The right to private property is slowly being eroded.

Perhaps the main weapon utilized in the battle is the
government's power to tax. As taxes increase, the public has
less and less ability to purchase property.

Another method that the attackers use to destroy private
property is inflation. This tool takes an ever increasing percentage of the earnings of the working class. Inflation, as has
already been discussed in this study, is defined as an increase in the money supply, resulting in a rise in the price
level. A deflation is caused by a decrease in the money supply, causing prices to drop. Therefore, the business cycle is
caused by those who control the money supply. And the purpose of the business cycle is to take property from some and

to give it to others. Those who know what course the money supply is going to take are certainly able to take advantage of their prior knowledge and can make exorbitant profits.

So inflation is a method of depriving some people of their private property without their knowledge.

That means that those who cause inflation can also prevent it. The controller of the money supply in the United States is the privately owned Federal Reserve, [called by this author the Private Reserve] and their purpose is to use their ability to cause business cycles through inflation and deflation to destroy the right of the people to own private property. But, few in America understand that that is their purpose.

So the plunder continues.

And the God-given, inalienable, "self-evident" right to private property continues to be slowly eroded.

Just like Karl Marx and the Humanists want.

Chapter 34
The Attack on Nationalism

One of the things that Lucifer did when he fell, according to the Bible, was to "weaken the nations."

The concept of national boundaries is one created by the creator God. The Bible says this in Acts 17:24, 26:

> "God that made the world and all things therein ... [and] hath determined ... the bounds of their habitation."

So, if the designer of national boundaries was God himself, it would follow that those who are out to dethrone the Creator would be anxious to abolish the nations of the world. And this is precisely what they are doing.

Professor John Robison, the exposer of the Illuminati, wrote that inside that secret society:

"... patriotism and loyalty were called narrow-minded prejudices ...." [636]

And the reason that they were so considered was because the founder, Adam Weishaupt, himself believed in the destruction of the nation. He wrote:

"With the origins of nations and peoples the worlds ceased to be a great family, a single kingdom ....
Nationalism took the place of human love ...." [637]

And he proposed a solution:

"Diminish patriotism, then men will learn to know each other again as such ... [and] the bond of union will widen out.
Nations shall vanish from the earth." [638]

About seventy years later, the Communists were quick to join those who desired the destruction of national boundaries. Karl Marx wrote in THE COMMUNIST MANIFESTO:

"The Communists are further reproached with desiring to abolish countries and nationalities." [639]

And the Humanists have also joined the chorus. They, too, have added their voice in the move to destroy nationalism. The Twelfth Principle of the HUMANIST MANIFESTO II reads as follows:

"We deplore the division of humankind on nationalistic grounds.
... the best option is to transcend the limits of national sovereignty and to move toward the building of a world community in which all sectors of the human family can participate.
Thus we look to the development of a system of world law and a world order based upon transnational federal government." [640]

Manly P. Hall, wrote that he shared the concerns of Marx and Weishaupt, and expressed the hope that someday soon national borders would be abolished. He wrote:

"... the existence of contiguous states or nations has been the excuse for their exploitation." [641]

"Patriotism is merely an accentuated egotism which embraces the members of the tribe or nation to which the egotist himself belongs.

Long regarded as a virtue, patriotism will yet demonstrate itself to be a most pernicious attitude." [642]

Someone more contemporary has also written about the need to eliminate national borders. Zbigniew Brzezinski, President Jimmy Carter's National Security Advisor, wrote this in his book entitled BETWEEN TWO AGES in a chapter entitled "International Prospects:"

"... the fiction of [national] sovereignty ... is clearly no longer compatible with reality." [643]

And Mr. Hall tells his readers that the future of the nation-state is bleak. The day is coming when they will be an obsolete remnant of the past. He wrote:

"... we are approaching a nobler era when nations shall be no more; when the whole earth shall be under one order, one government, one administrative body." [644]

So, the ultimate purpose of all of this attack on nationalism is to tear down national borders so that they can be replaced with a borderless world, a one world government.

The New Agers/Humanists/Communists/Masons want a one world government. They are confident that their goal will be achieved soon because they are creating the conditions that will persuade the people that they should adopt the world government when it is offered.

The family unit; the right to own private property; the national borders; the right to believe in a creator God; these beliefs will all be destroyed because the world must receive a world government supported by the planners inside the secret societies and the new religious groups.

The enemy has been identified. It is not the churches, the family, nationalism or patriotism, or the right to worship a God.

It is simply the belief in Lucifer.

Lucifer, the god of the New World Order, the New Age, some of the Communists and some of the Masons, wants to bring the world a one world religion, based upon a belief in man, and the unbridled power of man's mind and reason.

It is now possible for the people to know just what the new world government and its supporting religion will offer the people of the world:

The abolition of the family. Children will be raised by the society through the government.

The abolition of the right to private property. All land and property will be owned by the government.

The right to worship will no longer exist. Religious people will be subject to rigorous deprogramming. Those who will not alter their belief system will be forced into concentration camps, or simply killed, because the act of worshipping a God will become a crime.

National borders will no longer exist. There will be a one world government instead of city, county, state, and national governments.

All of the individual's private decisions will be made by others. The individual will no longer decide whom he or she will associate with, either in employment, voluntary associations, or in social organizations.

The New World Order is coming.

And the inception date has been revealed.

It will begin in the year 2000.

All that is remains to be done is to sort out those who will not accept it. Only believers will be around to live in it.

Unless men of good will everywhere act to prevent it.

Chapter 35
Answering the Skeptic

What if the reader does not believe all of this evidence of the scheduled inception of the New World Order? What if the unbeliever says that all of the writings offered in this study were just the thoughts of individual authors and that they are not connected to the writings of any other individual? What if it is claimed that it is simply not correct to draw that single conclusion from the material presented? Quite possibly there are many who will believe that it is not possible to reach that conclusion unless it was done in error.

In other words, what if the skeptic says that the author's interpretations of all of the evidence have lead to the wrong conclusion.

That is a reasonable position and one that the author is willing to discuss. But not for the obvious reason.

The reader is reminded of the admonition contained in the first chapters of this book.

The reader was warned that the conclusions drawn by the author would be too difficult to believe, and it was anticipated that the average reader would not believe them.

However, there is one piece of evidence that has not been placed into the puzzle, and the skeptics should hold their final opinion until it has been considered.

That evidence is contained in the following chapter.

Chapter 36
Reagan and Bush

The New Age Magazine is, as has been mentioned before, the official publication of the Supreme Council, 33rd degree, Ancient & Accepted Scottish Rite of Freemasonry of the Southern Jurisdiction. This Council claims to be the Mother Council of the World, or the Mother Jurisdiction of the World.

It appears from these self-applied titles that this Council is claiming to be the leading organization inside the world-wide Masonic organization.

The cover of the April, 1988 issue of that magazine has a rather interesting picture on it. It shows the then President Ronald Reagan along with three other Masons. The President is holding a framed certificate that had been presented to him by the three Masons in the picture: C. Fred Kleinknecht, Sovereign Grand Commander of the Southern Jurisdiction; Francis G. Paul, the Sovereign Grand Commander of the Northern Jurisdiction; and Voris King, the Imperial Potentate of the Ancient Arabic Order of Nobles of the Mystic Shrine of North America [the Shriners.].

The certificate that the President is holding is too small in the photograph to read, but what it says on it is described in a column written by Mr. Kleinknecht inside the New Age magazine. He wrote that the framed certificate that was given to President Reagan was a Certificate of Honor thanking him for "working for the common good." He then stated that he and Grand Commander Paul presented the President with another certificate, this one being a Certificate that conferred the title of Honorary Scottish Rite Mason. Then Imperial Potentate King gave the President a third Certificate, this one making him a Honorary Member of the Imperial Council.

President Ronald Reagan has become a honorary member of the Southern Jurisdiction of the Scottish Rite of Freemasonry.

The magazine then reproduced a letter that the President had written to "Illustrious Brother Kleinknecht." It reads, in part:

"Please accept my sincere gratitude for the framed certificate of membership and the other tokens of friendship which you and Illustrious Brother Paul presented to me.

I am honored to join the ranks of the sixteen former Presidents in their association with Freemasonry." [645]

The President's letter appears to indicate that he considered himself to be a full member of the Scottish Rite, rather than a "honorary member." Notice that he used the phrase "certificate of membership," and that he said he had joined "the ranks of the sixteen former Presidents" in their association with the Freemasons.

Also, he addressed both Mr. Kleinknecht and Mr. Paul as a "Brother." It is presumed that one can only call another Mason a "brother" if one is truly a member.

So, the question of the degree of the President's involvement is open to debate. Some could fairly say that the President had actually joined the Masonic Lodge, just as any other member would do in a formal lodge in their home town. But, the Masons claim that his membership is Honorary.

But, in any event, and no matter how involved the President is or will be, the degree of his membership is not the important thing to consider. The main concern is that this man who claims to be a Christian had joined an organization that many Christians have said should not be joined by any believer. In other words, other Christians have warned the President about not joining it in any capacity. But the President was not listening.

Later that year, in August of 1988, the President said some rather cryptic things in his address to the Republican Convention that met in New Orleans to select their Presidential and Vice Presidential candidates. On Monday night, the President gave the keynote speech, the opening speech of the convention.

A transcript of that speech has been printed in the New York Times and a perusal of those words is very revealing. The President spoke about George Bush, his Vice President, and the individual who was seeking the Presidential nomination of the Republican Party. The President said:

> "With George Bush, I'll know, as we approach the new millennium ...." [646]

The President did not explain what he meant by the phrase "the new millennium," (a millennium is a thousand year period) but one can get a clue by reviewing his use of two other phrases in that speech. He ended that paragraph with these words:

> "With George Bush ... we'll have a ... nation confidently willing to take its leadership into the uncharted reaches of a new age." [647]

Here he actually used the phrase "a new age."

But perhaps the President actually explained what he meant by these phrases when he ended his speech with these words:

> "That's a new day -- our sunlit new day --." [648]

The President chose to refer to the "new day" as being a "sunlit" new day. As has been illustrated, the Masons know that the sun has been a symbol of Lucifer for 6000 years. Did the President know that when he referred to the new day as being "sunlit?"

One can only wonder what he meant by the use of these words, since he did not explain them. But it is certain that he used them. It should be expected that he knew what he was saying when he gave that speech. And it is improbable that some clever speech writer had him say these words without his knowledge or approval. It is also improbable that he read them without a realization of what he was saying. The only conclusion that is fair is that he had to know.

Three nights later, on Thursday night, Vice President George Bush accepted the Republican nomination for the Presidency of the United States. He also spoke to the convention and the American people on national television. His speech has also been recorded in the New York Times, and a perusal of that speech reveals that he too used some rather cryptic language.

During that speech, the Vice-President spoke about the thousands and tens of thousands of volunteer organizations in America. He said that they constituted the true meaning of a "community." He contrasted that understanding with that of the "liberals," whom he said had a rather narrow definition. His exact words were:

> "And there is another tradition. And that is the idea of community -- a beautiful word with a big meaning, though liberal Democrats have an odd view of it. They see 'community' as a limited cluster of interest groups, locked in odd conformity. In this view, the country waits passive while Washington sets the rules.
>
> But that is not what community means, not to me. For we are a nation of communities, of thousands and tens of thousands of ethnic, religious, social, business, labor union, neighborhood, regional organizations, all of them varied, voluntary and unique.
>
> This is America |and then the Vice President named a group of volunteer organizations, like the Disabled American Veterans.|"

And then he ended that paragraph with this statement:

> "... a brilliant diversity spread like stars, like a thousand points of light, in a broad and peaceful sky." [649]

The President was referring to a large number of volunteer organizations (he referred to them by the unspecified numbers "thousands and tens of thousands." That meant that he didn't know how many there were.) He later referred to these organizations, so numerous that he admitted that he didn't know the exact number of them, by the precise number of "a thousand," The only explanation that makes sense is that he was referring to something else when he used the phrase "a thousand points of light."

Notice that he also referred to these organizations as if they were "light" in a broad and peaceful sky.

As has been illustrated, "light" has been regarded as the "truth" from the sun-god Lucifer for six thousand years. The number "[a] thousand" is the precise number of years that the millennium is predicted to last under the leadership of Lord Maitreya.

Was George Bush referring to the thousand years of the millennium led by Lord Maitreya?

One can only wonder. George Bush continues to explain that he was referring to "thousands and tens of thousands" of volunteer organizations.

And it is extremely unlikely that he will confirm these interpretations, if he is referring to the thousand year reign of Lord Maitreya, because he obviously would not want the American people to know.

However, he referred to that phrase again at the end of his speech. He said:

> "I will keep America moving forward, always forward -- for a better America, for an endless, enduring dream and a thousand points of light.
> That is my mission. And I will complete it." [650]

George Bush used that phrase repeatedly during his debates with the Democrat nominee Michael Dukakis. He referred to it again during his campaign across the United States. And he used it again in his inaugural address after he was sworn in as President of the United States in 1989.

But there are other clues.

On March 16, 1989, a radio station played a part of a speech the President delivered somewhere in the United States. The President said:

"What are we doing to prepare ourselves for the
new world coming just 11 short years from now?"

Here the President linked the "new world" coming in the
year 2000, just "eleven short years from now" to his previous
comments. He was saying that he was aware that the New
World Order was on its way, and would be here in eleven
years.
1989 plus eleven is the year 2000.
But the final piece of the puzzle was an article that appeared in the Arizona Daily Star on January 3, 1989. The
headline written by the Associated Press read:

"Millennium group expects Bush at '99 Egypt
bash"

The article reported that:

"President-elect Bush is spending this New Year's
holiday at Camp David, Maryland, but in 10 years he
may be in Egypt.
Organizers of the Millennium Society say he's
already committed to ushering in the next century at
the Great Pyramids of Cheops in Giza."

The article then reported that Mr. Bush had sent the
society a telegram that they quoted:

"'Barbara [Mr. Bush's wife] and I wish you the
best of luck in the next year, and we're looking forward
to your celebration in Egypt in 1999,' Bush said." [651]

The organization that Mr. Bush sent the telegram to was
called the Millennium Society. As was pointed out elsewhere,
a millennium is a period of 1000 years. So the Society is
going to the Great Pyramid to bring in, not the next century
as the article reported, but the next millennium, the next
1000 years. And lastly, the location of the big party is the
Great Pyramid of Cheops, the site of the ancient initiation
ceremony into Lucifer worship.
This party was mentioned in an article that appeared in
the June 27, 1988 Wall Street Journal. That article's headline
read:

"To Mark Year 2000, Some Events Will Be Out of
This World"

The article was about the "imminent arrival of the new
millennium," and some of the plans that were being made by
a variety of people and organizations. It went on to report:

"One group has booked the Great Pyramid of
Cheops in Egypt for a monumental bash on the eve of
the new millenium."

The article identified the group that had arranged the
party as the "Millennium Society."

George Bush is going to the Great Pyramid in the year
1999 to bring in the millennium reign of Lucifer, a period
called the New Age, or the New World Order.

Is that conclusion a misreading of the evidence? Can one
say that this interpretation of all of this evidence is incorrect?
Is there another possible interpretation?

The only way to know the answer to those questions for
sure is to wait until the year 1999.

However, if one does not like what the signs are saying,
one can attempt to prevent the inauguration of the New
World Order.

One thousand years of this world's future is in the hands
of the reader.

Let us pray that those who read this study will correctly
read the signs.

And choose to inform others.

And assist the world in preventing the reign of Lord
Maitreya and the New World Order.

Chapter 37
"Eleven Short Years"

"A lie well believed is just as good as the truth."

That anonymous statement of truth is an excellent reminder of the fact that a lie repeated often enough will become the truth.

The evidence is abundant that this nation is turning away from the God of creation. Others have warned America what the future will hold if that trend continues.

One of those voices is that of Alexander Solzhenitsyn, the ex-Russian who is now living in America. His words of warning are:

> "Over a half century ago, while I was still a child,
> I recall hearing a number of old people offer the fol-
> lowing explanation for the great disasters [meaning
> the disasters of the Communist Revolution that killed
> up to 42,000,000 Russians] that had befallen Russia:

'Men have forgotten God; that's why all this has happened.'

Since then I have spent well-nigh 50 years working on the history of our revolution.

But if I were asked today to formulate as concisely as possible the main cause of the ruinous revolution that swallowed up some 60 million of our people, I could not put it more accurately than to repeat:

'Men have forgotten God; that's why all this has happened.'" [652]

In 1832, a Frenchman named Alexis de Tocqueville was sent to America by his government to discover why America as a nation had constructed only a few prisons to house its criminals while his native France could not build them fast enough to house their growing prison population. He wrote back to his nation that he had discovered the answer. There was a reason that America did not need prisons.

America was basically good.

He wrote:

"I sought for the greatness and genius of America in her commodious harbors and her ample rivers, and it was not there. I sought for the greatness and genius of America in her fertile fields and boundless forests, and it was not there.

I sought for the genius and greatness of America in her rich mines and her vast world commerce, and it was not there. I sought for the greatness and genius of America in her public school system and her institutions of learning, and it was not there.

I sought for the greatness and genius of America in her democratic congress and her matchless constitution, and it was not there.

Not until I went into the churches of America and heard her pulpits flame with righteousness did I understand the secret of her genius and power.

America is great because America is good, and if America ever ceases to be good, America will cease to be great."

America is no longer great because it is no longer good. America's churches and synagogues are no longer aflame with righteousness.

America's people are not heeding the warnings nor understanding the signs that are telling them that there are dangers ahead.

Pope Felix III wrote his warning to the world back in the early 6th century:

> "Not to oppose error is to approve it, and indeed
> to neglect to confound evil men, when we can do it, is
> no less a sin than to encourage them."

It is time to oppose error.

America's people must become aflame with righteousness.

America's churches and synagogues must preach against the coming "New World Order."

If they don't, it will surely come to the shores of America.

The year 2000 lies just "eleven short years" ahead.

Chapter 38
The Summation

Perhaps the one statement that best summarizes just what the New World Order is, is this one offered by Pierre Joseph Proudhon, the French writer and socialist:

> "Our principle is:
> atheism in religion,
> anarchy in politics,
> no property in the economic sphere." [653]

He had figured it out.

But the tragic thought is that he believed in it.

Just like all of the other Socialists, Humanists, Illuminati members, Communists, Masons and New Agers who believe in the New World Order.

But it might have been George Orwell in his book 1984 that best summarized what the "New World Order" had in store for the world when he wrote:

CHAPTER 38 THE SUMMATION

"If you want a picture of the future, imagine a boot stamping on a human face -- forever." [654]

Chapter 39
The Solution

The Bible teaches that "a prophet hath no honor in his own country." The reason for this is obvious: no one wants to hear bad news.

I do not claim to be prophet, but it would be fair to presume that the majority of those who have just completed a reading of this book would conclude that the information imparted would be considered to be "bad news."

The solution is clear: all thoughtful people must act together to prevent the imposition of the "New World Order."

This will not be the place to offer the concerned reader any courses of action. There are abundant sources of material on the necessary solutions to this problem.

I will just offer this great thought in closing for those who are seeking a solution. This promise is found in II Chronicles 7:14.

"If my people, which are called by my name, shall humble themselves, and pray, and seek my face, and

301

turn from their wicked ways; then will I hear from heaven, and will forgive their sin, and will heal their land."

God has promised to heal sick nations.
America is sick, and the sickness is getting worse.
It is time to do some seeking.
He will do the healing when we find Him.

Questions Answered

The question that I am most frequently asked as I make public appearances or speeches in connection with my book entitled THE UNSEEN HAND, is why I am still alive after publishing my revelations about this Conspiracy. I continue to answer that question with basically the same answer I gave in 1985 at the end of that book. That answer was:

"I am frequently asked by students or friends who agree with me that this Conspiracy exists, why I believe I am allowed to continue teaching and writing about its existence. They cite the deaths of [President] Abraham Lincoln, [Secretary of Defense] James Forrestal, [Senator] Joseph McCarthy and [Congressman] Louis McFadden, [who all died under mysterious circumstances or were killed by this Conspiracy because it appeared that they had discovered its existence] among others, as evidence that those who expose the Conspiracy do so at their own risk.

I have no answer to that question.

I can only say that I am absolutely convinced that the Conspiracy exists and that they have a great deal to gain by the death of anyone who has figured it out.

I live in Arizona where a few years ago an investigative reporter [named Don Bolles] had his car blow-up as he started it because he was reporting on corruption in that state.

Why his enemies picked on him, and why mine have chosen not to pick on me, I do not know.

I will emphatically say this: if you hear about my car exploding because I rigged it so that it would explode, or that I suddenly 'attempted to fly' from the top of a sixteen story building [like they claim James Forrestal did,] please accept my pre-death statement: I did not do it!

If either of these circumstances occur or any other mysterious thing happens to me, all I can do is ask that you double your efforts in exposing this conspiracy ..... in my memory."

I continue to stand by that statement.

The author

INTRODUCTION TO FOOTNOTES

The author is once again taking an unprecedented step in an attempt to assist the reader.

The following listing of the documentation utilized in this book is different from the majority of listings used by authors in the past.

First of all, I have not used the traditional words "op cit," and "ibid," to show references to a previously cited book.

I have also altered somewhat the lengthy reference information traditionally used by authors in the past. What I have done is to list the major works cited in this book first, with all of the information normally placed there. In addition, I have provided a brief introduction to the contents of the book, in an attempt to induce the reader to read the book themselves.

Then I have simply listed the book by title, and the page where the reference in my book may be found. I have only used this method where the book is cited more than once, or where the book cited is important enough for the reader to know about it and its contents.

This list of books will also serve as a bibliography.

It is hoped that these changes will meet with the approval of those who read this book.

BOOKS UTILIZED

A BRIDGE TO LIGHT by Rex R. Hutchens
The Masons believe that "the publication of this work could truly be the dawning of a new day in our [meaning the Southern Jurisdiction]" of Freemasonry. An important "esoteric" book, written by a 32nd degree Mason.
Published by the Supreme Council in 1988.

A GIFT OF PROPHECY, THE PHENOMENAL JEANNE DIXON by Ruth Montgomery
The back cover of the book reports that "Jeanne Dixon has demonstrated the uncanny ability to see into the future of people, of nations, to forecast great international events." One of those "events" she "saw" was the arrival of a "all-knowing" child "full of wisdom," in 1962.
Published by Bantam Books, New York in 1965.

AMERICA'S SECRET ESTABLISHMENT by Antony C. Sutton
The author explains that this volume will explain "why the West built the Soviets and Hitler, why we go to war and lose, why Wall Street loves Marxists and Nazis, why the kids can't read, [and] why politicians lie ...."

AN ENCYCLOPAEDIA OF FREEMASONRY by Albert G. Mackey,
This two volume encyclopaedia is described by the publisher as "a work which would furnish every Freemason ... the means of acquiring a knowledge of all matters connected with the science, the philosophy, and the history of his Order."
Published by The Masonic History Company, New York, 1873.

A PLANNED DECEPTION by Constance Cumbey
This book "builds on and amplifies" Mrs. Cumbey's earlier book, THE HIDDEN DANGERS OF THE RAINBOW.
Published by Pointe Publishers, Inc., East Detroit, Michigan, in 1985.

AQUARIAN CONSPIRACY, THE, by Marilyn Ferguson
The Foreword of the book describes Marilyn Ferguson as "the best reporter today" on the subject of the New Age Movement. It says that "she has proven to be a whirlwind of information, thought, activity, a whole explatory 'network' in herself."
Published by J.P. Tarcher, Los Angeles, in 1980.

BEHIND THE LODGE DOOR by Paul A. Fisher
This book "traces the secret machinations of American Freemasonry from its early days in this country, concentrating on its unrelenting warfare against Christianity."
Published by Shield Publishing, Inc., Washington D.C., in 1988.

BETWEEN TWO AGES by Zbigniew Brzezinski
This book claims to be "one of the most original books on political and social thought." Mr. Brzezinski glorifies Marxist Communism, the greatest fraud ever conceived by man!
Published by Penguin Books, New York, in 1970.

BRAVE NEW WORLD and BRAVE NEW WORLD REVISITED, by Aldous Huxley
Two books about the "future" of the world, where controllers use "brain-washing" to control the minds and behavior of entire populations.
BRAVE NEW WORLD was published by Harper & Row, Inc., New York, in 1932.
BRAVE NEW WORLD, REVISITED, was published by Bantam Books, New York, in 1958

CLAUSEN'S COMMENTARIES ON MORALS AND DOGMA
by Henry C. Clausen
"For years each new member of the Scottish Rite of the Southern Jurissdiction was presented with a copy of MORALS AND DOGMA, by Albert Pike. The supply of the volumes being exhausted, and recognizing that today few members would tackle the reading of so formidable a volume, Henry C. Clausen, grand commander of the Scottish Rite, Southern Jurisdiction, wrote a fine book entitled COMMENTARIES ON MORALS AND DOGMA."

COMMUNIST MANIFESTO, THE by Karl Marx
A complete reprinting of the original Manifesto, issued in 1848, by the Communist League, also called the League of The Just Men. The book also includes an introduction by William P. Fall.
Published by American Opinion, now in Appleton, Wisconsin, in 1974.

CONSPIRACY AGAINST GOD AND MAN, by Rev. Clarence Kelly
This book presents vital information about the nature of the enemy that confronts America today. Included are discussions on the Illuminati, Freemasonry, and the French Revolution.
Published by Western Islands, now in Appleton, Wisconsin, in 1974.

COSMIC CONSPIRACY, THE, by Stan Deyo
This author discusses, amongst other things, the "4000 year glimpse into the history of the Illuminati, and the secret codes hidden in the Great Seal of the United States by the Illuminati."
Published by the West Australian Texas Trading, Kalamunda, Western Australia, in 1978.

DANCING IN THE LIGHT, by Shirley MacLaine
Miss MacLaine claims to be a "seeker of spiritual destiny," and she ends her foreword with this comment: "Love and Light."
Published by Bantam Books, Inc., New York, 1985.

DARK SECRETS OF THE NEW AGE by Texe Marrs
This book exposes the "Plan" for establishing a "New Age Messiah to lead a One-World Religion and a global government."
Published by Crossway Books, Westchester, Illinois in 1987.

DEADLY DECEPTION, THE, by Jim Shaw
This book was written by a 33rd degree Mason, and are his thoughts about how he saw that they were "victimizing multitudes of sincere men."
Published by Huntington House, Lafayette, Louisiana in 1988.

EXTERNALISATION OF THE HIERARCHY, THE, by Alice A. Bailey
An important book written by one inside the New Age Movement.
Published by the Lucis Publishing Company, New York.

FIRE IN THE MINDS OF MEN, ORIGINS OF THE REVOLUTIONARY FAITH, by James H. Billington
The book has been described as "a widely acclaimed history of the modern revolutionary spirit from the French Revolution of 1789 to the Bolshevik [Communist] Revolution of 1917."
It was written by James Billington, who received his doctorate as a Rhodes Scholar at Oxford, and who has previously taught history for seventeen years at Harvard and Princeton Universities.
Published by Basic Books Inc., of New York, in 1980.

5/5/2000 by Richard W. Noone
This author presents his theory that a giant catastrophe will occur to the world on May 5, 2000. This is not the place to debate the merits of this author's contentions, but he does present some excellent information on the Great Pyramid of Giza, which is pertinent to the subject of THE NEW WORLD ORDER.
Published by Harmony Books, New York, in 1982.

FREEMASONRY EXPOSED by Capt. William Morgan

This book was published in 1826 and was an apparent attempt by a Mason who had been a member for 30 years to reveal some of the secrets of the Masonic Lodge. It has been variously reported that he was murdered, or not murdered, by the Masons soon after its publication date. In any event, whether or not he was murdered because he published the book, one thing that resulted from the story was the creation of America's first "third party" in 1832 in an attempt to expose some of the dealings of the Order.

The copy circulating today shows no publisher's name but it shows that it was published in Batavia, New York, in 1826.

HIDDEN DANGERS OF THE RAINBOW, THE, by Constance Cumbey

This excellent book was one of the first written about the New Age Movement from someone not in favor of it. The author has "read hundreds of books on the subject," and her extensive research shows that to be true.

Published by Huntington House, Inc., Shreveport, Louisiana in 1983.

HUMANIST MANIFESTOS I AND II, edited by Paul Kurtz

This book is a reprinting of both of the two manifesto issued by those who believe in this religion. They were called the Humanist Manifesto I, issued in 1933, and the Humanist Manifesto II, issued in 1973. Mr. Kurtz, the editor of the Humanist Magazine, also provides a brief introduction to the reprinting.

Published by Prometheus Books, Buffalo, New York, in 1973.

INTRODUCTION TO FREEMASONRY by Carl H. Claudy

This is a series of three books given by the Grand Lodge of Massachusetts to "all candidates as an important part of their initiation into the Masonic Fraternity."

Published by the Temple Publishers, Washington D.C., in 1931.

LECTURES ON ANCIENT PHILOSOPHY, by Manly P. Hall
This book is a "commentary and expansion" of Mr. Hall's book entitled THE SECRET TEACHINGS OF ALL AGES.
Published by The Philosophical Research Society, Inc., of Los Angeles, in 1984.

LOST KEYS OF FREEMASONRY, THE, by Manly P. Hall
The foreword to this book reports that "the leading Masonic scholars have agreed that the symbols of the Fraternity are susceptible of the most profound interpretation and thus reveal to the truly initiated certain secrets concerning the spiritual realities of life." One of those "secrets" is revealed to the reader on page 48: "The seething energies of Lucifer are in his hands ...."
Published by the Macoy Publishing and Masonic Supply Company, Inc., Richmond, Virginia, in 1976.

MAGIC OF OBELISKS, THE, by Peter Tompkins
The author "explores their magical and physical properties."
Published by Harper & Row, New York, in 1981.4

MARX AND SATAN by Richard Wurmbrand
This book examines the evidence that Karl Marx was "led to a deep personal rebellion against God and all Christian values." That anger led him to a Satanic cult.
Published by Crossway Books, Westchester, Illinois, in 1986.

MASTER'S CARPET, THE, by Edmond Ronayne
This book reviews the similarity between Masonry, Romanism and 'the Mysteries,' and comparing the whole with the Bible." It was written by a "Past Master of Keystone Lodge, Chicago."
It appears that the book has been re-published since its original publication date. There is no publication information in the volume owned by the present author.

MEANING OF MASONRY, THE, by W.L. Wilmshurst
This book claims to disclose "the real purpose of modern Freemasonry and clearly states the true body of

311

teaching and practice concerning the esoteric meanings of Masonic ritual."

Published by Bell Publishing Company, New York, in 1927.

MORALS AND DOGMA by Albert Pike

This "esoteric" book [it has secret meanings] is "specially intended to be read and studied by the Brethern" of the of the Scottish Rite of Freemasonry. It was written by the Sovereign Grand Commander of the Scottish Rite from 1859 to 1891.

Published by The Supreme Council of the Southern Jurisdiction of the Scottish Rite of Freemasonry in Washington D.C. in 1871.

MYSTERIES OF THE GREAT PYRAMIDS, THE by Andre Pochan

This book suggests that the "Great Pyramid was a solar astronomical instrument."

Published in Avon Books, New York, in 1971.

MYSTERY MARK OF THE NEW AGE, by Texe Marrs

This book details plans by New Age enthusiasts to initiate people into Lucifer worship.

Published by Crossway Books, Westchester, Illinois, in 1988.

NEA: [the National Education Association] TROJAN HORSE IN AMERICAN EDUCATION by Samuel Blumenfeld

The author discusses the evidence that the NEA is "on the march toward total political power with the aim of converting America into a socialist society."

1984 by George Orwell

This book is described as a "great modern classic of 'Negative Utopia,' not a drama of what life might be ... but nightmares of what it is becoming."

Published by The New American Library, Inc., New York, 1961.

OCCULT AND THE THIRD REICH, THE, by Jean-Michel Angebert

This book reveals how strange and mystical cults, including the Thule Society, influenced the thinking of Adolf Hitler. As he once said, "he who has seen in National Socialism only a political movement has seen nothing."

That which the reader is to see is that the Thule Society worshipped Lucifer, also known as Satan, or the devil.

Published by McGraw-Hill Book Company, New York, in 1971.

OCCULT THEOCRASY by Edith Starr Miller

The author claims that her book exposes "some of the means and methods used by a secret world ... to penetrate, dominate and destroy ...."

The book was apprently self-published for "private circulation only" in 1933.

OUT ON A LIMB by Shirley MacLaine

Miss MacLaine says "This book is about ... the connection between mind, body, and spirit."

Published by Bantam Books, Inc., New York, in 1983.

PARADE TO GLORY by Fred Van Deventer

"The story of the Shriners and their caravan to destiny."

Published by Pyramid Books, New York, in 1959.

PROOFS OF A CONSPIRACY by John Robison

This is possibly the finest book ever written on the secret society known as the Illuminati, by a professor who was asked to join the organization. This book was read by President George Washington in 1798.

Originally published in 1798, but it was re-published in 1967 by Western Islands, now in Appleton, Wisconsin.

PYRAMID POWER by Max Toth

"The prophecies of the ancient masters are locked into the pyramid form ...."

Published by Warner Destiny Books, New York, in 1979.

ROYAL MASONIC CYCLOPAEDIA, THE, by Kenneth Mackenzie
This encyclopaedia has been "highly esteemed by occultists."
Published by The Aquarian Press, Wellingborough, Northamptonshire, England in 1987.

SAY NO TO THE NEW WORLD ORDER, by Gary Allen
One of the first books to explore the subject of the New World Order. However, Mr. Allen sees it only as an "attack on U.S. sovereignty," because it is to be "created by a merger of the United States and the Soviet Union into a one-world government.
Published by Concord Press, Seal Beach, California in 1987.

SECRET SOCIETIES AND SUBVERSIVE MOVEMENTS by Nesta Webster
Perhaps one of the finest works ever written on the history of Socialism, Communism and the Illluminati that have plagued mankind since their introduction centuries ago. Originally published in 1923, it has been re-published by the Christian Book Club of America.

SECRET SYMBOLISM IN OCCULT ART by Fred Gettings
This is a "tour of occult art and its symbolism from prehistoric times ... up to the present."
Published by Harmony Books, New York, in 1987.

SECRET TEACHINGS OF ALL AGES, THE, by Manly P. Hall
The book is described as "an Encyclopedic Outline of Masonic, Hermetic, Qabbalistic and Rosicrucian Symbolical Philosophy," and "an Interpretation of the Secret Teachings concealed within the Rituals, Allegories and Mysteries of all Ages."
Published by The Philosophical Research Society, Inc., Los Angeles, in 1977.

SERPENT IN THE SKY by John Anthony West
This book discusses the thesis that "the builders of ancient Egypt had far more sophisticated understand-

ing[s] of metaphysics ... than most Egyptologists have been unwilling to admit."

Published by The Julian Press, Inc., New York, in 1987.

SOCIALIST NETWORK, THE, by Nesta Webster

The object of this book is to "provide a history of the Socialist organizations of modern times."

Published in London in 1926.

SPEAR OF DESTINY, THE, by Trevor Ravenscroft

"In this book, you may find the ultimate explanation of the evil genius and ascent to power: The Occult Power behind the amazing Spear which pierced the side of Christ."

Published by G.P. Putnam's Sons, New York, in 1973.

TWISTED CROSS, THE, by Joseph J. Carr

This book is about "the occultic religion of [Adolf] Hitler and the New Age Nazism of the Third Reich." The author shows that "Nazism was an occultic religion in which Adolf Hitler was the messiah ...." "Nazism and the New Age Movement are one in the same: they are merely different manifestations of the same evil root."

Published by Huntington House Inc., Shreveport, Louisiana in 1985.

TWO BABYLONS, THE, by Rev. Alexander Hislop

This book discusses, amongst other things, the Coin of Tyre which appears to illustrate the premise of THE NEW WORLD ORDER: that Lucifer is attempting to establish his reign on this earth.

Published by Loizeaux Brothers, Neptune, New Jersey, in 1916.

WAS KARL MARX A SATANIST? by Richard Wurmbrand

The earliest book of the two written by Reverend Wurmbrand. It first exposed the evidence that Karl Marx had joined a Satanic cult.

WHAT THE ANCIENT WISDOM EXPECTS OF ITS
DISCIPLES by Manly P. Hall
This book is a "study concerning the mystery
schools," "a road leading to the understanding of life's
purpose."
Published by The Philosophical Research Society,
Inc., Los Angeles, 1982.

WORLD REVOLUTION by Nesta Webster
This book discusses the notion that "the revolution
through which we are now passing is not local but
universal, it is not political but social, and its causes
must be sought not in popular discontent, but in a deep-
laid conspiracy that uses the people to their own
undoing."
Published by Constable and Company, Inc., London,
England, in 1921.

FOOTNOTES

INTRODUCTION

1.   Associated Press, July 26, 1968
2.   Review of the News, (March 3, 1976), p. 38
3.   Seattle Post-Intelligence (April 18, 1975), p. A-2
4.   Arizona Daily Star, (May 12, 1989)
5.   American Opinion, (January, 1976), p. 91
6.   THE OCCULT AND THE THIRD REICH, p. 155
7.   THE OCCULT AND THE THIRD REICH, p. 120
8.   THE OCCULT AND THE THIRD REICH, p. 192
9.   THE OCCULT AND THE THIRD REICH, p. 174
10. HUMANIST MANIFESTOS I AND II, p. 22
11. Richard N. Gardner, Foreign Affairs, (April, 1974), as
     quoted in Review of the News, (January 16, 1974), p. 52
12. Angela Davis, People's Daily World, (March 9, 1989), p.
     21-A
13. Alexei Kovylov, quoted by Kathleen Hayes and Samantha
     Smith, Grave New World, (Golden, Colorado: self-
     published), p. 7
14. THE COMMUNIST MANIFESTO, p. 36
15. SECRET SOCIETIES AND SUBVERSIVE
     MOVEMENTS, p. 337

INTRODUCTION continued

16. CONSPIRACY AGAINST GOD AND MAN, p. 215
17. Pope Pius IX, Encyclical: The Dangers and Evils of the Times, as quoted in CONSPIRACY AGAINST GOD, p. 210
18. Dr. Jose Arguelles, (from a pamphlet published by the International Sacred Rites Festival, Haiku, Maui, Hawaii), p. 4-5
19. THE AQUARIAN CONSPIRACY, p., 412
20. FIRE IN THE MINDS OF MEN, p. 3
21. SAY NO TO THE NEW WORLD ORDER, p. 6
22. Alvin Toffler, quoted by the New American, (October 12,1987), p. 6
23. Gary North, Conspiracy, a Biblical View, (Ft. Worth: Dominion Press, 1986), p. 47
24. LECTURES ON ANCIENT PHILOSOPHY, p. 463
25. LECTURES ON ANCIENT PHILOSOPHY, p. 464
26. LECTURES ON ANCIENT PHILOSOPHY, p. 383
27. BRAVE NEW WORLD REVISITED, p. 115
28. Tucson Citizen, (November 3, 1988), p. C-1
29. BRAVE NEW WORLD REVISITED, p. 25
30. BRAVE NEW WORLD REVISITED, p. 116
31. BETWEEN TWO AGES, P. 258

CHAPTER ONE: TOMORROW'S RULERS

32. MYSTERY MARK OF THE NEW AGE, p. 233
33. CONSPIRACY AGAINST GOD AND MAN, p. 200
34. BEHIND THE LODGE DOOR, p. 240
35. INTRODUCTION TO FREEMASONRY, p. 105
36. MORALS AND DOGMA, p. 817
37. Albert Pike, Legenda XIX-XXX, p. 160, as quoted in A BRIDGE TO LIGHT, p. 291
38. MORALS AND DOGMA, p. 817
39. A BRIDGE TO LIGHT, p. 325
40. DARK SECRETS OF THE NEW AGE, p. viii
41. THE HIDDEN DANGERS OF THE RAINBOW, p. 40
42. THE EXTERNALISATION OF THE HIERARCHY, p. 511
43. quoted by Kathleen Hayes in her article on Masonry
44. DARK SECRETS OF THE NEW AGE, p. 195
45. LECTURES ON ANCIENT PHILOSOPHY, p. 454
46. quoted by Kathleen Hayes in her article on Masonry

CHAPTER ONE: TOMORROW'S RULERS continued

47. Don Bell Reports, (November 12, 1965), p. 1
48. MORALS AND DOGMA, p. 715
49. LECTURES ON ANCIENT PHILOSOPHY, p. 455
50. THE EXTERNALISATION OF THE HIERARCHY, p. 510
51. Ruth Montgomery, Herald of the New Age, p. 265, quoted in MYSTERY MARK OF THE NEW AGE, p. 197
52. THE HIDDEN DANGERS OF THE NEW AGE, p. 20
53. Time magazine, (December 7, 1987), p. 62
54. The New American, (October 12, 1982), p. 6
55. THE HIDDEN DANGERS OF THE RAINBOW, p. 17

CHAPTER TWO: THE NEW AGE MOVEMENT

56. Friedrich Nietzsche, quoted in THE SPEAR OF DESTINY, p. 28
57. DARK SECRETS OF THE NEW AGE, p. 153
58. DARK SECRETS OF THE NEW AGE, p. 177
59. THE SOCIALIST NETWORK, p. 23
60. DARK SECRETS OF THE NEW AGE, p. 63
61. DARK SECRETS OF THE NEW AGE, p. 141
62. THE HIDDEN DANGERS OF THE RAINBOW, p. 190
63. Ruth Montgomery, as quoted in DARK SECRETS OF THE NEW AGE, p. 136
64. Ruth Montgomery, as quoted in DARK SECRETS OF THE NEW AGE, p. 142
65. MYSTERY MARK OF THE NEW AGE, p. 153
66. MYSTERY MARK OF THE NEW AGE, p. 153
67. MYSTERY MARK OF THE NEW AGE, p. 153
68. full page advertisement that appeared on April 25, 1982, in various newspapers all over the world
69. MYSTERY MARK OF THE NEW AGE, p. 234
70. MYSTERY MARK OF THE NEW AGE, p. 32
71. THE OCCULT AND THE THIRD REICH, p. 225
72. George Bernard Shaw, The Intelligent Woman's Guide to Socialism, p. 470
73. MORALS AND DOGMA, p. 833
74. WORLD REVOLUTION, p. 13
75. PROOFS OF A CONSPIRACY, p. 78
76. CONSPIRACY AGAINST GOD AND MAN, p. 200-201
77. PROOFS OF A CONSPIRACY, p. 85
78. 1984, p. 142

CHAPTER THREE: LORD MAITREYA

79. LECTURES ON ANCIENT PHILOSOPHY, p. 101
80. MYSTERY MARK OF THE NEW AGE, p. 13
81. A GIFT OF PROPHECY, p. 185-187
82. A GIFT OF PROPHECY, p. 185-187
83. A GIFT OF PROPHECY, p. 178-181
84. A GIFT OF PROPHECY, p. 181
85. A GIFT OF PROPHECY, p. 181
86. New York Times, (February 4, 1962), p. A-1
87. New York Times, (February 4, 1962), p. A-1

CHAPTER FOUR: THE ANCIENT MYSTERIES

88. THE EXTERNALISATION OF THE HIERARCHY, p. 514
89. AN ENCYCLOPAEDIA OF FREEMASONRY, p. 497
90. AN ENCYCLOPAEDIA OF FREEMASONRY, first page opposite the portrait of Albert Mackey
91. INTRODUCTION TO FREEMASONRY, p. 44
92. INTRODUCTION TO FREEMASONRY, p. 44
93. WHAT THE ANCIENT WISDOM EXPECTS OF ITS DISCIPLES, p. 23
94. THE SECRET TEACHINGS OF ALL AGES, p. CLXIX
95. THE SECRET TEACHINGS OF ALL AGES, p. XX
96. THE SECRET TEACHINGS OF ALL AGES, p. XX
97. WHAT THE ANCIENT WISDOM EXPECTS OF ITS DISCIPLES, p. 56
98. THE SECRET TEACHINGS OF ALL AGES, p. CXCVII
99. THE SECRET TEACHINGS OF ALL AGES, p. XVII
100. MORALS AND DOGMA, p. 373
101. MORALS AND DOGMA, p. 428
102. WHAT THE ANCIENT WISDOM EXPECTS OF ITS DISCIPLES, p. 1
103. THE ROYAL MASONIC ENCYCLOPAEDIA, p. 124
104. FREEMASONRY EXPOSED, p. 80-85
105. MORALS AND DOGMA, p. 274
106. WHAT THE ANCIENT WISDOM EXPECTS OF ITS DISCIPLES, p. 58
107. George Steinmetz, Freemasonry, Its Hidden Meaning, p. 123
108. THE SECRET TEACHINGS OF ALL AGES, p. XXI
109. THE ENCYCLOPAEDIA OF FREEMASONRY, p. 497
110. THE MASTERS CARPET, p. 7

CHAPTER FOUR: THE ANCIENT MYSTERIES
continued

111. MORALS AND DOGMA, p. 363

CHAPTER FIVE: SECRET SOCIETIES

112. Arthur Edward Waite, Real History of the Rosicrucians, (Blauvelt, N.Y.: Steinerbooks, 1977), p. A
113. AMERICA'S SECRET ESTABLISHMENT, p. 117
114. MORALS AND DOGMA, p. 817
115. PROOFS OF A CONSPIRACY, p. 112
116. PROOFS OF A CONSPIRACY, p. 91
117. ENCYCLOPAEDIA OF FREEMASONRY, p. 574

CHAPTER SIX: CONCEALED MYSTERIES

118. MORALS AND DOGMA, p. 246
119. MORALS AND DOGMA, p. 331
120. PROOFS OF A CONSPIRACY, p. 129
121. MYSTERY MARK OF THE NEW AGE, p. 119
122. MORALS AND DOGMA, p. 849
123. LECTURES ON ANCIENT PHILOSOPHY, p. 21
124. Max Toth, Pyramid Prophecies, (New York: Warner Press, 1979), p. 239
125. Alice Bailey, The Reappearance of the Christ, pp. 121-123, as quoted in MYSTERY MARK OF THE NEW AGE, p. 241
126. INTRODUCTION TO FREEMASONRY, p. 9
127. A BRIDGE TO LIGHT, p. 100
128. SECRET SOCIETIES AND SUBVERSIVE MOVEMENTS, p. iv
129. INTRODUCTION TO FREEMASONRY, p. 172
130. MARX AND SATAN, p. 59

CHAPTER SEVEN: SERPENTS, STARS AND SUNS

131. THE SECRET TEACHINGS OF ALL AGES, p. LXXXVIII
132. THE SECRET TEACHINGS OF ALL AGES, P. LXXXVIII
133. WHAT THE ANCIENT WISDOM EXPECTS OF ITS DISCIPLES, p.29

CHAPTER SEVEN: SERPENTS, STARS AND SUNS
continued

134. WHAT THE ANCIENT WISDOM EXPECTS OF ITS DISCIPLES, p. 26
135. 5/5/2000, p. 111
136. THE SECRET TEACHINGS OF ALL AGES, p. LXXXVIII
137. THE SECRET TEACHINGS OF ALL AGES, p. LV
138. SERPENT IN THE SKY, p. 71
139. THE ROYAL MASONIC CYCLOPAEDIA, p. 67-68
140. THE TWO BABYLONS, p. 227
141. "Satan's Master Plan," The Good News magazine, (September, 1986), p. 10-12
142. PROOFS OF A CONSPIRACY, p. 93
143. AN ENCYCLOPAEDIA OF FREEMASONRY, p. 107
144. AN ENCYCLOPAEDIA OF FREEMASONRY, p. 106
145. A BRIDGE TO LIGHT, p. 95
146. MORALS AND DOGMA, p. 593
147. MORALS AND DOGMA, p. 77
148. MORALS AND DOGMA, p. 591
149. MORALS AND DOGMA, p. 13
150. MORALS AND DOGMA, p. 776
151. AN ENCYCLOPAEDIA OF FREEMASONRY, p. 736-737
152. INTRODUCTION TO FREEMASONRY, p. 97
153. A BRIDGE TO LIGHT, p. 205
154. MORALS AND DOGMA, p. 548, 550
155. AN ENCYCLOPAEDIA OF FREEMASONRY, p. 540
156. INTRODUCTION TO FREEMASONRY, p. 27
157. INTRODUCTION TO FREEMASONRY, p. 31
158. INTRODUCTION TO FREEMASONRY, p. 31
159. FREEMASONRY EXPOSED, p. 46
160. AN ENCYCLOPAEDIA OF FREEMASONRY, p. 518
161. MORALS AND DOGMA, p. 592
162. THE ROYAL MASONIC CYCLOPAEDIA, p. 171
163. A BRIDGE TO LIGHT, p. 288
164. INTRODUCTION TO FREEMASONRY, p. 107
165. A BRIDGE TO LIGHT, p. 145
166. AN ENCYCLOPAEDIA OF FREEMASONRY, p. 227
167. A BRIDGE TO LIGHT, p. 251
168. AN ENCYCLOPAEDIA OF FREEMASONRY, p. 152
169. AN ENCYCLOPAEDIA OF FREEMASONRY, p. 153

CHAPTER SEVEN: SERPENTS, STARS AND SUNS
continued

170. Jack Harris, Freemasonry: The Invisible Cult in Our Midst, (Chattanooga, Tennessee: Global Publishers, 1983), p. 34
171. AN ENCYCLOPAEDIA OF FREEMASONRY, p. 655
172. AN ENCYCLOPAEDIA OF FREEMASONRY, p. 153
173. A BRIDGE TO LIGHT, p. 80
174. A BRIDGE TO LIGHT, p. 58
175. A BRIDGE TO LIGHT, p. 64
176. THE MASTERS CARPET, p. 306
177. DARK SECRETS OF THE NEW AGE, p. 197-198
178. THE OCCULT AND THE THIRD REICH, p. 4

CHAPTER EIGHT: THE AUTHOR'S CLARIFICATION

No footnotes

CHAPTER NINE: LUCIFER WORSHIP

179. MORALS AND DOGMA, p. 859
180. MORALS AND DOGMA, p. 102
181. MORALS AND DOGMA, p. 697
182. OCCULT THEOCRASY, p. 220-221
183. THE SECRET TEACHINGS OF ALL AGES, p. XXI
184. THE LOST KEYS OF FREEMASONRY, p. 48
185. MARX AND SATAN, p. 26-27
186. DARK SECRETS OF THE NEW AGE, p. 76
187. DARK SECRETS OF THE NEW AGE, p. 74
188. THE MEANING OF MASONRY, p. 47
189. THE MEANING OF MASONRY, p. 94
190. THE MEANING OF MASONRY, p. 140-141
191. SERPENT IN THE SKY, p. 145
192. CONSPIRACY AGAINST GOD AND MAN, p. 194
193. CONSPIRACY AGAINST GOD AND MAN, p. 194
194. John Denver, quoted by Samantha Smith and Kathleen Hayes, Grave New World, (self-published paper, 1986), p. 4
195. LECTURES ON ANCIENT PHILOSOPHY, p. 64
196. DANCING IN THE LIGHT, p. 104
197. DANCING IN THE LIGHT, p. 112
198. DANCING IN THE LIGHT, p. 42

CHAPTER NINE: LUCIFER WORSHIP continued

199. DANCING IN THE LIGHT, p. 117
200. OUT ON A LIMB, p. 14
201. Parade Magazine, (December 18, 1988), p. 23
202. OUT ON A LIMB, p. 16
203. OUT ON A LIMB, p. 23
204. Newsweek magazine, (July 27, 1987)
205. Newsweek magazine, (July 27, 1987)
206. Newsweek magazine, (July 27, 1987)
207. Newsweek magazine, (July 27, 1987)
208. Time magazine, (December 7, 1987), p. 64
209. SECRET SOCIETIES AND SUBVERSIVE MOVEMENTS, p. 30

CHAPTER TEN: BECOMING A GOD

210. SECRET SYMBOLISM IN OCCULT ART, p. 117
211. LECTURES ON ANCIENT PHILOSOPHY, p. 63
212. THE SECRET TEACHINGS OF ALL AGES, p. CXCVII
213. THE SECRET TEACHINGS OF ALL AGES, p. CCIII
214. LECTURES ON ANCIENT PHILOSOPHY, p. 413
215. LECTURES ON ANCIENT PHILOSOPHY, p. 405
216. HUMANIST MANIFESTOS I AND II, p. 17
217. PROOFS OF A CONSPIRACY, p. 64
218. WORLD REVOLUTION, p. 9
219. Harold Bolen, New Age magazine, as quoted by Everett C. de Velde, Jr., Christianity and Civilization, p. 280
220. MORALS AND DOGMA, p. 437
221. MORALS AND DOGMA, p. 17
222. MORALS AND DOGMA, p. 737
223. MORALS AND DOGMA, p. 718
224. MORALS AND DOGMA, p. 810

CHAPTER ELEVEN: SONS OF LIGHT

225. AN ENCYCLOPAEDIA OF FREEMASONRY, p. 447
226. DARK SECRETS OF THE NEW AGE, p. 121
227. PROOFS OF A CONSPIRACY, p. 78
228. A PLANNED DECEPTION, p. 246
229. MORALS AND DOGMA, p. 252
230. MORALS AND DOGMA, p. 248
231. MORALS AND DOGMA, p. 32

CHAPTER ELEVEN: SONS OF LIGHT continued

232. THE ROYAL MASONIC CYCLOPAEDIA, p. 682
233. Henry Rugg, editor, The Freemasons' Repository, Volume XII, 1882-1883, (Providence, Rhode Island: E.L.Freeman & Co., undated), pps. 102-103
234. as above, p. 100, 102
235. AN ENCYCLOPAEDIA OF FREEMASONRY, p. 446
236. MORALS AND DOGMA, p. 275
237. MORALS AND DOGMA, p. 321
238. THE LOST KEYS OF FREEMASONRY, p. 48
239. THE LOST KEYS OF FREEMASONRY, p. 55
240. MORALS AND DOGMA, p. 287

CHAPTER TWELVE: EAST AND WEST

241. FREEMASONRY EXPOSED, p. 15
242. MORALS AND DOGMA, p. 366
243. AN ENCYCLOPAEDIA OF FREEMASONRY, p. 227

CHAPTER THIRTEEN: THE PYRAMID OF GIZA

244. AN ENCYCLOPAEDIA OF FREEMASONRY, p. 540
245. New Age magazine, (October, 1953), as quoted by Don Bell Reports, (March 5, 1965), p. 2
246. THE SECRET TEACHINGS OF ALL AGES, p. XII
247. THE SECRET TEACHINGS OF ALL AGES, p. XLIV
248. 5/5/2000, p. 126-127
249. Pyramid Prophecies, p. xii
250. 5/5/2000, p. 231
251. THE TWISTED CROSS, p. 11
252. 5/5/2000, p. 109
253. 5/5/2000, p. 188
254. THE MYSTERIES OF THE GREAT PYRAMID, p. 28
255. 5/5/2000, p. 111
256. 5/5/2000, p. 153
257. 5/5/2000, p. 149
258. 5/5/2000, p. 149
259. 5/5/2000, p. 150
260. 5/5/2000, p. 150
261. 5/5/2000, p. 165
262. AN ENCYCLOPAEDIA OF FREEMASONRY, p. 60-61
263. 5/5/2000, p. 231

CHAPTER THIRTEEN: THE PYRAMID OF GIZA
continued

264. THE AQUARIAN CONSPIRACY, p. 19
265. THE HIDDEN DANGERS OF THE RAINBOW, p. 227

CHAPTER FOURTEEN: OBELISKS

266. The Freemasons' Repository, p. 220
267. THE MAGIC OF OBELISKS, p. 1
268. THE COSMIC CONSPIRACY, p. 73
269. INTRODUCTION TO FREEMASONRY, p. 82
270. INTRODUCTION TO FREEMASONRY, p. 78
271. INTRODUCTION TO FREEMASONRY, p. 82
272. INTRODUCTION TO FREEMASONRY, p. 82
273. MORALS AND DOGMA, p. 460
274. THE ROYAL MASONIC CYCLOPAEDIA, p. 521
275. AN ENCYCLOPAEDIA OF FREEMASONRY, p. 525
276. Time magazine, (February 2, 1981), p. 9
277. Time magazine, (January 21, 1985)

CHAPTER FIFTEEN: THE ILLUMINATI

278. Winston Churchill, Illustrated Sunday Herald, (February 8, 1920), quoted by Review of the News, (January 26, 1972), p. 57
279. Adam Weishaupt, quoted by Gary North, Conspiracy, A Biblical View, (Ft. Worth: Dominion Press, 1986), p. 57
280. PROOFS OF A CONSPIRACY, p. 64
281. PROOFS OF A CONSPIRACY, p. 4
282. CONSPIRACY AGAINST GOD AND MAN, p. 125
283. MORALS AND DOGMA, p. 367
284. FIRE IN THE MINDS OF MEN, p. 97
285. CONSPIRACY AGAINST GOD AND MAN, p. 118
286. PROOFS OF A CONSPIRACY, p. 3
287. SECRET SOCIETIES AND SUBVERSIVE MOVEMENTS, p. 219
288. PROOFS OF A CONSPIRACY, p. 91-92
289. SECRET SOCIETIES AND SUBVERSIVE MOVEMENTS, p. 215, 216
290. PROOFS OF A CONSPIRACY, p. 123
291. PROOFS OF A CONSPIRACY, p. 6-7
292. PROOFS OF A CONSPIRACY, p. 74

CHAPTER FIFTEEN: THE ILLUMINATI continued

293. WORLD REVOLUTION, p. 9
294. PROOFS OF A CONSPIRACY, p. 106
295. WORLD REVOLUTION, p. 13
296. Diedre Manifold, Karl Marx, True of False Prophet?, (Galway, Ireland: Firinne Publications, 1985), p. 77
297. WORLD REVOLUTION, p. 22
298. PROOFS OF A CONSPIRACY, p. 84
299. THE MAGIC OF OBELISKS, p. 314-315
300. PROOFS OF A CONSPIRACY, p. 7
301. PROOFS OF A CONSPIRACY, p. 8
302. PROOFS OF A CONSPIRACY, p. 8
303. THE ROYAL MASONIC CYCLOPAEDIA, p. 133
304. PARADE TO GLORY, p. 51
305. AN ENCYCLOPAEDIA OF FREEMASONRY, p. 843
306. AN ENCYCLOPAEDIA OF FREEMASONRY, p. 628
307. AN ENCYCLOPAEDIA OF FREEMASONRY, p. 63
308. THE ROYAL MASONIC CYCLOPAEDIA , p. 608
309. CONSPIRACY AGAINST GOD AND MAN, p. 176
310. "Thomas Jefferson," Freemen Digest, (Salt Lake City: The Freemen Institute, 1981), p. 83
311. as above, p. 83
312. AN ENCYCLOPAEDIA OF FREEMASONRY, p. 347
313. AN ENCYCLOPAEDIA OF FREEMASONRY, p. 842
314. THE ROYAL MASONIC CYCLOPAEDIA, p. 329-330
315. WORLD REVOLUTION, p. 78
316. WORLD REVOLUTION, p. 78
317. THE UNSEEN HAND, p. 133
318. Captain Michael Shaack, Anarchy and Anarchists, (publisher not mentioned, 1889)
319. Review of the News, (December 21, 1977), p. 39
320. Review of the News, (December 21, 1977), p. 39

CHAPTER SIXTEEN: KARL MARX, SATANIST

321. MARX AND SATAN, p. 11
322. MARX AND SATAN, p. 22
323. WAS KARL MARX A SATANIST?, p. 19
324. WAS KARL MARX A SATANIST?, p. 4
325. WAS KARL MARX A SATANIST?, p. 7
326. MARX AND SATAN, p. 59
327. THE COMMUNIST MANIFESTO, p. 22

CHAPTER SIXTEEN: KARL MARX, SATINIST
continued

328. MARX AND SATAN, p. 32
329. J. Edgar Hoover, Masters of Deceit, (New York: Pocket Books, Inc., 1958), p. 15
330. WAS KARL MARX A SATANIST?, p. 20-21
331. WAS KARL MARX A SATANIST?, p. 20-21
332. MARX AND SATAN, p. 29
333. MARX AND SATAN, p. 59
334. quoted by G. Edward Griffin, This Is the John Birch Society, (Thousand Oaks, California: American Media, 1972), p. 46
335. Two Worlds, (Bensenville, Illinois: Flick-Reedy Education Enterprises, 1966), p. 107
336. quoted by J. Edgar Hoover, Masters of Deceit, (New York: Pocket Books, 1958), p. 300
337. as above, p. 299
338. Dr. Fred Schwarz, You Can Trust the Communists, (Englewood Cliffs, New Jersey: Prentice-Hall, Inc., 1960), p. 155
339. Masters of Deceit, p. 299
340. Zbigniew Brzezinski, Between Two Ages, (New York: Penguin Books, 1970), p. 72, 73, 74, 83, 123
341. "From A China Traveller," David Rockefeller, New York Times, (August 10, 1973), p. L 31
342. WORLD REVOLUTION, p. 13
343. Whittaker Chambers, Witness, (New York: Random House, 1952), p. 16

CHAPTER SEVENTEEN: ADOLF HITLER, SATANIST

344. THE OCCULT AND THE THIRD REICH, p. 91
345. THE OCCULT AND THE THIRD REICH, p. 164
346. THE OCCULT AND THE THIRD REICH, p. 164
347. THE OCCULT AND THE THIRD REICH, p. 167
348. THE SPEAR OF DESTINY, p. 102
349. THE SPEAR OF DESTINY, p. 159
350. THE TWISTED CROSS, p. 108
351. THE SPEAR OF DESTINY, p. 23
352. THE OCCULT AND THE THIRD REICH, p. 156
353. THE SPEAR OF DESTINY, p. 153
354. THE SPEAR OF DESTINY, p. xxi

CHAPTER SEVENTEEN: ADOLF HITLER, SATANIST
continued

355. THE SPEAR OF DESTINY, p. 91
356. THE TWISTED CROSS, p. 116
357. THE SPEAR OF DESTINY, p. 91
358. THE SPEAR OF DESTINY, p. 92
359. THE TWISTED CROSS, p. 102-103
360. THE OCCULT AND THE THIRD REICH, p. 168
361. LECTURES ON ANCIENT PHILOSOPHY, p. 37
362. THE OCCULT AND THE THIRD REICH, p. 169

CHAPTER EIGHTEEN: THE GREAT SEAL

363. THE SECRET DESTINY OF AMERICA, p. 9
364. THE SECRET DESTINY OF AMERICA, p. 11
365. THE SECRET DESTINY OF AMERICA, p. 130
366. THE SECRET DESTINY OF AMERICA, p. 134
367. THE SECRET TEACHINGS OF ALL AGES, p. XCI
368. THE SECRET DESTINY OF AMERICA, p. 177-178
369. Pyramid Prophecies, P. 24
370. THE SECRET TEACHINGS OF ALL AGES, p. XC
371. THE SECRET TEACHINGS OF ALL AGES, p. XCI
372. THE SECRET DESTINY OF AMERICA, p. 181
373. THE SECRET TEACHINHGS OF ALL AGES, p. XC
374. FIRE IN THE MINDS OF MEN, p. 6
375. THE SECRET TEACHINGS OF ALL AGES, p. CXL
376. A BRIDGE TO LIGHT, p. 150, 142
377. THE ROYAL MASONIC ENCYCLOPAEDIA, p. 168
378. MORALS AND DOGMA, p. 426, 291
379. Robert Hieronimus, The Two Great Seals of America, Baltimore: Savitriaum, 1976), p. 19
380. E. Raymond Capt, Our Great Seal, (Thousand Oaks, California: Artisan Sales, 1979), p. 42
381. Stan Deyo, The Cosmic Conspiracy, (Kalamunda, Western Australia: West Australian Texas Trading, 1978), p. 73
382. H.L. Haywood, Freemasonry and the Bible, (Great Britain: William Collins Sons and Co., Ltd.), p. 16
383. AN ENCYCLOPAEDIA OF FREEMASONRY, p. 47-48
384. THE ROYAL MASONIC ENCYCLOPAEDIA, p. 31
385. INTRODUCTION TO FREEMASONRY, p. 148
386. INTRODUCTION TO FREEMASONRY, p. 48
387. MORALS AND DOGMA, p. 375

CHAPTER EIGHTEEN: THE GREAT SEAL
continued

386. THE SECRET TEACHINGS OF ALL AGES, p. XLV
387. MORALS AND DOGMA, p. 375
388. THE SECRET TEACHINGS OF ALL AGES, p. XLV
389. A BRIDGE TO LIGHT, p. 247
390. MORALS AND DOGMA, p. 506
391. Robert Keith Spencer, The Cult of the All-Seeing Eye, (city not shown: Monte Carlo Press, 1964), p. 24
392. Our Great Seal, p. 59
393. THE LOST KEYS OF FREEMASONRY, p. 62
394. THE MASTER'S CARPET, p. 153
395. The New Age magazine, (The Supreme Council, Washington D.C.), April, 1960
396. The Cosmic Conspiracy, p. 73
397. The Cult of the All-Seeing Eye, p. 23
398. Our Great Seal, p. 39
399. "Thoughts About America," pamphlet published by the Supreme Council of the Scottish Rite of Freemasonry, 33rd Degree, (January, 1986).
400. Henry C. Clausen, Masons Who Have Shaped Our Nation, (Washington D.C.: The Supreme Council, 1976), p. 84
401. Masons Who Have Shaped Our Nation, p. 12
402. Manly P. Hall, Freemasonry of the Ancient Egyptians, (Los Angeles: The Philosophical Research Society, 1982), p. 70
403. C. William Smith, God's Plan In America, an article in the New Age magazine, (September, 1950), p. 551

CHAPTER NINETEEN: THE FREEMASONS

404. "What About Today?," article in the New Age magazine, (November, 1946), p. 667
405. LECTURES ON ANCIENT PHILOSOPHY, p. 451
406. THE EXTERNALISATION OF THE HIERARCHY, p. 511
407. Henry C. Clausen, pamphlet entitled "What is the Scottish Rite?," published by the Scottish Rite Supreme Council, 33rd Degree, Washington D.C.
408. INTRODUCTION TO FREEMASONRY, p. 17

CHAPTER NINETEEN: THE FREEMASONS continued

409. Arthur M. Schlesinger, Jr., History of U.S. Political Parties, Vol. 1, 1789-1960, (New York: Chelsea House Publishers, 1973), p. 634
410. William Preston Campbell-Everden, Freemasonry and Its Etiguette, (New York: Weathervane Books, 1978), p. 10
411. George Steinmetz, Freemasonry, Its Hidden Meaning, p. 5
412. MORALS AND DOGMA, p. 819
413. MORALS AND DOGMA, p. 104-105
414. THE ROYAL MASONIC CYCLOPAEDIA, p. 18
415. LECTURES ON ANCIENT PHILOSOPHY, p. 433
416. THE LOST KEYS OF FREEMASONRY, p. 14
417. THE ROYAL MASONIC CYCLOPAEDIA, p. 206
418. MORALS AND DOGMA, p. 218-219
419. MORALS AND DOGMA, p. 7
420. MORALS AND DOGMA, p. 526
421. LECTURES ON ANCIENT PHILOSOPHY, p. 434
422. MORALS AND DOGMA, p. 213
423. Bill Mankin, quoted in "The Masonic Lodge," a pamphlet produced by the John Ankerberg Show, Chattanooga, Tennessee, (1986), p. 34-35
424. Quoted on page 6 of the pamphlet entitled "The Masonic Lodge," produced by the John Ankerberg Show, Chattanooga, Tennessee, (1986).
425. pamphlet, "The Masonic Lodge," p. 6
426. pamphlet, "The Masonic Lodge," p. 26
427. pamphlet, "The Masonic Lodge," p. 7
428. CLAUSEN'S COMMENTARIES ON MORALS AND DOGMA, p. 75
429. pamphlet, "The Masonic Lodge," p. 13
430. MORALS AND DOGMA, p. 411, 548
431. MORALS AND DOGMA, p. 407
432. MORALS AND DOGMA, p. 781
433. MORALS AND DOGMA, p. iv
434. MORALS AND DOGMA, p. 324
435. MORALS AND DOGMA, p. 324
436. AN ENCYCLOPAEDIA OF FREEMASONRY, p. 618-619
437. THE MASTER'S CARPET, p. 50
438. THE MYSTERIES OF THE GREAT PYRAMID, p. 206
439. MORALS AND DOGMA, p. 624
440. MORALS AND DOGMA, p. 22

CHAPTER NINETEEN: THE FREEMASONS continued

441. THE SECRET TEACHINGS OF ALL AGES, p. XXII
442. SERPENT IN THE SKY, p. 123
443. Henry C. Clausen, pamphlet on Freemasonry, published by the Supreme Council, 33rd Degree, Scottish Rite of Freemasonry

CHAPTER TWENTY: THOSE WHO OBJECT

444. The Freemason's Repository, p. 17
445. FREEMASONRY EXPOSED, p. iii
446. AN ENCYCLOPAEDIA OF FREEMASONRY, p. 492
447. William Preston Vaughn, The Antimasonic Party in the United States, (Kentucky: The University Press of Kentucky, 1983), p. 13
448. CONSPIRACY AGAINST GOD AND MAN, p. 57-58
449. Jack Harris, Freemasonry: The Invisible Cult In Our Midst, (Global Publishers: Chattanooga, Tennessee, 1983), p. 128
450. Pamphlet, Presidents United States, (Chicago National Christian Association, 1953), p. 6
451. as above, pamphlet, p. 7
452. as above, pamphlet, p. 8
453. Everett C. De Velde, Jr., A Reformed View of Freemasonry, in Christianity and Civilization, p. 278
454. William Preston Vaughn, The Anti-Masonic Party in the United States, (Kentucky: University Press of Kentucky, 1983), p. 29
455. Charles G. Finney, Why I Left Freemasonry, (National Christian Association, 1868)
456. Pope Leo XIII, The Church Speaks fo the Modern World, (Garden City, N.Y.: Image Books, 1954), p. 122
457. as above, p. 123
458. as above, p. 127
459. as above, p. 128-129
460. Time magazine, (June 18, 1984), p. 52
461. Bernard Fay, Revolution and Freemasonry, 1680-1800, (Boston: Little, Brown, and Company, 1935), p. 111
462. Arthur Edward Waite, The Encyclopaedia of Freemasonry, (New York: Weathervane Books, 1920), p. 32
463. Christ or The Lodge, (Philadelphia: Great Commission Publications, undated), p. 22-23

CHAPTER TWENTY: THOSE WHO OBJECT continued

464. Arizona Daily Star, (July 14, 1987), p. 8-a
465. THE MASTER'S CARPET, p. 25

CHAPTER TWENTY-ONE: ALBERT PIKE

466. INTRODUCTION TO FREEMASONRY, p. 95-96
467. THE SECRET TEACHINGS OF ALL AGES, p. CXCVII
468. Dr. Robert B. Watts, pamphlet published by the Masonic Order, the Supreme Council, 1978, p. 3
469. A BRIDGE TO LIGHT, p. 2
470. A BRIDGE TO LIGHT, p. 2
471. CLAUSEN'S COMMENTARIES ON MORALS AND DOGMA, p. xvii
472. AN ENCYCLOPAEDIA OF FREEMASONRY, p. 564
473. BEHIND THE LODGE DOOR, p. 210
474. FREEMASONRY EXPOSED, p. 75

CHAPTER TWENTY-TWO: HIRAM ABIF

475. AN ENCYCLOPAEDIA OF FREEMASONRY, p. 329-330
476. THE MASTER'S CARPET, p. 339
477. A BRIDGE TO LIGHT, p. 10
478. A BRIDGE TO LIGHT, p. 66
479. A BRIDGE TO LIGHT, p. 73

CHAPTER TWENTY-THREE: THE HIERARCHY

480. THE EXTERNALISATION OF THE HIERARCHY, p. 521-522
481. THE EXTERNALISATION OF THE HIERARCHY, p. 521-522
482. THE EXTERNALISATION OF THE HIERARCHY, p. 522
483. THE EXTERNALISATION OF THE HIERARCHY, p. 519
484. THE EXTERNALISATION OF THE HIERARCHY, p. 515
485. SECRET TEACHINGS OF ALL AGES, p. CLXIV
486. THE LOST KEYS OF FREEMASONRY, p. 100
487. MORALS AND DOGMA, p. 817
488. THE SECRET TEACHINGS OF ALL AGES, p. CCIV
489. SAY NO TO THE NEW WORLD ORDER, p. 7

CHAPTER TWENTY-FOUR: MASONIC OBLIGATIONS

490. Malcolm C. Duncan, Duncan's Masonic Ritual and Monitor, (New York: David McKay and Company, Inc., not dated), p. 95
491. Pastor Earl Jones, Christian Crusade For Truth Intelligence Newsletter, (May-June, 1989), (Deming, New Mexico: Pastor Earl Jones, 1989), p. Seven
492. FREEMASONRY EXPOSED, p. 75
493. INTRODUCTION TO FREEMASONRY, p. 138-139
494. AN ENCYCLOPAEDIA OF FREEMASONRY, p. 525

CHAPTER TWENTY-FIVE: THE THIRTY-THIRD DEGREE

495. THE SECRET TEACHINGS OF ALL AGES, p. CCI
496. THE DEADLY DECEPTION, p. 156
497. THE SECRET TEACHINGS OF ALL AGES, p. 14
498. THE SECRET TEACHINGS OF ALL AGES, p. XC
499. SECRET SYMNBOLISM IN OCCULT ART, p. 150
500. A BRIDGE TO LIGHT, p. 188
501. A BRIDGE TO LIGHT, p. 144
502. A BRIDGE TO LIGHT, p. 289
503. A BRIDGE TO LIGHT, p. 287
504. A BRIDGE TO LIGHT, p. 283
505. A BRIDGE TO LIGHT, p. 321
506. A BRIDGE TO LIGHT, p. 292
507. THE ROYAY MASONIC ENCYCLOPAEDIA, p. 7
508. BEHIND THE LODGE DOOR, p. 29
509. THE DEADLY DECEPTION, p. 102-103
510. THE DEADLY DECEPTION, p. 104
511. E.M. Storms, Should a Christian Be A Mason?, (Fletcher, North Carolina: New Puritan Library, 1980), foreward page
512. OCCULT THEOCRASY, p. 363-364
513. A BRIDGE TO LIGHT, p. 319

CHAPTER TWENTY-SIX: THE HUMANISTS

514. Homer Duncan, Secular Humanism, (distributed by Christian Focus on Government, Inc.: Lubbock, Texas, 1979), p. 13
515. Secular Humanism, p. 13
516. HUMANIST MANIFESTOS I AND II, p. 7, 8

CHAPTER TWENTY-SIX: THE HUMANISTS continued

517. HUMANIST MANIFESTOS I AND II, p. 10
518. THE COMMUNIKST MANIFESTO, p. 20
519. Saturday Review magazine, (August 10, 1974), p. 84
520. HUMANIST MANIFESTOS I AND II, p. 13
521. THE COMMUNIST MANIFESTO, p. 47
522. THE UNSEEN HAND, p. 225-226
523. Review of the News, (July 16, 1975), p. 57
524. Arizona Daily Star, (September 2, 1977)
525. The Houston Chronicle, (NOvemvber 16, 1977)
526. The Review of the News, (June 27, 1979), p. 11
527. The Tucson Citizen, (Aigist 13, 1987), p. 8A
528. William J. Murray, letter in possession of author
529. Karl Marx, Economic Politique et Philosophie, Vol. I, p 38-40
530. Review of the News, (October 24, 1973), p. 49
531. 367 U.S. Reports, p., 495, as cited by Barbara Morris, Change Agents in the Schools, (Upland, California: The Barbara M. Morris Report, 1979), p. 19
532. United States v. Seeger, 1965, as cited by Claire Chambers, The SIECUS Circle, (Appleton, Wisconsin: Western Islands, 1977), p. 93
533. quoting Lloyd Morain, as cited by Claire Chambers, The SIECUS Circle, p. 92
534. Dr. Henry Morris, "The Gospel of Creation and the Anti-Gospel of Evolution," Institute of Creation Research Impact No. 25, p. iii
535. Arizona Daily Star, (March 5, 1987), p. A-1

CHAPTER TWENTY-SEVEN: SITUATION ETHICS

536. HUMANIST MANIFESTOS I AND II, p. 17
537. Time magazine, (December 7, 1987), p. 72
538. The SIECUS Circle, p. 37
539. John Stormer, Death of a Nation, (Florissant, Missouri: Liberty Bell Press, 1968), p. 97
540. PROOFS OF A CONSPIRACY, p. 78
541. PROOFS OF A CONSPIRACY, p. 61
542. DANCING IN THE LIGHT, p. 203
543. H.L. Haywood, quoted by pamphlet entitled "Christ or the Lodge?," (Philadelphia: Great Commission Publications, 1942), p. 14

CHAPTER TWENTY-SEVEN: SITUATION ETHICS
continued

544. W.L. Wilmshurst, The Meaning of Masonry, (New York: Bell Publishing Company, 1927), p. 96
545. MORALS AND DOGMA, p. 37
546. LECTURES ON ANCIENT PHILOSOPHY, p. 407
547. THE SPEAR OF DESTINY, p. 28
548. CONSPIRACY AGAINST GOD AND MAN, p. 203
549. Diedre Manifold, Karl Marx, True of False Prophet,(Galway, Ireland: Firinne Publications, 1985) 9, p. 66
550. Two Worlds, p. 107
551. quoted by G. Edward Griffin, This Is the John Birch Society, (Thousand Oaks, California: American Media, 1972), p. 38
552. Nikolai Lenin, Collected Works, Volume XVII, p. 321-323
553. MARX AND SATAN, p. 58-59
554. MARX AND SATAN, p. 108
555. MARX AND SATAN, p. 96
556. MARX AND SATAN, p. 97
557. Aldous Huxley, Brave New World Revisited, (New York: Harper & Brothers, 1958), p. 23

CHAPTER TWENTY-EIGHT: THE ATTACK ON RELIGION

558. Dr. Everett Sileven, America's First Padlocked Church, (Louisville, Nebraska: Fundamentalist Publications, 1983), p. 39
559. America's First Padlocked Church, p. 25

CHAPTER TWENTY-NINE: THE ATTACK ON
THE FAMILY

560. THE AQUARIAN CONSPIRACY, p. 397
561. THE AQUARIAN CONSPIRACY, p. 397-398
562. Tucson Citizen, (July 6, 1989), p. 6A
563. THE COMMUNIST MANIFESTO, p. 47-48
564. CONSPIRACY AGAINST GOD AND MAN, p. 121
565. The New American, (June 20, 1988), p. 22-23
566. The New American, (June 20, 1988), p. 22
567. Death of a Nation, p. 132
568. Review of the News, (February 12, 1970)
569. Fusion magazine, (July, 1981), p. 52

CHAPTER TWENTY-NINE: THE ATTACK ON
THE FAMILY continued

570. quoted in the John Birch Society Bulletin, (March, 1989)
571. Fusion magazine, (July, 1981), p. 52
572. Review of the News, (May 22, 1985), p. 37
573. Parage magazine, (December 11, 1988), p. 19
574. Review of the News, (March 21, 1979), p. 25
575. William E. Simon, Should We Bail Out Gorbachev?, Reader's Digest, (September, 1988), p. 67
576. The Conservative Digest, (March/April), p. 5
577. American Opinion, (June, 1985), p. 39
578. Tucson Citizen, (November 14, 1988), p. 9A
579. Human Events, (October 18, 1986), p. 919
580. A PLANNED DECEPTION, p. 165
581. A PLANNED DECEPTION, p. 165
582. A PLANNED DECEPTION, p. 165
583. Karl Marx, True or False Prophet?, p. 118-119
584. The New American, (November 9, 1987), p. 49
585. The New American, (January 30, 1989), p. 7
586. The New American, (January 30, 1989), p. 7
587. The New American, (January 30, 1989), p. 7
588. Arizona Daily Star, (July 13, 1987), p. 10-A
589. Newsweek magazine, (January 12, 1981), p. 15
590. Arizona Daily Republic, (June 7, 1980), p. 1
591. Parage magazine, (February 26, 1989), p. 14
592. The Review of the News, (July 14, 1984), p. 30

CHAPTER THIRTY: THE RIGHT OF ASSOCIATION

593. Arizona Daily Star, (May 5, 1987), p. 1-A
594. Action Newsletter, (November, 1988), p. 5
595. The Review of the News, (November 16, 1983), p. 57
596. Tucson Citizen, (September 24, 1987)
597. Senator John McCain's press release of April 13, 1989
598. The Arizona Daily Star, (April 14, 1989), p. A-6

CHAPTER THIRTY-ONE: THE ATTACK ON EDUCATION

599. PROOFS OF A CONSPIRACY, p. 111
600. PROOFS OF A CONSPIRACY, p. 109
601. PROOFS OF A CONSPIRACY, p. 75
602. THE COMMUNIST MANIFESTO, p. 56

CHAPTER THIRTY-ONE: THE ATTACK ON EDUCATION
continued

603. The New American, (March 13, 1989), p. 12
604. The New American, (March 13, 1989), p. 11
605. The New American, (March 13, 1989), p. 11
606. Henry C. Clausen, "Devilish Danger," pamphlet published by the Supreme Council of the Scottish Rite of Freemasonry
607. NEA: TROJAN HORSE IN AMERICAN EDUCATION, p. 254
608. NEA: TROJAN HORSE IN AMERICAN EDUCATION, p. 257
609. HUMANIST MANIFESTOS I AND II, p. 119
610. Mel and Norma Gabler, What Are They Teaching Our Children?, (Wheaton, Illinois: Victor Books, 1985), p. 119
611. What Are They Teaching Our Children?, p. 121-122
612. Secular Humanism, p. 18
613. DARK SECRETS OF THE NEW AGE, p. 233-234
614. James C. Hefley, Are Textbooks Ruining Your Children?, (Milford, Michigan: Mott Media, 1976), p. 31
615. Education USA, (September 24, 1979), p. 29
616. Education USA, (February 11, 1980), p. 179
617. Arizona Daily Star, (May 31, 1984), p. A-2

CHAPTER THIRTY-TWO: RUSSIAN LAWS

618. BEHIND THE LODGE DOOR, p. 130
619. BEHIND THE LODGE DOOR, p. 284
620. U.S. Congressional Record, Vol. 77, p. 1539-1540, as quoted in the Naked Communist, p. 308
621. Selected Essays of Karl Marx, p. 16, as quoted in The Naked Communist, p. 50
622. Alexander Solshenitsyn, as quoted by David Balsiger, Liberation Theology, p. 15
623. THE HIDDEN DANGERS OF THE RAINBOW, p. 65
624. THE HIDDEN DANGERS OF THE RAINBOW, p. 64
625. LECTURES ON ANCIENT PHILOSOPHY, p. 150
626. HUMANIST MANIFESTOS I AND II, p. 13
627. HUMANIST MANIFESTOS I AND II, p. 16
628. HUMANIST MANIFESTOS I AND II, p. 8

CHAPTER THIRTY-TWO: RUSSIAN LAWS continued

629. The Crisis in Religious Freedom newsletter, published by the Coalition For Religious Freedom, (Washington D.C.: 1987), p. 1

CHAPTER THIRTY-THREE: THE ATTACK ON PROPERTY

630. CONSPIRACY AGAINST GOD AND MAN, p. 10
631. PROOFS OF A CONSPIRACY, p. 61
632. Karl Marx, Capital and Other Writings, (New York: The Modern Library, 1932), p. 2
633. Capital and Other Writings, p. xi
634. THE COMMUNBIST MANIFESTO, p. 19
635. HUMANIST MANIFESTOS I AND II, p. 10

CHAPTER THIRTY-FOUR: THE ATTACK ON NATIONALISM

636. PROOFS OF A CONSPIRACY, p. 61
637. SECRET SOCIETIES AND SUBVERSIVE MOVEMENTS, p. 214
638. CONSPIRACY AGAINST GOD AND MAN, p. 198
639. THE COMMUNIST MANIFESTO, p. 23
640. HUMANIST MANIFESTOS I AND II, p. 21
641. LECTURES ON ANCIENT PHILOSOPHY, p. 466
642. LECTURES ON ANCIENT PHILOSOPHY, p. 109
643. Between Two Ages, p. 274
644. LECTURES ON ANCIENT PHILOSPHY, p. 463

CHAPTER THIRTY-FIVE: ANSWERING THE SKEPTIC

No footnotes

CHAPTER THIRTY-SIX: REAGAN AND BUSH

645. New Age magazine, (April, 1988)
646. New York Times, (August 16, 1988), p. 12
647. New York Times, (August 16, 1988), p. 12
648. New York Times, (August 16, 1988), p. 12
649. New York Times, (August 19, 1988), p. 8-Y
650. New York Times, (August 19, 1988), p. 8-Y

CHAPTER THIRTY-SIX: REAGAN AND BUSH
continued

651.   The Arizona Daily Star, (January 3, 1989), p. A-5

CHAPTER THIRTY-SEVEN: "ELEVEN SHORT YEARS"

652.   quoted by Dr. David Noebel, Summit Journal, (December, 1987), p. 8

CHAPTER THIRTY-EIGHT: THE SUMMATION

653.   CONSPIRACY AGAINST GOD AND MAN, p. 66
654.   George Orwell, 1984, (New York: Harcourt Brace Jovanovich, Inc., 1949), p. 220

CHAPTER THIRTY-NINE: THE SOLUTION

no footnotes

INDEX

B.

Bacchus 76
Bailey, Alice
    about the Masons 148
    on ancient mysteries
        25, 37
    on the 20th century 8
    on the hierarchy 177
    on three channels 4
Bailey, Foster
    on hidden symbols 36
Bakunin, Mikhail
    evil and good gods 67
    on Satan 121
Baphomet 43
Barruel, the Abbe 113
Bavaria 2
Bazot, Etienne Francois 52
Beatles, the 12
BEHIND THE LODGE
    DOOR 2
Bel 46
Belin or Belinis 46
Belsky, Jay, Dr. 245
Bertrand, Michel 55
Besharov, Douglas 239
BETWEEN TWO AGES
    fiction of nationalism 285
    on 1976 or 1989 xix
    on Marxism 124
BEYOND FREEDOM AND
    DIGNITY
    force and slavery xvii
    on freedom 251
Billington, James H.
    on Great Seal 138
    on overthr'g authority
        xvii
Birth control
    acc'd'g to Humanists 204
Blanchard, Paul 266
Blavatsky, Helena Petrovna
    and Henry Wallace 145
    "dragon of wisdom" 23

Lucifer Publ'g Co. 80
Blue Lodge, the 6
Blumenfeld, Sam 265
Bolen, Harold J. 75
Born again, def'n of
    according to Pike 29
Bowlby, John 244
Boy Scouts, the 257
Brahma 46
Brainard, W.F. 149
BRAVE NEW WORLD
    REVISITED xviii
    situation ethics 223
BRIDGE TO LIGHT
    on death of Hiram 175
    on the ax 187
Brotherhood of Spirits 67
Brzezinski, Zbigniew
    fiction of nationalism 285
    on 1976 or 1989 xix
    thoughts: Marxism 124
Bush, George
    Millenium Society 294
    on "world order" xiii
    Reagan's speech about 291
    "thousand points" 292

C.

Calhoun, Arthur W. 240
Candles, yellow 54
Capt, E. Raymond
    on eagle symbol 139
    on pyramid symbol 142
Carr, Joseph
    on Aleister Crowley 92
    on Thule Society 129
Carter, Jimmy
    about Brzezinski xix
    on BETWEEN TWO AGES
        124
    on Humanism 197
Castro, Fidel 71
CELESTIAL LODGE
    ABOVE, THE 157

M.

Mackenzie, Kenneth
  concealed secrets 153
  eagle as symbol 139
  eye of Osiris 141
  on adepts 151
  on Illuminati 112, 115
  on Knights Templar 43
  on North darkness 51
  on Robison, John 113
  on sons of light 81
  on suns, obelisks 101
Mackey, Albert Gallatin 52, 53
  "all-seeing eye" 141
  ancient myst's 25, 31
  comments on Robison 113
  north is "darkness" 50
  obelisks, sun-gods 101
  on Albert Pike 170
  on all seeing eye 140
  on blazing star 45
  on circumambulation 52
  on Hiram Abif 173
  on Illuminati 114
  on light worship 79
  on mason religion 159
  on obedience 184
  on Osirus, the sun 89
  on revolution 34
  on shooting star 44
  on sons of light 82
  on sun worship 46
  on year of light 95
  Osirus, the sun 49
  praise of Weishaupt 113
  the symbolic east 88
  thoughts by Claudy 26
  "we are ... God" 70
MacLaine, Shirley 70
  '87 window of light 72
  AIDS 72
  biography of Marx 71

cancer of abdomen 72
earth mov'g axis 72
money to buy 71
no "reality" 70
Situation Ethics 219
tour 71
waivers 72
we "choose parents" 70
with Castro 71
with Khrushchev 71
Magical Blend 13
Maharishi Mahesh Yogi 12
Maitreya, Lord 8, 20, 40
  and world government 14
  Bush's speech 293
  "dragon of wisdom" 23
  hoped by Eckart 130
  London; July, '77 19
Malkarth 46
Mankin, Bill 154
Manning, Henry Edward, Archbishop 117
Marrs, Texe 4, 11, 13, 20, 79
Marshall, John 164
Marx, Karl
  forcible overthrow xv
  "from each ... to each" 200, 205, 280
  his own family 121
  in Churchill's quote 105
  on education 205, 263
  on family 232
  on Feuerbach 69
  on his own family 120
  on nationalism 284
  on private property 200, 280
  on religion 274
  the family 120
  the humanist 211
  the Luciferian 118
  thoughts: religion 119
  worship of Satan 121, 122
MASONIC HANDBOOK 182

Dr. Hewish's star 94
on grand gallery 94
on line of 6000 " 91
Pyramid of Giza 93
North, symbolic 50, 51
Novus Ordo Seclorum
138, 144-146,
Novus Ordo Seclorum,
def'n on the dollar bill
197

O.

O'Hair, Madlyn Murray 211
city counc. prayer 209
Comm. of Sep. of Ch'h
& St. 211
edit FREE HUMANIST
208
"In God We Trust"
208-209
on FCC petition 208
on In God We Trust 208
on nativity scene 208
on religion 208
on Soc. of Separation-
ists 209
on son Wm. Murray 210
son: "a Marxist" 211
Oath of office, Constit'l
senators 259
OCCULT AND THE THIRD
REICH, THE 55
OCCULT THEOCRASY
on 33rd degree 193
Old Testament
1st Kings 7:13 174
Deut. 17:2-4,7 56
Exodus 20:13 16
Exodus 20:15 280
Ezekiel 8:15-16 56
Genesis 2:16-17 61
Isaiah 14: 12-14 42
Isaiah 14:12 45, 60
Isaiah 14:13 51

Isaiah 43:10 69
Isaiah 45:5 70
Isaiah 5:20-21 224
Proverbs 1:7 77
Proverbs 3:5 77
ONCE AND FUTURE STAR,
THE 94
Order of the Quest 133
ORDO AB CHAO 191
Orthodox Presb. Church 167
Orwell, George
on The Brotherhood 17
Osiris 46, 49
"all-seeing eye" of
140, 141
ancient mysteries 31
built pyramid Giza 89
changed name:
Adoni 31
Bacchus 31
connected: pyramid 90
future return 146
Mackey: "the sun" 89
Masonic light,
as sun 49
the sun 157
on tomb, white
apron 157
one of Egyptian trinity
160
Pike: "the sun" 141
representative: sun 49
worshipped as sun 46
Osiris, worship of
ancient mysteries 31
OUR GREAT SEAL
and Henry Wallace 145
by E. Ray. Capt 139
OUT ON A LIMB 71, 73
Owen, Robert (socialist)
on the family 232
Oxford University xvii

P.

PADLOCKED CHURCH,
   THE 227
PARADE TO GLORY 112
Participatory democracy 204
Paul, Francis G. 289
Pedagogy, defined 268
People's Daily World xv
PHI DELTA KAPPAN
   Feb. 1980 issue 270
Phoenicia 43
Phoenix bird, the 186
Pike, Albert 7, 35, 46
   All-seeing eye 141
   and And. Johnson 171
   author: MOR. & DOG.
      170
   Holy Masonic Empire 4
   July 1889 letter 63
   Masonic great lights 157
   Mor. & Dog. "not
      intended" 158
   no "rebellious evil" 62
   on disc'g secrets 153
   on East & West 88
   on eternal truths 219
   on god of light 81
   on good force 62
   on Hydra, serpent 84
   on intentional misleading
      150, 151
   on light 84
   on light overc'g dark-
      ness 83
   on Lucifer 159
   on Lucifer, light-
      bearer 83
   on Masonic relig'n 154
   on Masonic 10
      Comm'd'ts 76
   on Masonic light: sun
      49
   on Masons; "anc.
      myst's." 160

on May 1st 106
on new born birth 28
on North darkness 51
on obelisk, sun 101
on past sun worship 46
on reason 30
on secret meanings 158
on symbol of eagle 139
on the Phoenix bird 186
on tiara 3
on truth 191
on two doctrines 33
on voluntary sun 47
Osiris, the sun 141
praise by Claudy 2, 169
   Hall 169
   Watts 170
reason is absolute 76
sacrificing one man 16
"sover's and pon-
   tiffs" 179
"superior and inferior"
   158
traces ancient
   mysteries 31
Pius IX, Pope xvi
Pius XI, Pope xvi
Plain Truth
   Sept. 1986 issue 43
Plan, The
   by Benjamin Creme 14
Plotinus 28
Pochan, Andre 93
Population explosion
   a fraud 206
   acc'd'g to Friends of
      Earth 242
   control by Humanists 206
   quote from THE UNSEEN
      HAND 206
Price, John Randolph 13
Prog. of the Comm. Int'l
   combatt'g religion 274
PROOFS OF CONSPIRACY
   on education 263

352

S.

RALPH EPPERSON is an historian, lecturer, and writer who has been researching the Conspiratorial View of History for over 27 years.

He is a graduate of the University of Arizona, but readily admits that the overwhelming majority of the material he was taught in college simply was not true. He claims that he has had to "re-educate" himself since college, and that is what he has done.

His first book was entitled THE UNSEEN HAND, AN INTRODUCTION TO THE CONSPIRATORIAL VIEW OF HISTORY. This best-selling book of some 488 pages, now in its ninth printing, is a documented expose of the conspiracy that has plagued America with a series of wars, depressions, and inflations for some 270 years. Many who have read it have praised the author's ability to make sense out of the often contradictory evidence of the past.

This is his second book, and provides the reader with the motive for the conspiracy exposed in his first book that has actively pursued their goal of THE NEW WORLD ORDER for some 6000 years.

It is his wish that those who read this book will be moved to reverse the trend of those who want to re-make the world.

Made in the USA
Monee, IL
20 September 2021